Globalization and the New Politics of Embedded Liberalism

Globalization and the New Politics of Embedded Liberalism

Jude C. Hays

OXFORD
UNIVERSITY PRESS
2009

OXFORD
UNIVERSITY PRESS

Oxford University Press, Inc., publishes works that further
Oxford University's objective of excellence
in research, scholarship, and education.

Oxford   New York
Auckland   Cape Town   Dar es Salaam   Hong Kong   Karachi
Kuala Lumpur   Madrid   Melbourne   Mexico City   Nairobi
New Delhi   Shanghai   Taipei   Toronto

With offices in
Argentina   Austria   Brazil   Chile   Czech Republic   France   Greece
Guatemala   Hungary   Italy   Japan   Poland   Portugal   Singapore
South Korea   Switzerland   Thailand   Turkey   Ukraine   Vietnam

Copyright © 2009 by Oxford University Press, Inc.

Published by Oxford University Press, Inc.
198 Madison Avenue, New York, New York 10016

www.oup.com

Oxford is a registered trademark of Oxford University Press

Library of Congress Cataloging-in-Publication Data
Hays, Jude C.
Globalization and the new politics of embedded liberalism / Jude C. Hays.
    p. cm.
Includes bibliographical references and index.
ISBN 978-0-19-536933-5; 978-0-19-536932-8 (pbk.)
1. Liberalism. 2. Globalization—Political aspects. I. Title.
JC574.H38 2009
320.51'3—dc22   2009003559

9 8 7 6 5 4 3 2 1
Printed in the United States of America
on acid-free paper

For Ivy Katherine

Preface

I have been working on this book for many years. (Most of my friends would say *too many* years.) When asked to describe the project, I used to respond that it is about how national institutions—primarily electoral and labor market institutions—shape the political and policy responses of governments to economic globalization. To clarify, I would add that it is about how domestic politics reacts to and interacts with the global economy and how institutions structure these relationships. These topics are central to the study of comparative and international political economy, my areas of specialization in political science. As a result of contemporary world events, I have changed the way I frame these issues and even changed the content of the book to a limited extent, hoping to reach a larger audience. Today I describe the book's topic as the political backlash against globalization in the Anglo-American democracies, and I say that the reason people who do not study political economy for a living should care about this, without trying to sound hyperbolic, is that the future of the global economy is at stake, and possibly international peace and stability as well. This is a more interesting description, even for political scientists.

When I started writing, the likelihood of a political backlash against globalization, one with the potential to undermine longstanding foreign economic policy commitments to economic openness and multilateralism, seemed remote. The idea that such a backlash would take hold in the Anglo-American democracies seemed even less likely. Economic historians were noting important similarities between the late 19th and early 21st centuries, but the possibility that the emerging discontent then and now would end the same way, that we would see a repeat of the 1930s when the international economy collapsed under the weight of global depression and beggar-thy-neighbor foreign economic policies, was dismissed, and rightfully so, by most as fanciful. This is no longer the case. The 1930s have become our new historical reference point. At the time of this writing, headlines warning the return of economic nationalism abound. The United Kingdom is preparing to undertake immigration reform, partly to save "British Jobs for British Workers," and the United States has just adopted a nearly $800 billion stimulus bill with a "Buy America" clause that has the international community crying foul. Recognizing the severity of the economic crisis, the head of U.S. intelligence recently announced that the global economy is now the number one threat to American national security, replacing Al Qaeda and global terrorism. I still believe that we are unlikely to see a 1930s-like scenario unfold, mainly because policymakers have learned important lessons from the interwar period, but the risks to the international economy are more serious today than at any other point since the end of World War II.

During the years I worked on this project, I took a tour of Big Ten political science departments, a journey that started in Minnesota and ended in Illinois by way of Michigan. My ideas were influenced significantly at each stop on the trip. The germ of this project surfaced in my dissertation, which I wrote at the University of Minnesota. John Freeman's passion for political economy and social science infected me at a very early stage in my graduate studies, and his imprint on the book is probably the largest. I was inspired by both his and Ethan Kapstein's research on globalization. John got me to think about the policy constraints that come with international capital mobility. Ethan Kapstein alerted me to the destructive potential of a globalization backlash. Both John and Diana Richards provided sage advice throughout the writing of my thesis. I received constructive comments from a number of my fellow graduate students as well. I am grateful to Glenda Morgan, Hans Nesseth, Darel Paul, and the other members of the international relations dissertation discussion group that met during my last few years in Minnesota.

The book began to take shape while I was an assistant professor at the University of Michigan. I owe a special debt of gratitude to Sean Ehrlich and Clint Peinhardt, political science graduate students at the time, who worked with me as coauthors on a paper that ultimately became chapter 2. It would be impossible to overstate the influence, both in terms of research methods and political economy substance, of Robert (Rob) Franzese. When it comes to political economy scholarship, Rob has been and remains my example of excellence. I also benefited from conversations with several of my colleagues at the Gerald R. Ford School of Public Policy including Rebecca Blank, Kerwin Charles, Alan Deardorff, John DiNardo, Katherine Terrell, David Thacher, and Marina Whitman. Moving to Illinois in the fall of 2005 allowed me to finish the project. As department head, Peter Nardulli made sure that I had the time that I needed to write. William Bernhard and Robert Pahre gave me valuable comments on chapter drafts. Many of my Illinois colleagues, past and present, provided advice and needed encouragement, particularly Jose Cheibub, Xinyuan Dai, Zachary Elkins, Brian Gaines, James Kuklinski, and Milan Svolik.

I benefited from several seminar presentations including ones at the University of Illinois in the summer of 2003, Yale University in the winter of 2005, Duke University and Pennsylvania State University in the fall 2006, and the University of Minnesota in the winter of 2007. I thank my hosts and

the participants for their suggestions. Others who have provided useful feedback over the years include Tim Büthe, William Clark, Jim Granato, Mark
Hallerberg, Nathan Jensen, William Keech, Judith Kelley, David Leblang,
Quan Li, Layna Mosley, Thomas Plümper, Frances Rosenbluth, Ken Scheve,
and Vera Troeger. I apologize to those whose names I have forgotten to men-
tion. I know there are many. I also want to thank David McBride for providing
comments that helped to make the book much more accessible to non-spe-
cialists. Finally, I want to thank my family and friends for all the support that
they have provided me. I know that they, more than anyone, have made it
possible for me to write this book.

Contents

Globalization and the New Politics of Embedded Liberalism

1

Economic Globalization and Domestic
Politics in the Developed Democracies

Around the world there is growing political opposition to the liberalization of trade, the rising levels of foreign investment, and increased inflows of foreign workers. This backlash against economic globalization is beginning to have an impact on public policy, particularly in the developed democracies. In Europe over the last few years, we have witnessed EU "enlargement fatigue," the rejection of a European constitution by French and Dutch voters, and, more recently, governmental attempts to limit cross-border mergers and acquisitions in a number of "strategic" sectors of the economy, such as the banking, steel, and energy sectors. On the other side of the Atlantic we see similar political developments. President George W. Bush had to fight an intense political battle early in his administration to win Trade Promotion Authority from Congress. During the 2004 campaign, presidential candidate John Kerry referred to CEOs who outsource production as traitors. The Central American Free Trade Agreement passed the U.S. House of Representatives by a single vote in the summer of 2005. Dozens of anti-China trade bills have been introduced in Congress in recent years. The collapse of the World Trade Organization's Doha round of multilateral trade negotiations is yet another manifestation of swelling discontent with globalization. Why do we observe this backlash, and where will it have the most significant and lasting policy consequences? What are the implications for the global economy and international relations more generally?

International and comparative political economists have argued that the domestic political foundation of the current liberal international economy rests on an implicit bargain between governments and their citizens called the bargain of embedded liberalism. According to this compact, governments are expected to protect their citizens from the vagaries of the global economy, primarily through the provision of social insurance and, more recently, with active labor market programs in return for political support for policies like free trade that drive economic globalization. Without this support, democratically elected politicians find it hard to endorse policies of economic openness.

Some believe that new revenue constraints arising from the globalization of production and finance are making it increasingly difficult for governments to live up to their end of the bargain, which, in turn, puts the future of the international economy in doubt. International bond markets "discipline" governments that borrow excessively, and multinational corporations shift production across borders to avoid taxation. This is troubling on economic grounds as expanding trade has been a source of growth and prosperity in core countries for many years and promises the same for countries in the developing periphery. There are potentially serious consequences for international peace and security as well. When globalization was reversed in the 1930s, political disintegration and world war followed closely behind. Hence, it is imperative that we better our understanding of these issues.

In this book, I argue that the combination of majoritarian democracy and decentralized labor markets exacerbates the political problems that governments committed to economic openness face, and that the countries with these institutions are the most susceptible to a backlash against globalization. Unfortunately, this list of countries includes the United States and United Kingdom, two pillars of the international economy, Australia, a country that plays a special role in multilateral trade talks because of its membership in the Cairns Group—a coalition of agricultural exporting nations that was organized to promote free trade in agricultural products—and Canada, also a member of the Cairns group as well as the G8. Moreover, Germany and Japan are undergoing market reforms that, if successful, will make their political economies much more similar to the American and British systems. I engage and occasionally challenge some of the most influential research on globalization in political science, which has focused almost exclusively on the small corporatist European economies with large welfare states, downplayed the policy constraints arising from increased international capital mobility, and ignored public attitudes toward the international economy. In the end, I conclude that a new bargain of embedded liberalism must be forged, particularly within the world's most powerful nations, to sustain economic globalization. This will require carefully crafted compensatory programs that are designed with an eye to their politically sustainability.

ALTERNATIVE VIEWS OF GLOBALIZATION AND DOMESTIC POLITICS

Political economists have studied the reciprocal relationship between economic globalization and domestic politics in the developed democracies for many years now.[1] Does the internationalization of financial markets lead to welfare state retrenchment? Is the international economy vulnerable to a political backlash against globalization? Can corporatist systems of industrial relations survive the multinationalization of economic production? These are just a few of the important topics debated in the globalization literature today. Based on the answers they provide to these and related questions, it is possible to separate most globalization scholars into one of two groups— those who view the relationship between domestic politics and economic globalization optimistically or, in other words, largely compatible; and those who take a more pessimistic outlook, emphasizing the tension between democratic politics at the national level and the growth of international markets.[2] I do not take sides in the debate between globalization optimists and pessimists.[3] Instead, I draw on the relative analytical strengths of both camps in an attempt to bridge the divide that separates them. I begin by outlining their respective positions.

Pessimists believe that the internationalization of markets presents national governments with a number of serious challenges. They emphasize the constraints that come with economic openness. Dani Rodrik (1997), for example, has argued in an influential monograph that globalization increases the political demands on governments to provide social insurance and other public goods at the same time that it undermines their ability to finance additional spending. According to this argument, which I refer to throughout the book as Rodrik's "globalization dilemma," the political and economic forces of globalization pull governments from different directions. Pessimists point to welfare state retrenchment and declining capital taxes as evidence of this dilemma.

The concern is that ultimately one of these opposing forces will win out— either we will see an erosion of popular sovereignty over the domestic economy and democracy will be severely vitiated, or a political backlash against globalization will cause governments to rethink their commitment to policies of economic openness. The latter fear has become more prevalent recently, particularly among economic historians. These scholars worry that a public backlash against international economic openness might lead to a repeat of the policies of the 1930s that ended the first great period of globalization (e.g., Kapstein 1996; Rodrik 1997; O'Rourke and Williamson 1999; Gilpin 2000; James 2001; Bordo, Taylor, and Williamson 2003). By contrast, much of the early research on globalization in political science argued that the internationalization of markets would force all countries to converge onto a single neoliberal political economic model (e.g., Freeman 1990; Kurzer 1993; Moses 1994; Steinmo 1994).[4] In other words, this work emphasized the domestic political consequences of economic globalization rather than the effects of politics on the international economy.[5]

The more optimistic view of globalization developed partly as a response to the convergence thesis, which was, and to some extent remains, ubiquitous in both academic journals and the popular press. The group of globalization optimists includes many of the scholars who contribute to the "varieties of capitalism" literature.[6] Optimists downplay globalization's constraints and emphasize democratic choice instead.[7] Most do not deny that globalization has important effects on domestic politics, but they see the relationship between the global economy and domestic politics as mutually reinforcing and supportive. Societies that prefer regulated economies, interventionist governments, and income equality will only see their preferences strengthened by economic globalization. Moreover, cross-national differences in domestic political and economic institutions create space for leftist governments to choose distinct policies in response to globalization. Therefore, significant variation in the forms of democratic capitalism will continue into the indefinite future and may even increase. Countries will pursue "divergent paths" in response to globalization. Kitschelt and colleagues (1999, 444) put it simply:

> The more organized market economies remain organized, interventionist, regulatory, and socially supportive, and they continue to seek to manage adaptation through cooperation and concertation among collective organizations and governments. The liberal market economies are becoming even more liberal, with a weakening of social supports and an increased emphasis on individual merit and markets.

Garrett (1998a, chapter 4) also concludes on the basis of careful empirical analysis that globalization increases the policy differences between governments in corporatist and liberal market economies: the former are spending more while the latter are spending less. The quantitative evidence in Swank (2002a, chapter 3, table 3.5) supports the divergent paths thesis as well. Increasing international capital mobility is associated with lower levels of social welfare effort in countries with liberal market economies and exclusive electoral systems (i.e., polities in which the interests of political "losers" are not represented in the policy-making process) and higher levels of social welfare effort in countries with corporatist economies and inclusive electoral systems that encourage accommodation between political "winners" and "losers."[8]

Because they argue that the constraints associated with globalization are exaggerated, some optimists believe the threat of a backlash is overstated as well. If globalization does not lead to neoliberal convergence, there is no reason for a backlash to emerge. Countries that have competitive markets and minimalist welfare states have freely chosen this path, so compensating market losers is politically unnecessary. These societies have elected right-wing and center-left governments that have pushed both economic openness and welfare state retrenchment. According to the optimists, these choices tell us something about societal preferences in the countries with liberal market economies: they prefer free markets, trade, small government, and economic growth.[9] Again, globalization will only reinforce the existing societal preferences. This position is implicit, if not explicit, in much of the "varieties of capitalism" research.[10]

For some purposes this division (optimists vs. pessimists) is a fruitful way to organize and think about the research on globalization, but it also obscures the fact that there are really two important and largely separate issues being debated. The first debate is about convergence. More specifically, does globalization cause a race-to-the-neoliberal-bottom? The second is about the likelihood of a political backlash against economic openness and the reversibility of globalization. Once we disconnect these debates, it is easier to see why globalization optimists and pessimists occasionally talk past each other, and the limitations of both camps become more apparent.

One problem with the standard "divergent paths" argument is that its assumptions about societal preferences in the liberal market economies are largely inconsistent with the public opinion research on globalization.[11] Consider the United States, everyone's exemplar of a liberal market economy.[12] The survey evidence from the United States is clear. Americans are worried about globalization, seemingly growing more so over time, and they expect their government to help them adjust to international competition. For example, here is a question from a recent (January 2004) PIPA/ Knowledge Networks Poll about government support for trade that was also asked in 1999.

> Overall, with regard to international trade, do you think that it should be a goal of the US to: try to actively promote it, simply allow it to continue, try to slow it down, or try to stop or reverse it?

From 1999 to 2004, the number of American respondents who said the United States should actively promote international trade dropped by 9% from 32% to 23%. The number who said the United States should either allow it to continue without promoting it or actively try to slow it down (67%) increased by 10%.[13] The numbers are similar when the question asks more generally about globalization. Moreover, the response to the following question suggests that Americans are not unconditional proponents of free trade.

> Which of the following three positions comes closest to your point of view? I favor free trade, and I believe that it is necessary for the government to have programs to help workers who lose their jobs. I favor free trade, and I believe that it is not necessary for the government to have programs to help workers who lose their jobs. I do not favor free trade.

A significant majority of respondents say their support for trade is conditional on the government providing programs to help displaced workers. In 2004, 60% of respondents agreed with the statement expressing conditional support for trade. This is 6% below the level of support in 1999. The number of respondents expressing unconditional support for trade also declined 5% from 18% to 13%. There was a large increase in the number of respondents who said they opposed free trade unconditionally (14% to 22%). Of those surveyed, 63% said that government efforts to retrain workers who have lost their jobs as a result of trade were inadequate, up from 57% in 1999 (PIPA 2004).[14]

These concerns have had some effect on policy. In the summer of 2002, the U.S. Congress ended an eight-year stalemate by granting trade promotion authority to President Bush. The authorizing legislation included an important concession made to free trade opponents—an increase in trade adjustment assistance to those who lose their jobs as a result of more intense international competition and an experimental wage insurance program for older workers.[15] More recently, in his nomination address at the 2008 Republican National Convention, presidential candidate John McCain embraced retraining programs and wage insurance as part of a comprehensive strategy for economic adjustment to trade-related job loss. In short, there seems to be little reason to dismiss the role of compensating losers when it comes to the politics of economic openness in the U.S. and other liberal market economies.[16]

Globalization optimists and other proponents of the "divergent paths" argument correctly point out that the liberal and coordinated (or corporatist) economies have responded differently to globalization. The problem is that there is almost no evidence that confirms the underlying assumptions about public attitudes in the liberal market economies. This suggests that it may be problematic to infer social preferences from observed policy choices. At the same time, the pessimists have largely ignored domestic institutions and therefore failed to show why the liberal market economies are uniquely vulnerable to globalization pressures or why the growing discontentment with economic openness might have future policy implications. This book addresses these important yet relatively neglected issues.

To sum, surprisingly little progress has been made in reconciling the views of globalization pessimists and optimists. The divide remains wide. Most importantly, for my purposes, they give two different explanations for why the liberal market economies are heading down a policy path that combines greater economic openness and smaller social safety nets. The "divergent paths" viewpoint is that the liberal market economies have freely chosen their course, which implies it is a politically sustainable trajectory (see figure 1.1). Others see this trend as evidence of a "globalization dilemma." Governments must provide social protection in order to maintain public support for economic openness, but the policy constraints that come with increased international capital mobility are pushing these countries off a stable equilibrium path (see figure 1.2). To restore political equilibrium, governments must

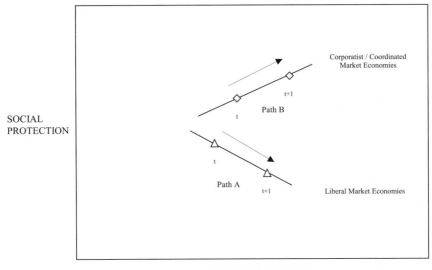

SOCIAL
PROTECTION

Corporatist / Coordinated
Market Economies

t+1

Path B

t

t

Path A

t+1

Liberal Market Economies

ECONOMIC OPENNESS

Figure 1.1 Divergent Paths Thesis

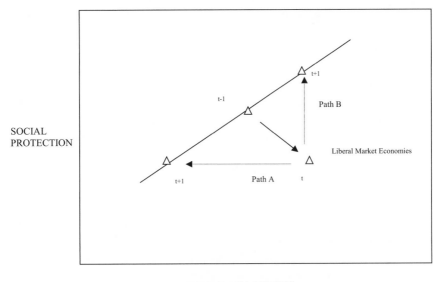

SOCIAL
PROTECTION

t-1

t+1

Path B

Liberal Market Economies

t+1

Path A

t

ECONOMIC OPENNESS

Figure 1.2 The Globalization Dilemma

either reduce levels of exposure to the international economy (Path A) or find new ways to provide effective social protection (Path B).

It is worth noting that there is a group of scholars who argue that the internationalization of markets has little, if any, effect on domestic politics and policymaking (e.g., Iversen and Wren 1998; Iversen and Cusack 2000; Pierson 2001). I refer to this group as the globalization *skeptics*. If pessimists believe that globalization creates both pressures and constraints on governments, and optimists accept the former but not the latter (countries must adjust to globalization pressures but they are not constrained to a single neoliberal response), skeptics argue that globalization produces neither. Iversen and Cusack, for example, contend that globalization pressures are unrelated to overtime and cross-national patterns in government spending. This position differs from arguments like Garrett's and other "divergent path" proponents who believe, not that globalization is causally irrelevant when it comes to variables like government spending, but rather, that globalization's effects are filtered through domestic political structures and institutions. I address the skeptics' case throughout the book.

In what remains of this introductory chapter, I briefly outline my theoretical argument for why the majoritarian democracies with liberal market economies are vulnerable to a political backlash against globalization and discuss the empirical evidence that supports this argument. Some would say my concerns about a globalization backlash are overly dire because (1) there are positive trends in the international economy that make openness less risky for workers than in the past, (2) globalization is largely irreversible, and (3) globalization's losers can be effectively compensated. I conclude the chapter by addressing each of these issues.

THE ARGUMENT

My argument does not fit neatly into any of the categories described above. I agree with the optimists (and disagree with many pessimists) that globalization does not lead to neoliberal convergence. I do not believe, at any time in the near future, the economies of Austria and Sweden will resemble that of the United States. Nor do I believe that these countries are vulnerable to a globalization backlash that could have adverse consequences for the international economy. Thus, I accept the divergent paths thesis as an accurate description of what we are observing empirically. Nevertheless, I argue that globalization creates new political pressures on governments in countries where trade is directly linked to levels of unemployment and associated with more labor market risk, and I argue that globalization constrains governments that are dependent on capital taxation. For these reasons, I contend that the political and economic conditions are ripe for a backlash against glo-balization in a particular subset of the developed democracies: the majoritar-ian democracies with liberal market economies. These countries are the ones that face Rodrik's globalization dilemma. Therefore, I share a concern held by some pessimists. I do not believe that the policy trajectory of these coun-tries is politically sustainable over the long term. I am particularly troubled because this subset includes some of the most important countries when it comes to governing the international economy (e.g., Canada, Britain, and the United States). If the leaders of any of these countries abandon their commit-ment to maintaining openness in the international economy, it would have grave consequences. My argument, which has three parts, begins with the connection between Ruggie's notion of embedded liberalism and Rodrik's globalization dilemma.

Globalization and the Crisis of Embedded Liberalism (Part I)

Building on the classic work of Polanyi (1944), John Ruggie (1982) introduced the concept of embedded liberalism into the political science mainstream with his seminal article on hegemony and international economic orders.[17] According to Ruggie, the international community learned two important lessons from the collapse of the gold standard and interwar global economy. First, the international economy would break down if states pursued unilat-eral, beggar-thy-neighbor trade policies. As a result, postwar governments around the Organisation for Economic Co-operation and Development (OECD), by and large, have committed themselves to pursuing free trade through multilateralism. Second, governments could not ignore the internal costs of adjusting to external economic shocks. Because trade causes eco-nomic dislocations and exposes workers to greater risk, it generates political opposition that democratically elected leaders ignore at their peril. Thus, one important implication of the commitment to free trade is that political lead-ers have had to be aware of and actively manage public support for economic openness. To do this, governments have exchanged welfare state policies that cushion their citizens from the vagaries of the international economy in return for public support for openness.

Embedded liberalism is the domestic social compact on which the post-World War II international economy was built. It recognized the importance of maintaining a liberal international economic order based on free trade and multilateral cooperation, but this commitment to liberalism was embed-ded within a more important obligation of governments to protect domes-tic social welfare. According to this story of postwar reconstruction, a link between trade and welfare state spending was established soon after World War II ended.

Ruggie's argument recognizes there is both a *demand* and *supply side* associated with the politics of international economic openness.[18] Workers exposed to fierce international competition *demand* protection. Governments, in turn, *supply* protection, which can come in a number of different forms—for example, tariffs, insurance, and adjustment assistance, to name a few of the most important kinds. Governments committed to economic openness prefer, if possible, to supply policies like insurance and adjustment assistance (rather than tariffs) in return for public support for trade. In chapter 2, I argue that the underlying factors that gave rise to the bargain of embedded liberalism are still in place, even in the liberal market economies: governments remain committed to free trade; workers in sectors of the economy exposed to foreign competition are still the strongest opponents; insurance and compensation programs remain the most effective means for governments to increase support for trade among those who are inclined to oppose it.

Starting with Ruggie's ideas, Rodrik (1997) identifies a significant globalization dilemma. He argues that growing international economic integration increases the *demand* on governments for protection at the same time it undermines their ability to *supply* policies that require significant government spending.[19] More workers are exposed to international competition through trade, and increased international capital mobility makes it difficult for governments to finance spending. This dilemma makes countries politically vulnerable to a backlash against globalization. The unfortunate possibility is that constrained governments will abandon their commitment to economic openness by adopting restrictions on international trade and capital flows. In this way, Rodrik's globalization dilemma can be viewed as a crisis of embedded liberalism (Keohane 1984; Garrett 1998b).

I argue that, because of important cross-national differences in domestic political and economic institutions, Rodrik's globalization dilemma is not equally severe for all countries. First, the degree to which globalization increases demands for protection depends on how, and the extent to which, shocks in international commercial markets are transmitted to domestic labor markets. This depends greatly on a country's labor market institutions. The strength of the political demand for protection also depends on how exposed the aggregate (national) labor market is to trade and the size of the shocks in international commercial markets. I argue that, *ceteris paribus*, trade generates more uncertainty and insecurity for workers who operate in competitive labor markets, and this leads them to pressure their governments for protection. Second, the constraints arising from international capital mobility primarily affect countries dependent on capital taxes to finance government spending. This dependence is a function of how majoritarian a country's polity is. Majoritarian democracies rely more heavily on capital taxes to finance public spending. Therefore, Rodrik's globalization dilemma applies most forcefully to countries that combine competitive labor markets with majoritarian political institutions, a combination found in the Anglo-American democracies.

Competitive Labor Markets and the Demand for Protection (Part II)

I argue in chapter 3 that governments in countries with relatively competitive labor markets will face stronger demands for protection from international competition.[20] The logic is mainly conventional and twofold. First, as Hall and Soskice (2001) have argued, firms in countries with liberal market economies are quick to hire and fire in response to changing prices. Therefore, in these countries, trade-related shocks to the economy (e.g., shocks to foreign demand or the competitiveness of foreign firms) are passed to workers in terms of employment levels. This is not true in the corporatist economies where the labor market institutions were designed in part to sustain full employment despite volatile conditions in the international economy. One of the strategies used in the corporatist economies to achieve this end is real wage moderation (Lange 1984; Garrett 1998a, 32). Given their dependence on trade, it is critical to keep wages low in order to maintain international competitiveness. In fact, Katzenstein has argued that terms-of-trade and balance-of-payments problems—or, more generally, the deterioration of a country's trade performance—are the key signals to labor unions that it is time to hold wages down.[21]

Second, trade increases the elasticity of the demand for labor in competitive market economies, exposing workers to greater risk (Rodrik 1997).[22] To the extent that it facilitates the multinationalization of production, either through outsourcing or foreign direct investment, trade flattens the labor demand curve by making it easier for firms to substitute foreign labor for domestic.[23] Exogenous shocks (domestic or international in origin) to a flat labor demand curve lead to greater changes in equilibrium levels of employment than shocks to a steep labor demand curve do.[24] Therefore, in countries with competitive labor markets, increased trade should be associated with more stochastic volatility in employment—that is, random, unpredictable changes in employment from year to year. Again, we would not expect this to be the case in corporatist economies where the labor market institutions were designed to stabilize employment and insulate workers from the risks associated with economic openness. However, the relative certainty under corporatism comes at a cost: there is less labor mobility across sectors of the economy, which can lead to long-term unemployment for a small group of workers. I argue that this is a trade-off many workers, particularly the politically powerful labor "insiders" who face very little if any risk of unemployment in corporatist systems, are willing to make. Even in a growing economy with opportunities for reemployment at high wages, losing one's job generates more risk and insecurity than real wage cuts. Thus, workers in non-corporatist economies are more likely to suffer trade-induced anxieties than their counterparts employed in corporatist systems.

Majoritarian Democracy and the Supply of Protection (Part III)

In chapter 4, I argue that countries with majoritarian political institutions face the strongest revenue constraints as a result of globalization because they are more dependent on capital taxes than countries with consensual polities. This makes it difficult for them to respond with increased spending to new globalization pressures without experiencing significant deterioration in their budget balances. To understand my argument, it is helpful to think about the tax policy preferences of the median voter (most likely a wage earner) and the influence of the median voter in different political contexts. The policy preferences of the median voter are important in majoritarian democracies because these policies will have majority support among the electorate. With respect to capital taxation, the median voter will prefer revenue-maximizing rates, and therefore, in majoritarian democracies, the capital tax rate will be set close to this level. In consensus democracies, where the polity is more inclusive in its representation of political minorities, the preferences of individuals with significant capital income are more likely to be incorporated into tax policy, and, importantly, parties that represent wage earners are able to make credible commitments to tax rates below their revenue-maximizing levels. To the extent that globalization reduces the cost of international capital mobility, it will shift the revenue-maximizing tax rate downward, and this will pressure governments in majoritarian countries to lower their capital taxes. It they do not lower tax rates, capital will flow out of the country, the tax base will shrink, and the revenue losses will be even greater.

THE EVIDENCE

In chapter 2, I provide micro-level evidence that connects exposure to trade, government spending, and individual support for tariff protection. The data set I use comes from two International Social Survey Programme (ISSP) surveys on national identity conducted in 1995 and 2003. It includes respondents from Australia, Austria, Canada, Germany, New Zealand, Norway, Spain, Sweden, the United Kingdom, and the United States. The results are consistent with the embedded liberalism thesis. The strongest opposition to trade comes from individuals employed in sectors of the economy that have the highest levels of imports. Yet, the results demonstrate that politicians can, in fact, build support for trade, even among these sectors. Politically feasible policy reforms can offset declines caused by increased exposure to international competition. Interestingly, I find that raising net replacement rates for unemployment insurance increases support for trade among those employed in tradable sectors of the economy while spending on active labor market programs does not.

At the macro-level, I show that aggregate exposure to import competition correlates strongly with levels of government spending across the OECD. As imports rise, so do levels of government spending, and the magnitude of this effect depends on the percentage of workers employed in tradable industries and, to a lesser extent, the average duration of unemployment spells. The macro-panel data set analyzed in chapter 2 (and later chapters) includes twenty OECD countries: Australia, Austria, Belgium, Canada, Denmark, Finland, France, Germany, Ireland, Italy, Japan, the Netherlands, New Zealand, Norway, Portugal, Spain, Sweden, Switzerland, the United Kingdom, and the United States. The sample period is 1960–2000. Taken together, the micro and macro findings suggest that the bargain of embedded liberalism is an important part of the contemporary politics of international economic openness, even in countries with strong right-wing parties and liberal market economies like the United States.

The empirical analyses in chapters 3 and 4 also utilize the macro-panel dataset. In chapter 3, I examine the relationship between wage and trade-related shocks, levels of trade openness, and employment. The results are more or less consistent with the conventional wisdom from comparative political economy. First, there is more evidence that shocks, in non-corporatist countries, are passed to workers in terms of employment levels; second, trade openness increases the elasticity of the demand for labor in the liberal market economies; and finally, trade generates more employment volatility in countries with competitive labor markets than it does in the corporatist economies.

The empirical evidence presented in chapter 4 shows that the tax policies of majoritarian democracies, richly endowed ones in particular, are most constrained by increasing levels of international capital mobility. These countries are the most dependent on capital taxes, and they have seen the largest declines in tax rates. A comparison of tax reform in Britain and the Netherlands beginning in the 1980s largely supports the theoretical argument. Britain, a majoritarian democracy, was at (or possibly above) its revenue-maximizing capital tax rate at the beginning of the 1980s. European economic integration, which made these tax rates very costly in terms of revenue generation, was a major impetus for reform. The British government could either lower its capital tax rate or see the tax base shrink to the point at which the capital taxes would generate very little revenue anyway. The Netherlands, a consensus democracy, also reformed its tax system, but the Dutch if anything increased their average effective capital tax rate. The Dutch tax system was less dependent on capital taxes than the British system for revenue generation, and therefore European economic integration did not present the same set of challenges for the Netherlands. In chapter 5, I examine the empirical consequences of the demand and supply sides of my argument jointly. The econometric evidence suggests that countries that have relied heavily on capital taxes to finance spending face substantial budgetary pressures when they experience an increase in employment volatility.

IS THERE A SILVER LINING?

There are at least three reasons that my concerns about a political backlash against globalization may be too pessimistic. First, because of structural changes in the economies of the developed democracies, primarily deindustrialization, workers are becoming less exposed to foreign competition and externally generated risk despite rising trade flows. A similar argument is that there is more price stability in international markets today than in previous decades. Second, it could be that globalization is more or less irreversible. The most sophisticated and persuasive version of this argument is that a coherent ideological alternative to globalism is a necessary and currently missing condition for globalization to be reversed, particularly in the liberal market economies. Finally, it is possible that a new bargain of embedded liberalism can be established, one that will allow governments in the Anglo-American democracies to rebuild popular support for economic openness.

I address these arguments in turn below. I am doubtful that the first two conditions make the probability of a political backlash significantly less likely, but I am hopeful that a new social compact with this effect can be established.

Economic Trends

Figures 1.3 and 1.4 plot the average (cross-national) values of four key economic variables throughout the post–Bretton Woods period. The first two in figure 1.3 are the average percentage of workers employed in "tradable" sectors of the economy (i.e., manufacturing and agriculture) and the terms of trade volatility. The terms of trade measure is the average five-year moving standard deviation for the log difference in the ratio of export to import prices. The variables plotted in figure 1.4 are the percentage of possible capital account transactions that are unrestricted and the value of imports

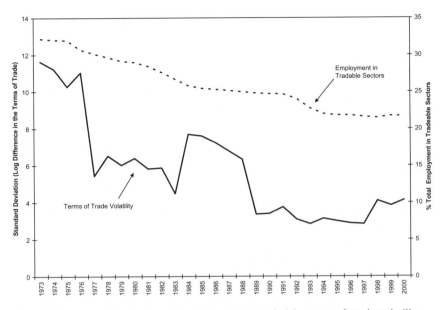

Figure 1.3 Average Exposure and Sensitivity to External Risk: Terms of Trade Volatility and Employment in Tradable Sectors (20 OECD Countries, Post–Bretton Woods)

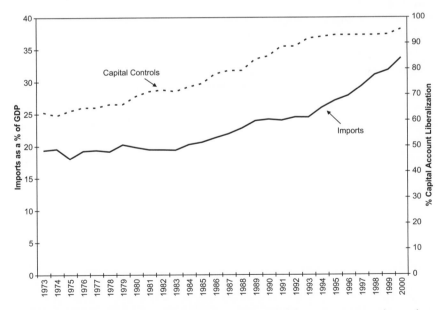

Figure 1.4 Average Exposure and Sensitivity to External Risk: Import Penetration and Capital Controls (20 OECD Countries, Post–Bretton Woods)

expressed as a percentage of GDP. From the graphs, it is clear that (on average) imports are rising; capital account restrictions are on the decline; fewer workers are employed in tradable sectors of the economy (deindustrialization); and terms-of-trade volatility is dropping. These trends are interesting because two of the changes—increased imports on the one hand and fewer capital account restrictions on the other—are making countries more susceptible to externally generated labor market risk, while the other two changes—declining terms of trade volatility and deindustrialization—are making countries less vulnerable.

Deindustrialization and the concomitant rise of the service economy represent one of the biggest changes underway in the OECD economies (Rowthorn and Ramaswamy 1999; Alderson 1999; Iversen and Wren 1998; Iversen and Cusack 2000; Alderson and Nielsen 2002). To the extent that services remain non-traded, this implies fewer workers exposed to trade competition and therefore lower levels of political opposition to free trade policies. This proposition receives substantial support from the empirical analysis in chapter 2, but there is an important caveat. Those employed in services sectors of the economy will become increasingly exposed to international competition over time.

Regarding the U.S. economy, trade in services is growing rapidly and the balance between exports and imports is shrinking (relative to the value of these flows). According to data from the Bureau of Economic Analysis, exports of private services were worth $197 billion and imports $130 billion in 1995. By 2005, these numbers were $360 billion and $281 billion, respectively. The recent American backlash against Indian phone centers is indicative of the increasingly competitive and global nature of service industries. Using measures of geographic industrial concentration, Jensen and Kletzer (2005) estimate that 13.7% of total U.S. employment is in *tradable service industries* and therefore, at least potentially, subject to international competition. In comparison, only 12.4% of total U.S. employment is in tradable manufacturing industries.

As for international prices, there is no reason to expect continued terms-of-trade stability. In fact, the oil price spike that occurred shortly after the U.S. invasion of Iraq sent a major terms-of-trade shock to most of the world's economies. International price stability may be a bygone feature of the global economy already.

Globalization Is Irreversible

Not everyone believes that globalization is reversible. Some contend that the degree of interdependence and its benefits are so great that reversal is unimaginable. Others argue that globalization is not simply the result of policy choices made by states, but is also driven by exogenous forces like technological and organizational change that are difficult for governments to shape (Skolnikoff 1993; Winner 1977). In this sense, the international economy is beyond the control of states and acts as a structural constraint upon them (Andrews 1994; Cerny 1995). Some would go so far as to argue that the nation-state has become obsolete (Wriston 1992; Ohmae 1995). Much of the comparative politics literature on globalization also treats international economic integration as an exogenous force that acts upon domestic politics (Kitschelt et al. 1999; Garrett 1998a).

While it may be useful to assume that globalization is exogenous for analytical purposes, the historical record strongly contradicts the view that globalization is truly irreversible and exogenous. Though we sometimes forget, globalization has been stopped and reversed before, and many of the same arguments that are being made today about technology and interdependence also were made in the years prior to World War I (Angell 1914). In fact, the scholars who are most concerned about the future of the international economy seem to be ones who study globalization from a historical perspective.[25] For these scholars, the analogy of the early twentieth century and interwar periods has much to tell us about contemporary political responses to globalization.

For example, Kevin O'Rourke and Jeffrey Williamson (1999, 287) contend that distributional consequences of globalization during the late nineteenth and early twentieth centuries fueled the political backlash that ultimately destroyed the global economy; they argue that "globalization, at least in part, destroyed itself" and that "the globalization experience of the Atlantic economy prior to the Great War speaks directly and eloquently to globalization debates today." Jeffry Frieden (2006, xvi) writes "As was the case a hundred years ago, many people now take an integrated world economy for granted, regard it as the natural state of things, and expect that it will last forever. Yet the bases on which global capitalism rests today are not very different from what they were in 1900, and the potential for their disruption is as present today as then." A similar theme is echoed in the Bordo et al. (2003) conference volume, *Globalization in Historical Perspective*. In the book's introduction, the editors advise, "if we fear that the violent political reaction to globalization seen recently in Seattle, Ottawa, Gothenberg, and Genoa might cause a political retreat from liberal policy, then it would pay to look carefully at the twenty years or so before World War I." Globalization's losers—landowners in Europe and workers in the New World—became the political opponents of economic openness later on. Today, low- to medium-skilled workers in the OECD have the most to lose from globalization. The fear is that globalization will produce labor market uncertainty and a feeling of economic insecurity, which, in turn, will generate support for protectionism. If this happens on a widespread basis, the possibility of a protectionist backlash becomes more likely (Kapstein 1996, 1999).

Harold James (2001) has a slightly more sophisticated understanding of the political backlash against globalization that occurred during the 1930s, one that includes but goes beyond economic self-interest. In *The End of Globalization,* James argues that a number of additional factors contributed to the de-globalization period of the interwar years. Importantly, the initial idealism of the 1920s about the efficacy of managing globalization problems through international institutions led to unreasonable expectations about their effectiveness. When these institutions failed to live up to expectations, they became targets of widespread resentment. This fostered the development of nationalist ideologies such as the Soviet brand of Communism and the Fascism of Germany and Italy, which provided coherent alternatives to the liberal internationalism of the day.

According to James, the interwar backlash against globalization was more than a response to global economic integration; it was a backlash against internationalism broadly defined. From his perspective, the economists may be correct about the economic parallels between the current and earlier period of globalization, but the political and social preconditions for a backlash are missing today. Interestingly, the "divergent paths" proponents make a similar argument about politics in the liberal market economies. Because of the relative strength of right-wing parties in these countries, and the social preferences revealed by this fact, these scholars see dramatic trade policy reversals as unlikely. There are no alternatives to the free trade policies of the status quo available to voters, and even if there were, no one would vote for candidates or parties that espoused them.

In some ways, these arguments are reassuring. There does not seem to be a common nationalist agenda that unites today's "opponents" of globalization. Clearly, the leaders of the anti-neoliberal globalization movement do not espouse nationalism (Elliott et al. 2004). But James's argument begs the question of causation. Did nationalism make it possible for governments to justify and adopt the beggar-thy-neighbor policies that ultimately led to the "end of globalization"? Or, did the failing international economy fuel the flames of nationalism? Sheri Berman (2006) argues that the latter is true in her explanation for the rise of Fascism and National Socialism. The Depression played an important role in discrediting liberal institutions and policies, and this created the necessary ideological space for radical nationalism to emerge. Moreover, the argument that there are no coherent nationalistic ideological alternatives to liberalism today, like fascism and communism were in the 1930s, is a straw man. Political change on a much smaller scale could produce a retreat from policies of economic openness.

Those who argue that globalization is irreversible because there are currently no alternatives to the policies of economic openness—at least not ones supported by major parties—underestimate the potential for political change.

As I argued earlier in this chapter, we already see the emergence of a back-lash against globalization that is beginning to influence foreign economic policy, particularly in the majoritarian democracies. In these cases, "critical realignments" are one possible mechanism of policy change. Nardulli (1995, 11) defines this concept, which comes out of the research on American politics, as an "abrupt, large, and enduring form of change in prevailing electoral patterns, one that is initiated by a critical election and results in a signifi-cantly different partisan balance in the electorate." These realignments over-come institutional checks and balances designed to stabilize policy in normal times.[26] Other scholars of American politics, particularly those who study macropartisanship, argue that change is more continuous than abrupt (Erikson et al. 2002). For my purposes, it matters little which of these models is the appropriate one. Most likely, both kinds of political change occur in majoritarian democracies. What does matter is that economic factors seem to drive both abrupt and continuous changes in the partisan balance of power by converting existing voters and mobilizing new ones.[27]

Careful studies of the New Deal realignment in the United States show convincingly that these are the kind of micro-level changes that brought Roosevelt to power. Brown (1988), for example, argues that both partisan conversion and participation by new voters explain the New Deal realign-ment. It started with conversion in the 1932 election. A large number of Republican voters in 1928 switched their votes in 1932 because, according to most accounts, the public became dissatisfied with the way the Hoover administration was handling the economy. The Democrats' hold on the pres-idency was cemented by an infusion of new "working class" voters in 1936. Interestingly, Brown argues that voters abandoned the Republican Party in 1932 not because the Democrats offered a coherent set of policy alternatives to end the Depression—this came later—but rather because the electorate was frustrated with ineffective Republican "solutions."

It is well beyond the scope of this book to present a complete model of political change in majoritarian democracies. My point is to challenge and make explicit what is frequently implicit in the varieties of capitalism lit-erature: that the underlying societal preferences driving policy divergence among the developed democracies are fixed. If this were true, the current policy trajectory of the liberal market economies would be stable, and glo-balization would be, for all intents and purposes, irreversible. In this book I show that, in majoritarian democracies with liberal market economies, glo-balization is generating the kind of conditions that historically have led to significant political change by making existing voters frustrated with status quo policies and by mobilizing new voters. We should not dismiss the poten-tial for a backlash against globalization because we discount the possibility of significant political change.

A New Bargain of Embedded Liberalism

The strongest safeguard for the international economy is a renewed commitment by politicians to policies of economic openness. This will require an updated version of the bargain of embedded liberalism, one that, at minimal cost, effectively protects workers in the liberal market economies from the new risks they face.

A number of policy recommendations have been made along these lines. Unfortunately, very little attention has been paid to the political sustainability of these recommendations. For example, one possible strategy for governments in the liberal market countries is labor market reform. These countries could "import" corporatism (Garrett 1998a, 155–157). This has been tried in two majoritarian democracies—Britain during the 1970s and Australia during the 1980s—and in both cases the experiment failed.[28] Simply put, these reforms are not robust to partisan changes in government. Unless these reforms follow a major realignment of New Deal proportions, they are unlikely to provide a solid foundation upon which a new bargain of embedded liberalism can be built.[29]

Another strategy that is frequently discussed and debated is the use of policies to improve the supply side of the labor market. If they work, active labor market programs keep unemployment low and generate income growth, which makes them cost effective. This strategy is the hallmark of third way social democracy. Tony Blair's and now Gordon Brown's Labour government in Britain is the test case, and the jury is still out. It is not yet clear whether this approach will spread elsewhere. If there is a downside to this strategy, at least for left-leaning governments, it may be in its political consequences over the medium to long term. What made Margaret Thatcher's economic reforms politically successful is that they helped cement the electoral dominance of the Tories. Privatization created a new set of property owners in Britain, and these individuals were more likely to vote Conservative in the next election (Garrett 1993, Boix 1998). Keynesian policies of demand management played a similar role for the Left throughout the OECD (Przeworksi 1985, chapter 5). Labour's new "supply side agenda" may be less effective in this respect and therefore less attractive to leftist governments. If one takes the literature on the economics of voting seriously, active labor market policies that generate human capital may actually undermine electoral support for leftist parties.

Moreover, active labor market policies benefit labor "outsiders" in ways that may undermine political support of "insiders," which some argue are the core constituency of leftist parties (Rueda 2005).[30] Also, the political reaction of firms, which matters greatly for the viability of active labor market policies, is highly contingent on the design of these programs (Mares 2003). Along these lines, recent work by Iversen and Soskice (2001) on the relationship between workers' skill sets and attitudes toward social policy suggests that the design of active labor market policies is critical in determining their effect on support for government spending and interventionist policies. Programs that increase workers' skill specificity are likely to increase support for government spending on things like unemployment insurance, health care, and pensions, while those that provide general skills are likely to undermine support for government spending.[31] This is because workers with sector-specific skills are much more likely than those with general skills to experience long spells of unemployment. Workers with general skills have more opportunities for reemployment since they can search for jobs across a large number of sectors.

Retraining programs that provide workers with general skills could also change the underlying nature of trade politics in a way that has unintended consequences for foreign economic policy making. Research in political science and economics on trade policy politics has identified the degree of intersectoral factor mobility as the key variable that determines the political cleavages over trade. If capital and labor are mobile across sectors of the economy, the political fault lines will divide classes, and, in the OECD countries, workers, particularly low-skilled workers, will be hurt the most by free trade. If capital and labor are immobile, the political cleavages will divide sectors of the economy. Those tied to export-oriented sectors will support free trade and those connected to import-competing sectors will oppose it. If they provided general skills to workers, retraining programs would increase the degree of intersectoral mobility, making it more likely that the major trade cleavages among producers would fall along class instead of sector lines (Hiscox 2001; Hiscox 2002). This could move trade policy from the realm of pressure politics to partisan politics (Verdier 1994), which, in turn, would make it more difficult for chief executive officers, particularly ones from leftist parties, to pursue free trade policies. Countries like the United States—where trade policy politics remains, to a significant degree, sector based—have delegated authority over trade policy to the executive branch of government as a way to depoliticize trade. Because they represent large diverse constituencies, chief executives are rarely dependent politically on one or two industries in the way that individual legislators frequently are. This strategy becomes much less effective when the degree of intersectoral mobility is high and trade becomes an issue around which the major (class-based) parties contest elections. My own individual-level empirical analysis in chapter 2 suggests that spending on active labor market programs may not increase support for free trade policies among those employed in tradable sectors of the economy.

Finally, countries with competitive labor markets could simply redesign (and boost) their unemployment insurance programs. The problem with unemployment insurance is that these programs create incentives for people to stay out of work and this makes them too costly. Therefore, these programs would need to be designed to minimize their labor market distortions (e.g., Shavell and Weiss 1979; Hopenhayn and Nicolini 1997; Acemoglu and Shimer 1999; Kletzer and Litan 2001). To a very limited extent, the United States has started down this path with the expansion of trade adjustment assistance and the new wage insurance experiment for older workers that accompanied the latest trade promotion authority bill. This is a positive development, and maintaining support for globalization will require further increases in government programs aimed at those who will be directly affected by greater competition. In order for these programs to be politically sustainable, however, they must be designed to minimize the forms of moral hazard that unemployment insurance can generate.

During the early postwar period, Keynesian policies of demand management were crucial to the bargain of embedded liberalism in the liberal market economies. Today, there is not yet a clear alternative to these policies. Labor market reform, retraining, and insurance all have political and economic costs that make them potentially problematic. Thus, the design of these programs is critical to their long-term success. I return to this topic—the possibility of a new bargain of embedded liberalism—in chapter 5.

SUMMARY

One of the most important debates in the globalization literature concerns the likelihood of a political backlash against policies of economic openness. Globalization optimists dismiss the possibility of a backlash because they believe the constraints that come with openness are exaggerated. They argue that countries that combine policies of economic openness with welfare state retrenchment—that is, the liberal market economies—have freely chosen this path and that the political forces giving rise to these policies are stable. Globalization pessimists disagree, but these scholars have failed to make a case for why globalization presents the liberal market economies with a unique set of political challenges.

I argue that the combination of competitive labor markets and majoritarian political institutions increases the vulnerability of countries like the United States, the United Kingdom, Canada, and Australia (the Anglo-American democracies) to globalization pressures and constraints that could lead them to abandon their policies of economic openness. The theoretical elaboration and empirical evaluation of this argument make up the core of this book (chapters 2–4). In chapter 5, I argue that the best guarantee against a return to autarky is a new bargain of embedded liberalism, one based on carefully crafted compensatory programs. I conclude in chapter 6.

2

Government Spending and Public Support
for Trade in the OECD

Governments learned from the collapse of the interwar global economy that they could not ignore the domestic costs of adjustment to external shocks. Trade causes economic dislocation, exposes workers to greater risk, and, therefore, generates political opposition to which democratically elected leaders must respond. In order to pursue free trade policies, politicians have had to monitor and manage public support for economic openness. To accomplish the latter, governments have provided welfare state policies that protect their citizens from the vagaries of the international economy. John Ruggie calls this exchange the bargain of *embedded liberalism*.[1]

According to Ruggie's story of postwar reconstruction, a link between trade and welfare state spending was established soon after World War II ended. Of course, the specific form this bargain takes is both geographically and historically contingent. The Keynesianism that emerged in the United States, for example, differed from the social democratic corporatism that developed in Sweden and Austria, and the demand management policies of the Bretton Woods era have given way to the active (supply-side) labor market policies of the so-called Third Way. But the idea that there is a more or less universal expectation held by citizens in the developed democracies that their governments will limit the costs and distribute the benefits of open markets through some kind of government intervention and spending, and that public support for liberalism depends on the willingness and ability of governments to do this successfully, is the core of the embedded liberalism thesis. This is what distinguishes the embedded liberalism of the postwar period from the ideology of pure laissez-faire that guided economic policy under the gold standard.[2]

Recently, the argument that trade and government spending go hand in hand because governments in the developed democracies have to compensate market losers has come under attack. Several studies claim that the observed country-level (macro-level) relationship between trade and spending is weak at best and largely attributable to omitted variable bias. In other words, the critics claim, the relationship is spurious not causal. I take a fresh look at this old controversy by using individual-level (micro-level) survey data to test the critical assumption underlying the embedded liberalism thesis: government-provided compensatory and protective programs increase support for free trade among those individuals who would oppose it otherwise.

The chapter is organized as follows. In the first section, I briefly review and critique the literature on trade and government spending. In the second, I examine the empirical determinants of individual support for protectionism. My results show that lesser educated individuals, unemployed individuals, and individuals employed in tradable industries, particularly import competing industries, are the strongest opponents of free trade, but unemployment insurance and, to a lesser extent, other government programs can moderate their opposition. There is some evidence that active labor market spending is counterproductive in the sense that these programs lower support for free trade among workers in tradable sectors of the economy. Based on these findings, I argue that the macro-level relationship between trade and government spending is a conditional one. More specifically, I argue that (1) politicians respond more strongly to surges in imports and less so to expanding trade if it is balanced or generating trade surpluses, and (2) the extent to which politicians respond to rising imports will be a function of how many workers are employed in tradable industries and the overall level of unemployment. I test these two macro-level hypotheses in the third section of the chapter as a way to check the significance of my micro-level results for the trade and welfare state debate. I conclude in the fourth section.

TRADE AND GOVERNMENT SPENDING IN THE
DEVELOPED DEMOCRACIES

It is well-known that countries with open economies have bigger governments.[3] It is also true that OECD countries have increased both their levels of trade and government spending for most of the post–World War II period. However, the debate remains unresolved as to whether these strong cross-national and over-time correlations reflect a ubiquitous causal relationship between trade and government spending, a politically conditioned relationship that exists in a small subset of OECD countries, or a completely spurious one. In addition to Ruggie, those who have argued recently that government policies, by neutralizing the negative effects of trade, can deliver pro-trade majorities are Rodrik; Adserà and Boix; Swank; and Mares.[4]

These scholars argue that there is a short-term causal, though conditional, relationship between trade and government spending throughout the OECD.[5] For example, Rodrik argues that exposure to external risk explains the empirical relationship between trade and government spending. According to this line of reasoning, the impact of trade openness on spending depends on the level of terms-of-trade volatility that a country experiences. Adserà and Boix argue that the political logic of embedded liberalism applies only to democracies and therefore the empirical effects of trade openness on government spending should be observed only in countries with democratic institutions. Mares argues that trade's losers will only demand protection and compensation from governments that can efficiently provide these goods. The effect of openness on government spending is, therefore, conditional on state capacity. For my purposes, the important connection between these arguments is that they all imply that the politics of embedded liberalism will be present, under the right economic conditions, in all of the high-capacity, democratic states of the OECD.

This position that there is a causal relationship between trade and the size of government across the OECD has been challenged in two ways. First, Garrett and Mitchell argue that the relationship between trade and welfare state effort is long-term and historically contingent.[6] For the small economies of Western Europe, trade dependence facilitated unionization, which, in turn, created strong social democratic parties that built large welfare states when they came to power. These historical forces molded a new type of political economy, what Garrett has called social democratic corporatism. Garrett and Mitchell distinguish this argument, which is in the varieties of capitalism tradition, from Ruggie's:

> With respect to trade, for example, Cameron (1978) and Katzenstein (1985) both argue that there is a historical relationship between trade and welfare state effort.... This is a very different argument from another perspective with which it is often conflated—Ruggie's (1983) notion of embedded liberalism. For Ruggie, the American welfare state expanded immediately after World War II because the government chose to liberalize trade, and realized they had to compensate market losers directly for the dislocations liberalization generated.[7]

Garrett and Mitchell contend that when country and year dummies (fixed unit and period effects) are added to regression models, the analyst can distinguish between the long-term historical argument of Cameron and Katzenstein on the one hand and Ruggie's notion of embedded liberalism on the other. They do this and show that the positive relationship between trade openness and government spending disappears.[8] To the extent that these short-term effects do exist, they are found in the social democratic corporatist economies (Garrett 1998a).[9]

The strongest challenge to the embedded liberalism thesis, however, has come from globalization skeptics who believe the pressures and constraints attributed to international economic integration have been grossly exaggerated. Iversen and Cusack, for example, argue that the post–World War II growth of the welfare state is a product of deindustrialization, not expanding trade.[10] They posit that workers who move from manufacturing and agriculture to services cross significant skill boundaries that make the transition difficult and uncertain. These problems, in turn, create new demands for government spending. Iversen and Cusack show that the relationship between trade and spending is either statistically or substantively insignificant after controlling for deindustrialization. Moreover, they claim that deindustrialization and globalization are largely independent processes.

Garrett and Mitchell and Iversen and Cusack raise serious questions about the validity of the embedded liberalism thesis. Thus, the causal mechanisms identified by Ruggie and others deserve closer empirical scrutiny. Before turning to this task, however, I note four important criticisms of the research described in this section.

First, it fails to adequately distinguish between imports and exports. Most of the research uses trade openness—the summed value of exports and imports as a percentage of GDP—as the key independent variable.[11] This variable constrains the effects of imports and exports on government spending to have the same magnitude and sign. Yet theory tells us that increasing imports and exports should have different effects on government spending.[12] Rising imports create losers—displaced workers in import competing industries—that may have to be compensated; rising exports do not. Similarly, falling exports are harmful to domestic employment in a way that declining imports are not. Thus, there should be a positive relationship between rising imports and government spending and a negative relationship between exports and government spending.

Of course, this argument ignores Rodrik's point about exposure to external risk, but adding risk to the equation does not change the basic story. The size of the negative effect from rising exports on government spending will be reduced if production for foreign markets is risky—even workers in export-oriented industries will want to maintain some protective and compensatory programs—but the positive relationship between rising imports and government spending should be magnified by high terms-of-trade volatility. This implies that balanced increases in trade will increase government spending, but by less than under expanding trade deficits (holding exports constant).

Second, the research also fails to recognize that the impact of trade flows on government spending depends on the underlying structure of the economy, in particular how many workers are employed in vulnerable traded industries and the ease with which displaced workers can find new employment. Because democratically elected governments are sensitive to numbers of votes, *ceteris paribus*, their response will be conditioned by the scope of threatened industries. If imports displace a large number of workers/voters who are unable to find new jobs quickly, governments will have little choice but to provide compensation. If a small numbers of workers are displaced and they are able to find employment quickly, politicians will face less pressure to respond.[13]

Third, the empirical analyses in these studies ignore the spatial interdependence in the data. This is not only inefficient from an econometric standpoint, but it could lead to biased estimates of the impact of imports on government spending. For example, if it is true that governments have been constrained by international capital mobility, particularly during the post–Bretton Woods era, then countries will be affected by levels of government spending in their neighbors. If imports cluster spatially as well, ignoring the spatial interdependence in spending will bias estimation. For example, hypothetically, a surge in U.S. exports to Canada will have, in the short run, positive and negative consequences for labor market performance in the two countries, respectively. In Canada, this will lead to increased demands on the government to provide compensation, but, to the extent that the Canadian government is constrained by the possibility that financing this spending will lead to capital flight, it will not respond as strongly as it would under other conditions. This is precisely the dilemma that globalization poses for politicians, and yet the analyst who ignores this spatial interdependence may overlook the evidence completely.

My final and most important criticism is that very few studies have tested the micro-foundations of the embedded liberalism thesis. The key assumption is that government policies can build public support for trade. Macro-empirical studies that put spending on the left-hand side of regression models will always be vulnerable to claims of omitted variable bias. To build a convincing empirical case for the free trade / welfare state linkage, it is necessary to examine data at a lower level of aggregation. In this chapter, I provide a micro-level test of the embedded liberalism thesis using individual-level survey data. The results have important and testable implications for the relationship between aggregate trade and government spending. If government spending on unemployment insurance, active labor market and other protective and (or) compensatory programs successfully reduces the level of opposition to trade, there is micro-level evidence that the embedded liberalism compromise is a viable solution to the political problems faced by democratically elected leaders who commit their countries to international economic openness.

UNEMPLOYMENT BENEFITS, EMPLOYMENT PROTECTION, AND INDIVIDUAL ATTITUDES TOWARD TRADE

A flurry of research on the determinants of individual support for trade has been published in the last couple of years. Most of it, drawing on international trade theory, focuses on how one's skill level and the competitiveness of one's sector of employment determine support for protectionism. Examples include Scheve and Slaughter, O'Rourke and Sinnot, and Mayda and Rodrik, among others.[14] The main conclusion of this research is that groups adversely affected by international economic competition are less likely to support policies of free trade. If government spending is driven partly by the need to generate public support for economic openness, this micro-level research has significant implications for the macro debate over trade and government spending. Yet none of these studies examines the impact of government programs on support for trade. It is surprising that very few scholars have tried to bridge the micro-macro divide.[15]

Data and Methods

The data that I use for my individual-level (micro) analysis is from the International Social Survey Programme's (ISSP) 1995 and 2003 surveys on national identity. These data sets provide information about individuals' attitudes toward free trade. The countries in my sample are Australia, Germany, the United Kingdom, the United States, Austria, Norway, Sweden, Spain, New Zealand, and Canada.[16] The dependent variable (FREETRADE) is constructed from respondents' answers to the following question asked in the survey:

> How much do you agree or disagree with the following statement: (Respondent's Country) should limit the import of foreign products in order to protect its national economy.

> 1) Agree strongly
> 2) Agree
> 3) Neither agree nor disagree
> 4) Disagree
> 5) Disagree strongly

I assigned a value of 1 to respondents who answered "agree strongly," a 2 to those who answered "agree," and so on. Thus, high values of FREE-TRADE reflect pro-trade attitudes, whereas low values reflect support for protectionism.

The sample contains substantial cross-national and over-time variation in support for trade. This variance is highlighted in table 2.1 where the distributions of respondents giving each of the five responses to the trade question are reported by country and year. Looking at the percentages of respondents who either support or strongly support limiting imports to protect the national economy, the greatest opposition to free trade is found in Australia, Austria, the United States, the United Kingdom, New Zealand, and Canada. These six countries have majorities that think limiting imports is a good idea.

Table 2.1 Cross-National Support for Trade

	freetrade = 1 (Support Protection)	freetrade = 2	freetrade = 3 (Indifferent)	freetrade = 4	freetrade = 5 (Oppose Protection)	X² statistic
Australia						
1995 Observed%	34.8	43.0	10.9	10.0	1.3	99.7***
2003 Observed%	25.0	41.1	19.4	12.7	1.8	
Total Observed%	30.2	42.1	14.9	11.3	1.5	
Austria						
1995 Observed%	38.9	32.9	11.2	13.0	4.0	46.6***
2003 Observed%	29.9	28.9	17.7	14.7	8.8	
Total Observed%	34.5	30.9	14.4	13.8	6.4	
Canada						
1995 Observed%	14.8	33.3	22.7	22.9	6.3	7.3
2003 Observed%	15.1	36.2	22.4	22.0	4.2	
Total Observed%	15.0	34.6	22.5	22.5	5.4	
Germany						
1995 Observed%	19.8	27.5	19.1	25.2	8.5	29.02***
2003 Observed%	12.9	31.4	22.7	25.6	7.4	
Total Observed%	17.0	29.0	20.5	25.4	8.0	
New Zealand						
1995 Observed%	18.4	35.6	20.2	20.7	5.2	10.6**
2003 Observed%	20.4	36.6	21.7	18.6	2.7	
Total Observed%	19.4	36.1	20.9	19.6	4.0	
Norway						
1995 Observed%	9.8	30.7	29.5	24.6	5.3	17.4***
2003 Observed%	9.7	25.5	28.5	28.9	7.5	
Total Observed%	9.8	28.1	29.0	26.7	6.4	

(*Continued*)

Table 2.1 (*Continued*)

	freetrade = 1 (Support Protection)	freetrade = 2	freetrade = 3 (Indifferent)	freetrade = 4	freetrade = 5 (Oppose Protection)	X^2 statistic
Spain						
1995 Observed%	22.9	54.2	11.9	10.0	1.1	936.8***
2003 Observed%	2.1	12.6	25.8	51.4	8.1	
Total Observed%	12.4	33.1	18.9	31.0	4.6	
Sweden						
1995 Observed%	13.3	30.0	31.2	18.7	6.8	63.9***
2003 Observed%	6.4	22.5	35.8	23.7	11.6	
Total Observed%	10.0	26.4	33.4	21.1	9.1	
United Kingdom						
1995 Observed%	24.2	42.0	19.4	12.9	1.5	13.6***
2003 Observed%	18.4	41.1	24.3	14.4	1.8	
Total Observed%	21.6	41.6	21.6	13.6	1.6	
United States						
1995 Observed%	22.7	46.0	17.1	11.1	3.1	25.8***
2003 Observed%	23.0	38.4	21.4	15.3	1.9	
Total Observed%	22.8	42.3	19.2	13.1	2.6	

Notes: Cell entries are sample percentages. Rows sum to 100%. The X^2 statistic tests the null hypothesis that year and the distribution of support for trade are independent. *** significant at 1%, ** significant at 5%, * significant at 10%.

Most countries experienced statistically significant pro-trade shifts in the mass of their distributions from 1995 to 2003. The exceptions are New Zealand, the only country to show a statistically significant shift in the opposite (anti-trade) direction, and Canada, whose sample distribution also shifts toward the anti-trade side of the scale, but by a smaller and statistically insignificant amount. Given the large pro-trade shift in Canadian public opinion over the 1990s (Mendelsohn and Wolfe 2001), this apparent loss of momentum in the early 2000s is notable. Interestingly, the United States shows a small but statistically significant increase in support from 1995 to 2003. This contrasts with the evidence from the PIPA surveys discussed in chapter 1. Although it is impossible to say definitively, support for trade in the United States likely reached its highest point in the late 1990s when the first PIPA survey was conducted and has declined since then. The countries with the largest percentage gains in respondents who said they either oppose or strongly oppose limiting imports to protect the domestic economy were Spain (+48.4%), Sweden (+9.8%), and Norway (+6.5%). What explains the variation we observe in trade attitudes? To answer this question, I turn to individual-level regression analysis.

My baseline regression is mostly grounded in trade theory.[17] The specific factors (Ricardo-Viner) model from international economics identifies sector of employment as crucial to determining an individual's attitudes toward trade. Individuals employed in export industries are likely to benefit from trade, whereas individuals employed in import industries are likely harmed. This contrasts with the mobile factors (Stolper-Samuelson) model, which highlights the importance of one's factor endowment. Regardless of their industry of employment, the owners of relatively abundant factors of production benefit from trade. For the countries in this OECD sample, the abundant factors are highly skilled labor and capital.[18] I also include the respondent's employment status in the baseline specification. Neither of the basic trade models, which assume full employment, have anything to say about this condition, but we know from other theoretical frameworks and empirical research that it is likely to be an important determinant of one's preferences regarding free trade (Scheve and Slaughter 2006) as well as one's preferred means of government protection and (or) compensation (Rueda 2005, 2006). To the baseline regression, I also add two policy variables: the net replacement rate for unemployment insurance (NRR) and the amount of government spending on active labor market programs per unemployed worker (ALM). In my extended analysis, which is primarily designed to see how robust the estimated effects are, I add two more policy related variables, fixed-country and year effects, and a battery of individual-level controls highlighted in the literature. Before turning to the regression results, I describe the construction of all these variables and my methods of empirical analysis.

As a proxy for one's capital endowment, I use an income dummy variable that takes a value of one for everyone in the sample whose annual family income is greater than \$35,000 (1995 \$) and a score of zero for everyone else.[19] Following Mayda and Rodrik (2005) and Scheve and Slaughter (2001), I use one's level of education as a proxy for skill endowment. The education variable uses a five-point scale. The median respondent in my data set has an education level of three, which represents a secondary-level education. An education level of five represents a completed university degree.

I identify a respondent's (or spouse's) industry of employment by their occupation using the reported 4-digit code from the International Labor Organization's *International Standard Classification of Occupations* (ISCO). Several countries in my data set use ISCO-68 for their 1995 samples, but all of the countries use ISCO-88 for their 2003 samples. I start by converting all of the occupation codes into the ISCO-88 codes, using the conversion tables provided by Cusack, Iversen, and Rehm (2006). I then assign each occupation to either a non-tradable category or one of eleven tradable sectors identified in the OECD's (STAN) *Industry Structural Analysis Database*.[20] This matching process is relatively straightforward, given the level of detail provided by the 4-digit ISCO codes. In many cases, the sector of employment is included in the occupational description. For example, the description for the ISCO-88 occupation 1221 is "production and operations department managers *in agriculture, hunting and fishing*." Table 2.2 provides a list of the occupations assigned to each of the tradable sectors. A random sample of the nearly 300 non-traded occupations is also provided.

After matching occupations to industries of employment, I used the values of each industry's ratio of exports and imports to value added to create an export and import variable for the respondents employed in tradable sectors. The export variable ranges from a low of zero for non-traded industries to a high of 4.403 for the Norwegian fabricated metals industry in 2003. The denominator in this ratio, value added, represents each sector's contribution to the country's GDP. The ratio can be greater than one for industries with costly inputs. The import variable ranges from zero for all non-traded industries to 9.656 for the Norwegian textile industry in 2003. I calculated a *net exports* variable by taking the difference between exports and imports and then used this difference to create a *net exports* dummy variable that takes a value of -1 for all country-sector-years below the 25th percentile (*net exports* < -0.41), +1 for all country-sector-years above the 75th percentile (*net exports* > 0.24), and 0 for the country-sector-years in the middle of the distribution. I refer to sectors below the 25th percentile of the *net exports* distribution as import-competing sectors and those above the 75th percentile as export-oriented sectors. To estimate the effects of one's employment status, I created an *unemployed* dummy variable that takes a value of one for all jobless respondents who are actively seeking work and zero for those who are not.

Table 2.2 Matching ISCO-88 Occupation Codes to OECD Sectors

(1) Agriculture, hunting, forestry and fishing

Production and operations department managers in agriculture, hunting, and fishing (1221); General managers in agriculture, hunting, and fishing (1311); Agronomists and related professionals (2213); Agronomy and forestry technicians (3212); Farming and forestry advisers (3213); Skilled agricultural and fishery worker (6000); Market-oriented skilled agricultural and fishery workers (6100); Market gardeners and crop growers (6110); Field crop and vegetable growers (6111); Tree and shrub crop growers (6112); Gardeners, horticultural and nursery growers (6113); Mixed-crop growers (6114); Market-oriented animal producers and related workers (6120); Dairy and livestock producers (6121); Poultry producers (6122); Apiarists and sericulturists (6123); Mixed animal producers (6124); Market-oriented animal producers and related workers not elsewhere classified (6129); Market-oriented crop animal producers (6131); Forestry and related workers (6140); Forestry workers and loggers (6141); Charcoal burners and related workers (6142); Fishery workers, hunters and trappers (6150); Aquatic-life cultivation workers (6151); Inland and coastal waters fishery workers (6152); Deep-sea fishery workers (6153); Aquatic-life cultivation workers (6154); Agricultural and other mobile-plant operators (8330); Motorised farm and forestry plant operators (8331); Agricultural, fishery and related labourers (9200, 9210, 9211); Forestry labourers (9212); Fishery, hunting and trapping labourers (9213).

(2) Mining and quarrying

Mining engineers, metallurgists and related professionals (2147); Mining and metallurgical technicians (3117); Miners and quarry workers (7111); Mining- and mineral-processing-plant operators (8110, 8111, 8112); Well drillers and borers and related workers (8113); Mining and quarrying labourers (9311).

(3) Food products, beverages, and tobacco

Food processing and related trades workers (7410); Butchers, fishmongers and related food preparers (7411); Bakers, pastry-cooks and confectionary makers (7412); Dairy-products makers (7413); Fruit, vegetable and related preservers (7414); Food and beverage tasters and graders (7415); Tobacco preparers and tobacco products makers (7416); Food and related products machine operators (8270); Meat- and fish-processing-machine operators (8271); Dairy-products machine operators (8272); Grain- and spice-milling-machine operators (8273); Baked-goods, cereal and chocolate-products machine operators (8274); Fruit-, vegetable- and nut-processing-machine operators (8275); Sugar production machine operators (8276); Tea-, coffee-, and cocoa-processing-machine operators (8277); Brewers-, wine and other beverage machine operators (8278); Tobacco production machine operators (8279).

(Continued)

Table 2.2 (*Continued*)

(4) Textiles, textile products, leather and footwear

Handicraft workers in textile, leather and related materials (7332); Silk-screen, block and textile printers (7346); Textile, garment and related trades workers (7430); Fibre preparers (7431); Weavers, knitters and related workers (7432); Tailors, dressmakers and hatters (7433); Furriers and related workers (7434); Textile, leather and related pattern-makers and cutters (7435); Sewers, embroiderers and related workers (7436); Upholsterers and related workers (7437); Pelt, leather and shoemaking trades workers (7440); Pelt dressers, tanners and fellmongers (7441, 7442); Textile-, fur- and leather-products machine operators (8260); Fibre-preparing-, spinning- and winding-machine operators (8261); Weaving- and knitting-machine operators (8262); Sewing-machine operators (8263); Bleaching-, dyeing- and cleaning-machine operators (8264); Fur- and leather-preparing-machine operators (8265); Shoemaking- and related machine operators (8266); Textile-, fur- and leather-products machine operators not elsewhere classified (8269).

(5) Wood and products of wood and cork

Handicraft workers in wood and related materials (7331); Wood treaters, cabinet-makers and related trades workers (7420, 7421, 7422, 7423); Wood-processing- and papermaking-plant operators (8140, 8141); Wood products machine operators (8240).

(6) Paper and paper products

Paper-pulp plant operators (8142); Papermaking-plant operators (8143); Paper products machine operators (8253).

(7) Publishing, printing and reproduction of recorded media

Printing and related trades workers (7340); Compositors, typesetters and related workers (7341); Stereotypers, and electrotypers (7342); Printing engravers and etchers (7343); Photographic and related workers (7344); Bookbinders and related workers (7345); Printing-, binding- and paper-products machine operators (8250); Printing-machine operators (8251); Bookbinding-machine operators (8252)

(8) Chemical, rubber, plastics and fuel products

Chemical engineers (2146); Pharmacologists, pathologists, and related professionals (2212); Chemical engineering technicians (3116); Chemical-processing-plant operators (8150); Crushing-, grinding- and chemical-mixing-machinery operators (8151); Chemical-heat-treating-plant operators (8152); Chemical-filtering- and separating-equipment operators (8153); Chemical-still and reactor operators except petroleum and natural gas (8154); Petroleum- and natural-gas-refining-plant operators (8155); Chemical-processing-plant operators not elsewhere classified (8159);

Chemical-products machine operators (8220); Pharmaceutical- and toiletry products machine operators (8221); Chemical-products machine operators not elsewhere classified (8229); Rubber- and plastic-products machine operators (8230); Rubber-products machine operators (8231); Plastic-products machine operators (8232).

(9) Other non-metallic mineral products

Stone splitters, cutters, and carvers (7113); Potters, glass-makers and related trades workers (7320); Abrasive wheel formers, potters and related workers (7321); Glass-makers, cutters, grinders and finishers (7322); Glass engravers and etchers (7323); Glass, ceramics and related decorative painters (7324); Glass, ceramics and related plant operators (8130); Glass and ceramics kiln and related machine operators (8131); Glass, ceramics and related plant operators, not elsewhere classified (8139); Cement and other mineral-products machine operators (8212).

(10) Basic metals

Metal moulders, welders, sheetmetal workers, structural-metal preparers, and related trades workers (7210); Metal moulders vand coremakers (7211); Precision workers in metal and related materials (7310); Metal worker general (7500); Metal worker n.e.c. (7510); Metal-processing-plant operators (8120); Ore ad metal furnace operators (8121); Metal melters, casters and rolling-mill operators (8122); Metal-heat-treating-plant operators (8123); Metal drawers and extruders (8124); Metal- and mineral-products machine operators (8210); Metal finishing-, plating- and coating-machine operators (8223).

(11) Machinery and equipment

Precision-instrument makers and repairers (7311); Electrical engineers (2143); Electronics and telecommunication engineers (2144); Electrical engineering technicians (3113); Electronics and telecommunications engineering technicians (3114); Mechanical engineering technicians (3115); Blacksmiths, tool-makers and related trades workers (7220); Blacksmiths, hammer-smiths and forging-press workers (7221); Tool-makers and related workers (7222); Metal wheel-grinders, polishers and tool sharpeners (7224); Mechanical-machinery assemblers (8281); Electrical-equipment assemblers (8282); Electronic-equipment assemblers.

(12) Non-traded sectors

Mathematicians, statisticians and related professionals (2120, 2121); Social science and related professionals (2440); Archivists, librarians and related information professionals (2430); Computer programmers (2132); Biologists, botanists, zoologists and related professionals (2211); Writers and creative or performing artists (2450); Civil engineering technicians (3112);

(Continued)

Table 2.2 (*Continued*)

Air traffic pilots (3144); Air traffic safety technicians (3145); Modern health associate professionals except nursing (3220); Medical assistants (3221); Dental assistants (3225); Pharmaceutical assistants (3228); Administrative secretaries and related associate professionals (3431); Statistical, mathematical and related associate professionals (3434); Administrative associate professionals not elsewhere classified (3439); Artistic, entertainment and sports associate professionals (3470); Religious associate professionals (3480); Secretaries and keyboard-operating clerks (4110); Word-processor and related operators (4112); Client information clerks (4220); Telephone switchboard operators (4223); Transport conductors (5112); Cooks (5122); Fashion and other models (5210); Shop salespersons and demonstrators (5220); Insulation workers (7134); Car, taxi and van drivers (8322); Lifting-truck operators (8334); Building caretakers, window and related cleaners (9140, 9141)

Notes: ISCO-88 occupations are assigned to one of eleven tradable sectors from the OECD's STAN Industrial Dataset. Parentheses contain ISCO-88 occupation codes. There are approximately three hundred occupations assigned to the non-traded sector. This table contains a random sample of those occupations.

I calculated each country's spending on active labor market (ALM) programs per unemployed worker using data from the OECD's Social Spending and Labor Force databases. These ALM programs, which are designed to improve job seekers' prospects of finding employment and increase the earning potential of workers, include spending on public employment, labor market training, and other policies intended to promote employment among the unemployed. The average spending per unemployed worker is roughly the amount of ALM expenditures that an unemployed (or underemployed) individual can expect to benefit from in times of need. I include the net replacement rate of each respondent's government-provided unemployment benefits (NRR). The 1998 edition of the OECD's *Benefit Systems and Work Incentives* provides the 1995 net replacement rates for four family types at two income levels; the 2004 edition of *Benefits and Wages* provides these rates for 2002.[21] The family types are single, married couple, couple with two children, and lone parent with two children. The income levels are average and two-thirds the average income level.[22] This gives up to eight different net replacement rates for each country in the sample.

I use marital status, number of persons in household, and the household cycle variables from the ISSP data set (v202, v293, and v294, respectively), as well as the family income dummy variable to identify each survey respondent's net replacement rate. The household cycle variable indicates whether there are children in the household. It is not a problem to identify singles and married couples without children. In many instances it is not difficult to identify lone parents and married couples with children because these family types are included in the household cycle variable. The difficult cases arise when singles live in households with more than one adult and couples live in households with more than two adults. In these cases, parental status is unknown. I gave all identified married respondents with children the married two-child net replacement rate. Similarly, I gave all lone parents the lone parent two-child net replacement rate. When I could not identify parental status, I gave the respondent the average value of their no dependent and two-child net replacement rate.

The household cycle variable is not available for the United Kingdom and Austria in the 1995 survey. For these British and Austrian respondents, I used the number of persons in household variable to identify cases where there are no children living in the household (e.g., a single respondent living in a household with only one person). When I could not determine whether or not children were living in the household, I used an average net replacement rate. In most countries, net replacement rates are higher for low-income individuals. I used the income dummy variable to assign average income and below average net replacement rates. The main advantage of the NRR variable is that, with eight replacement rates, it provides variation within a country in unemployment insurance coverage. Nevertheless, most of the variation in net replacement rates in the sample is still between countries.[23]

I include two additional policy variables in the extended analysis: the strictness of a country's employment protection legislation (EPL) and each respondent's subjective evaluation of the social security system. The EPL index comes from the OECD's Employment Outlook publication.[24] The subjective evaluation variable is based on a question that asks respondents how proud they are of the social security system in their country. Respondents can answer "very proud," "somewhat proud," "not very proud," or "not proud at all." I scored these responses from 1 to 4, giving those who were not proud at all a 1 and those that were very proud a 4. I included a subjective measure out of concern that respondents might not be aware of the details of the unemployment insurance, active labor market, or employment protection policies in their countries. I assume that respondents who are "very proud" of their social security system feel that they are well protected by it and those who are "not proud at all" feel that they are not.[25]

I also use an extensive list of individual-level controls in the analysis, including Iversen and Soskice's measure of skill specificity and several demographic and ideological variables used by Hiscox and Burgoon.[26] An individual's skill specificity determines how easily she or he can adjust to trade-related dislocations. High degrees of skill specificity make workers more vulnerable to unemployment during economic downturns. Hiscox and Burgoon identify gender, age, employment status, and marital status as important determinants of trade preferences. They also focus on an individual's political ideology and whether or not the respondent self-identifies with a particular religious faith. For ideology I use a five-point party affiliation scale provided in the ISSP data set that ranges from far left (1) to far right (5). For the religion variable, I use a dummy that takes a value of one for individuals who self-identify with a religious denomination and zero for everyone else. One important demographic characteristic that Hiscox and Burgoon do not include in their analysis is whether the respondent has a dependent child living in his or her household. When it is possible to identify parental status from the survey, I include it as a control variable. I also include whether one holds nationalist attitudes, which was found by both Mayda and Rodrik and O'Rourke and Sinnott to be an important determinant of trade policy preferences. In their analysis, Mayda and Rodrik use four separate questions that gauge whether one holds patriotic, nationalistic, and/or chauvinistic attitudes. Using factor analysis, I extract from the answers to these four questions a single component that measures the degree to which an individual holds nationalist attitudes.

I estimate ordered probits because my dependent variable, FREETRADE, is ordinal. Ordinal dependent variables can create problems for the standard linear model because it assumes that the intervals between adjacent categories are equal. This implies, for instance, that the difference in support for trade between a 2 (agree) and a 3 (neither agree nor disagree) is equivalent to the difference between a 4 (disagree) and a 5 (strongly disagree). This is a strong assumption, and if it does not hold, the estimated coefficients and the predicted probabilities they generate will be biased and misleading.[27] Also, since individuals sampled from the same country are likely to be influenced by common contextual factors, they should not be treated as independent of one another. This systematic country-level heterogeneity either needs to be modeled directly, or the standard error estimates for the regression coefficients need to take this clustering into account. I use fixed country and period effects and robust clustered standard errors to address this problem.[28]

Results

The regression results are presented in table 2.3.[29] Model 1 is the baseline regression, which includes all the trade-theory variables, one's employment status, the respondent's net replacement rate (NRR) from unemployment insurance, and the amount of ALM expenditures from which she or he can expect to benefit in times of need. Note that I use the trichotomous *net exports* dummy variable in the regressions because the relationship between sector net exports and support for trade is nonlinear.[30] One of the drawbacks of the ordered probit model is that the *size* of effects from changes in the independent variables on an individual's propensity to support free trade policies

Table 2.3 Ordered Probit Models of Individual Support for Trade

	(1)	(2)	(3)	(4)	(5)
Tradable	−.204***	−.327**	−.443***	−.262	−.401*
	(.051)	(.167)	(.168)	(.344)	(.207)
Net Exports	.117**	.132***	.101***	.123*	.091**
	(.048)	(.031)	(.031)	(.068)	(.039)
Education	.119***	.148***	.155***	.106***	.112***
	(.026)	(.006)	(.006)	(.018)	(.008)
Income	.238***	.246***	.233***	.302***	.253***
	(.050)	(.017)	(.017)	(.045)	(.024)
Unemployed	−.022	−.406*	−.537*	−.846*	−.826**
	(.052)	(.313)	(.315)	(.500)	(.419)
NRR	1.679***	1.001***	−.122*	1.186***	.099
	(.407)	(.250)	(.104)	(.297)	(.151)
NRR × Tradable		.164	.475*	−.055	.181
		(.278)	(.250)	(.419)	(.311)
NRR × Unemployed		.043	.261	1.049*	1.149*
		(.522)	(.450)	(.624)	(.600)
ALM	.118**	.062		.105**	
	(.045)	(.054)		(.048)	
ALM × Tradable		−.118***	−.117***	−.126***	−.131***
		(.043)	(.024)	(.045)	(.031)
ALM × Unemployed		.064	.107**	.034	.074
		(.093)	(.045)	(.093)	(.061)
EPL		.234**		.180**	
		(.091)		(.078)	
EPL × Tradable		.104	.038	.123	.091**
		(.084)	(.036)	(.089)	(.046)
EPL × Unemployed		.012	−.050	−.081	−.151**
		(.078)	(.055)	(.087)	(.071)
Social Security		.015	.023**	.078**	.094***
		(.036)	(.010)	(.031)	(.013)
Soc. Sec. × Tradable		−.030	−.016	.011	.022
		(.033)	(.027)	(.040)	(.034)
Soc. Sec. × Unemp.		.104*	.125***	.048	.047
		(.059)	(.041)	(.081)	(.057)
Skill Specificity				−.060**	−.044***
				(.026)	(.011)
Male				.265***	.262***
				(.036)	(.020)
Age				−.002**	−.003***
				(.001)	(.001)
Single				.120***	.051**
				(.039)	(.024)

(Continued)

Table 2.3 (*Continued*)

	(1)	(2)	(3)	(4)	(5)
No Kids				.124***	.059**
				(.035)	(.024)
Ideology				.045***	.043***
				(.014)	(.010)
Religious				−.065	−.090***
				(.056)	(.025)
Nationalism				−.298***	−.295***
				(.029)	(.010)
Fixed Effects Country/Period	No/No	No/No	Yes/Yes	No/No	Yes/Yes
Clustered S.E.s	Yes	Yes	No	Yes	No
Observations	20,811	19,979	19,979	12,680	12,680
Log Likelihood	−30055.5	−28647.4	−28217.3	−17214.4	−16971.3
Pseudo R2	.027	.035	.049	.068	.082

Notes: The dependent variable, support for free trade, is ordinal with values ranging from 1 to 5. Low values represent support for limiting imports and high values represent opposition. The models' cut-point estimates are omitted to save space. Parentheses contain standard errors. The standard-error estimates for models 1, 2, and 4 are clustered by country-year.
*** significant at 1%, ** significant at 5%, * significant at 10%.

cannot be read directly from the coefficient estimates. The *sign* of these coefficient estimates are meaningful, however, in the sense that a positive coefficient on an independent variables implies that the probability of observing the extreme (disagree strongly) pro–free trade response increases with this variable, while the probability of observing the extreme (agree strongly) anti–free trade response decreases. The effects on the probability of observing the intermediate responses are ambiguous and depend on the values of the other independent variables, but the coefficients do tell us whether the variables strengthen or weaken attitudes that are pro–free trade.

The coefficients on all of the model 1 variables except *unemployed* are correctly signed and statistically significant. Individuals in tradable industries are less supportive of free trade policies than those employed in non-tradable industries. However, because of the positive coefficient on the *net exports* dummy variable, this difference is smaller (and statistically insignificant) for individuals employed in export-oriented industries, implying that individuals employed in import-competing industries are more likely to support tariffs to protect the economy than individuals who are employed in either high-export or non-tradable industries. The size of the coefficient on the tradable dummy variable should be viewed as conditional on the value of net exports. The tradable coefficient for an individual employed in an export-oriented sector of the economy is −.087 (−.204 + .117), −.204 for an individual employed in a sector with balanced imports and exports, and $-.321$ ($-.204 + -.117$) for an individual employed in an import-competing sector of the economy. Note that being employed in an export-oriented sector of the economy does not make one an ardent supporter of free trade (at least, not relative to those employed in non-tradable sectors). Why not? The likely explanation is that no sector in any country exists solely to supply goods to foreign markets. Even in export-oriented sectors, firms sell to both foreign and domestic buyers. Therefore, even workers in export-oriented sectors may see limiting imports as providing some degree of protection against job loss.[31] This is particularly true if these respondents do not anticipate retaliatory responses from their country's trading partners. Turning to the factor endowment variables, as expected, individuals with high levels of education (skills) and income (capital) are less likely to support protectionism. The estimated coefficient on the *unemployed* variable is correctly signed (negative), but statistically insignificant.

With respect to the policy variables, the higher an individual's net replacement rate, the less likely he or she is to support protectionism. Note that these effects are identified from cross-national and over-time differences in net replacement rates for the various household types (e.g., single parent with below average income). The coefficient on the ALM policy variable is also correctly signed and statistically significant. For these regressions, the standard error estimates assume clustering by country-year (e.g., New Zealand-1995). These results confirm an important element of the embedded liberalism argument: government policies that remedy the negative effects of trade increase support for economic openness.[32]

In the second regression, I add the two other policy-related variables, EPL and the respondent's subjective evaluation of his or her social security system, and allow for interaction effects between all the policy variables and the respondent's labor market status variables (i.e., *tradable* and *unemployed*). The interaction effects are important because trade's likely opponents are a heterogeneous group with conflicting preferences over public policy alternatives. Most importantly, the insider-outsider division highlighted in the work of David Rueda (2005, 2006) suggests that individuals employed in tradable sectors of the economy benefit more from employment protection policies than unemployed individuals, and unemployed individuals are likely to benefit more from ALM expenditures than individuals who are already employed. The model 2 estimates are very similar to the model 1 estimates. Again, the standard error estimates are clustered by country-year. One of the main differences is that the estimated coefficient on *unemployed* is now statistically significant at the .10 level. Support for the insider-outsider distinction is mixed. The positive effects on support for free trade from ALM expenditures are larger for the unemployed than for those employed in tradable sectors, but the effect of EPL strictness on support for trade, while positive and statistically significant, does not seem to depend on one's employment status. This is likely due to the estimates picking up substantial cross-national variation in support for free trade. The within-country insider-outsider divisions are likely to be more pronounced when we allow for country-specific cut-points. Finally, positive evaluations of the social security system seem to increase support for trade primarily among the unemployed.

In the third regression, I add fixed country and year effects. Most of the estimated coefficients on the baseline variables are similar to those previously reported. Note that we can no longer estimate a general effect for ALM spending and the EPL index since there is no within-country-year variation in these variables. The within-country divisions with respect to policy effects on support for trade are more evident in this model, however. The effect of NRR on support for free trade is positive and statistically significant for individuals employed in tradable sectors of the economy. The positive effects of ALM expenditures are much larger for the unemployed than for individuals employed in tradable sectors. Positive evaluations of the social security system have general effects, but the largest effects are still among the unemployed.

In the fourth and fifth regressions, I add the full battery of control variables. The final regression includes country and year fixed effects while the penultimate regression does not. All of the additional controls are statistically significant and have the anticipated signs. Individuals with specific skills are more likely to support limiting imports to protect the domestic economy. Young, single men without children, right-wing partisans, and individuals with cosmopolitan attitudes are stronger supporters of free trade, all else equal. Unfortunately, because of missing data on the additional variables, I lose almost 40% of the original sample, and this makes it difficult to identify whether differences in coefficient estimates are due to changes in the model specification or changes in the sample. Nevertheless, all of the baseline coefficient estimates are robust to the addition of the new control variables and changes in the sample. The effects of NRR and ELP show up primarily among the unemployed. In the former case the effects are positive and in the latter they are negative. NRR still has a positive and statistically significant effect on support for trade among those employed in tradable sectors of the economy, though the magnitude of the effects are considerably smaller (see the counterfactual analysis below). ALM expenditures have a negative and statistically significant effect on support for free trade among those employed in tradable sectors of the economy. Positive evaluations of the social security system now have a large positive, general, and statistically significant correlation with pro–free trade attitudes.

In order to demonstrate the size of the effects that the key variables have on individual support for free trade, I conduct several counterfactual experiments using the estimates for models 1 and 5. The results are reported in terms of predicted probabilities and changes in predicted probabilities in Table 2.4. As the benchmark, I use an individual employed in an import-competing industry with median scores on all of the other variables. This individual has the equivalent of a high school level education, government-provided unemployment insurance with a net replacement rate of 70%, can expect to benefit from $189 worth of government spending on active labor market programs in the case of job loss, and supports protectionism as a means to bolster the domestic economy with an approximate probability of .69 and .59 according to the model 1 and model 5 estimates, respectively. This representative respondent opposes protection with an approximate probability of .13 (model 1) and .19 (model 5).

According to the model 1 estimates, if the respondent were employed in an export-oriented sector of the economy instead of an import-competing sector, the probability of support for protectionism would decrease by a little less than .09. This number is calculated by summing the first two columns of table 2.4. If this respondent had a college degree instead of a high school degree, support for protectionism would drop again by approximately .09. Increasing this respondent's unemployment insurance from the median net replacement rate of 70% to the maximum rate of 92% would lower the probability of strong support for protection by .14. Finally, raising the level of active labor market spending from the median of $189 to the maximum level of $3,393 would lower the probability of support for protectionism by more than .14.

The model 5 estimates of the counterfactual effects from increasing NRR's and ALM spending, which are quite different from the model 1 estimates, are presented in the last two rows of table 2.4. Model 5 includes country and year fixed effects and a complete set of control variables. The effects of NRR on support for trade have the same sign as previously and remain statistically significant, but the size of the effects is considerably smaller. Support for protectionism decreases by about 2.5%, while support for trade increases by almost 2%. These estimates should be viewed as conservative, however. The fixed effects take care of unobservable or otherwise omitted country-level factors that correlate with a country's average net replacement rate, which makes it a useful model for convincing skeptics that a causal relationship exists, but it also suffers from attenuation bias since the NRR variable is measured with error and most of the sample variance in replacement rates is between countries (see note 24).

The model 5 estimates for ALM spending effects on support for trade change signs. These estimates should also be viewed as "worst case" since the common effect of ALM spending on support for trade in a given country in a given year is completely absorbed by the country-year fixed effects. If we give ALM spending no credit for differences in average levels of support for

Table 2.4 Estimated Effects of Key Variables on Support for Trade

	Pr(freetrade=1) (Support Protection)	Pr(freetrade=2)	Pr(freetrade=3) (Indifferent)	Pr(freetrade=4)	Pr(freetrade=5) (Oppose Protection)
Benchmark, Import Industry	.298	.392	.176	.117	.017
Model 1 Estimates	(.038)	(.013)	(.008)	(.001)	(.005)
Predicted Probability					
1) Effect of changing from import to export industry	−.075** (.038)	−.011*** (.001)	.030*** (.002)	.045*** (.001)	.012** (.006)
2) Effect of college degree	−.077*** (.020)	−.012*** (.001)	.030*** (.002)	.046*** (.001)	.013*** (.003)
3) Effect of raising NRR from 70% to 92%	−.114*** (.020)	−.026*** (.002)	.044*** (.003)	.074*** (.002)	.023** (.011)
4) Effect of raising ALM from $189 to $3,393	−.116** (.046)	−.027*** (.002)	.044*** (.003)	.075*** (.002)	.023** (.009)
Benchmark, Import Industry	.176	.415	.223	.168	.018
Model 5 Estimates	(.056)	(.006)	(.003)	(.001)	(.010)
Predicted Probability					
5) Effect of raising NRR from 70% to 92%	−.014 (.014)	−.011*** (.000)	.006*** (.000)	.015*** (.000)	.004 (.005)
6) Effect of raising ALM from $189 to $3,393	.131*** (.042)	.019*** (.001)	−.061*** (.001)	−.075*** (.002)	−.011** (.006)

Notes: Parentheses contain standard errors, calculated using the delta method. For each counterfactual, I report the *change* in predicted probabilities based on the Model 1 and Model 5 estimates.

*** significant at 1%, ** significant at 5%, * significant at 10%

trade across country-years, individuals employed in import-competing industries in countries with high ALM spending are less supportive of free trade (relative to their respective country-year mean levels of support) than their counterparts in countries with low ALM spending. Why might high NRRs increase support for trade among workers in import-competing industries while high ALM expenditures decrease support? One explanation is that individuals who lose their jobs in countries that invest heavily in ALM programs are expected to find employment in new sectors of the economy, and this is something that workers would like to avoid if possible (e.g., Iversen and Cusack 2000). In countries that provide generous unemployment insurance, the individual is not being pushed to seek employment in a new industry. Individual workers may ultimately choose to seek employment elsewhere, but a benefits system based primarily on unemployment insurance does not incentivize labor mobility to the same extent that a system based on ALM programs does. In chapter 5, where I explore the possibility of rebuilding the bargain of embedded liberalism, I discuss these and related issues in more detail.

Overall, the results are very supportive of the embedded liberalism thesis. The strongest opposition to trade comes from individuals employed in sectors of the economy that have the highest levels of imports. Yet, the analysis also demonstrates that politicians can, in fact, build support for trade, even among these sectors. Politically feasible policy reforms can offset declines caused by increased exposure to international competition. Are these findings unique to the ISSP surveys and my particular sample of countries? Fortunately, my findings are consistent with and add to a growing collection of evidence which suggests that governments can effectively manage support for trade. For example, in their analysis of data from the Asia-Europe Survey, Mayda et al. (2007) find that generous social safety nets reduce the marginal effect of risk aversion on opposition to trade. Similarly, using Eurobarometer data, Scheve (2000) finds that welfare state spending shrinks the skill gap in support for European integration, which he interprets as evidence that compensatory programs can build support for international economic openness among those who are likely to oppose it otherwise. Finally, in a larger sample of ISSP countries, Scheve and Slaughter (2004) find that labor market spending reduces aggregate levels protectionist opinion.

One possible problem with my estimates is that question framing can have an effect on respondents' attitudes toward trade, particularly among lesser educated individuals (Hiscox 2006). Hiscox argues the ISSP question wording (a negative frame) exaggerates the differences in support for trade between individuals with high and low levels of education. This implies that the coefficient estimates for variables correlated with education may be inflated or attenuated. Since education is correlated with employment in tradable sectors of the economy—highly educated individuals are more likely to work in non-traded sectors of the economy (e.g., Jensen and Kletzer 2005)—the negative effect of working in a tradable industry on support for free trade policies may be inflated by framing. More importantly for my purposes, however, is the fact that the respondents who qualify for high net replacement rates, low-income single parents, have less education on average, so the estimated effect of the net replacement rate (NRR) variable on support for trade is likely attenuated.

IMPORTS AND GOVERNMENT SPENDING IN POST-INDUSTRIAL ECONOMIES

The micro results confirm the significance of the tradable/non-tradable, import/export, and employed/unemployed distinctions. Politicians who want to maintain support for trade will have to respond to surges in imports. This is particularly true if there are a large number of individuals employed in tradable sectors of the economy and the macroeconomy is performing poorly. However, as individuals move out of tradable industries and/or the macroeconomic environment improves, it becomes less important for politicians to respond to increased imports. Thus, the micro results suggest that the movement of workers from tradable to non-tradable sectors and improvements in the employment performance of the economy will increase support for trade. Therefore, globalization, deindustrialization, and level of unemployment should have interdependent effects on government spending.[33] In post-industrial high-employment economies, the effect of imports on spending should be smaller in magnitude. I test this hypothesis below.

Data and Methods

The sample, which spans from 1960 to 2000, includes twenty OECD countries: Australia, Austria, Belgium, Canada, Denmark, Finland, France, Germany, Ireland, Italy, Japan, the Netherlands, New Zealand, Norway, Portugal, Spain, Sweden, Switzerland, the United Kingdom and the United States. The key independent variable is the natural log of imports measured in millions of 1995 U.S. dollars.[34] The size of the effect that imports will have on spending depends on how many workers are employed in tradable industries and the rate of unemployment. I use Iversen and Cusack's measure of deindustrialization as a measure of the number of workers exposed to import competition.[35]

I include two dependent variables in the analysis, both of which are common in the literature: government consumption as a percentage of GDP and social benefits as a percentage of GDP.[36] Some have criticized research using government consumption and social benefits as dependent variables (for example, see Burgoon 2001; Mares 2004). Mares argues that all expenditure-based measures are problematic because they do not reflect politically salient aspects of policy design. I disagree, since expenditures are driven partly by the generosity of benefit payments, which is both discretionary and politically salient, and the non-discretionary component of spending can be addressed with controls. Moreover, with respect to the program scope of the dependent variable, it is important not to be too narrowly focused. Constrained governments might respond in less direct ways to demands for compensation and insurance. For example, in the United States, much of the insecurity associated with losing one's job comes from the fear of losing one's health insurance. In theory, the U.S. government could respond to globalization pressures by providing better health care for its poorest citizens.

I add five control variables to the analysis: GDP per capita; the percentage of the population above the age of sixty-five; the percentage of cabinet seats held by left-wing parties; union density; and exports.[37] The first variable controls for Wagner's law, which predicts that governments will spend a higher proportion of GDP as per-capita real income rises. It also correlates with the business cycle and therefore may control for some of the nondiscretionary changes in government spending. (In this case, we would expect the coefficient to be negative.) Pierson and others have identified an aging population as the key demographic change driving government spending in the OECD today.[38] One would expect government spending to be higher where the political left and/or organized labor is strong. Since imports and exports are highly correlated, the log of exports is also included as a control variable. I expect the coefficients on imports and exports to have opposite signs.

I estimate four panel regressions, two for each of the dependent variables. One model includes the controls and year dummies; the other does not. Like many political scientists, I include a temporal lag of the dependent variable and country dummies in all of the models to control for persistence and unit heterogeneity, respectively. I also include a spatial lag in the analysis as a way to model the cross-sectional interdependence in the data. This not only improves estimation efficiency, but also helps guard against bias. For example, if it is true that governments have been constrained by international capital mobility, particularly during the post–Bretton Woods era, then countries will be affected by levels of government spending in their neighbors. If imports cluster spatially as well, ignoring this interdependence in spending will bias estimation of the impact of imports on government spending.[39] The spatial lags are generated with a row-standardized binary contiguity weighting matrix using shared territorial borders as the criterion.[40] Spatio-temporal lag models are discussed extensively in Franzese and Hays (2007, 2008) and more briefly in the methodological appendix to this chapter. Formally, the model is written as

$$y = \rho\,\mathbf{Wy} + \phi\mathbf{My} + \mathbf{X\beta} + \varepsilon \qquad (2.1)$$

Where $\mathbf{y}$, the dependent variable, is an $NT \times 1$ vector of cross sections stacked by periods (i.e., the N first-period observations, then the N second-period ones, and so on to the N in the last period, T). The parameter ρ is the spatial autoregressive coefficient and $\mathbf{W}$ is an $NT \times NT$ block-diagonal spatial-weighting matrix. More specifically, we can express this $\mathbf{W}$ matrix as the Kronecker product of a $T \times T$ identity matrix and an $N \times N$ weights matrix $(\mathbf{I}_T \otimes \mathbf{W}_N)$, with elements w_{ij} of $\mathbf{W}_N$ reflecting the relative degree of connection from unit j to i. $\mathbf{Wy}$ is thus the spatial lag; that is, for each observation y_{it}, $\mathbf{Wy}$ gives a weighted sum of the y_{jt}, with weights, w_{ij}, given by the relative connectivity from j to i. The parameter ϕ is the temporal autoregressive coefficient, and $\mathbf{M}$ is an $NT \times NT$ matrix with ones on the minor diagonal, that is, at coordinates $(N+1, 1)$, $(N+2, 2)$,..., $(NT, NT - N)$, and zeros elsewhere, so $\mathbf{My}$ is the (first-order) temporal lag. The matrix $\mathbf{X}$ contains $NT \times k$ observations on k independent variables, and $\mathbf{\beta}$ is a $k \times 1$ vector of coefficients on them. The final term in (2.1), ε, is an $NT \times 1$ vector of disturbances, assumed to be independent and identically distributed.

I estimate the model using maximum likelihood. This estimator is discussed in the appendix as well. All of the right-hand-side variables, with the exception of the spatial lag, are serially lagged one period to address potential problems of endogeneity.[41]

Results

The regression estimates are reported in table 2.5. In short, I find that the effect of imports on a country's level of government spending depends on how exposed the domestic labor market is to trade.[42] The estimated coefficients on the imports and deindustrialization interaction variables are correctly signed in all the regressions. An increase in a country's imports is associated with an increase in government spending. This effect is magnified when a large portion of the working-age population is employed in tradable industries. I find more limited support for the argument that a healthy labor market reduces the size of the import effect. The unemployment variable and the unemployment-imports interaction term are jointly statistically significant and correctly signed in the baseline social benefits regression, but not in any of the other models. The estimated coefficients on both the temporal and spatial lag variables are positively signed and statistically significant.

What do these results tell us of the substantive magnitude that import shocks in OECD countries have on government spending over time and across space? To answer this question we need to calculate the so-called

Table 2.5 Trade and Government Spending

	Government Consumption		Social Benefits	
	(1)	(2)	(3)	(4)
Temporal Lag	.890***	.905***	.961***	.962***
	(.018)	(.021)	(.019)	(.020)
Spatial Lag	.022***	.010***	.017***	.003
	(.004)	(.004)	(.005)	(.005)
Imports	2.132***	1.860***	2.286***	1.810***
	(.343)	(.496)	(.359)	(.589)
Deindustrialization	.152***	.132**	.144**	.113
	(.053)	(.060)	(.060)	(.076)
Unemployment	−.124	−.106	−.080††	−.128
	(.104)	(.118)	(.117)	(.134)
Imports × Deindustrialization	−.023***	−.014**	−.024***	−.013*
	(.005)	(.006)	(.005)	(.007)
Imports × Unemployment	.012	.010	.011††	.013
	(.010)	(.011)	(.011)	(.012)
Exports		−.544*		−1.062***
		(.282)		(.280)
RGDP per capita		.006		.022
		(.018)		(.019)
Old Age		8.080***		8.900**
		(2.856)		(3.528)
Leftist Government		.130*		−.018
		(.068)		(.070)
Union Density		−.117		−.053
		(.363)		(.395)
Fixed Effects Country / Year	Yes/No	Yes/Yes	Yes/No	Yes/Yes
Observations	706	706	650	650
Log Likelihood	−596.6	−487.14	−533.5	−433.3
R-squared	.977	.985	.984	.988

Notes: The fixed effect coefficient-estimates are suppressed to conserve space. Standard errors are in parentheses. The spatial lags are generated with a binary contiguity weighting matrix using shared territorial borders as the criterion, excepting that France, Belgium, and the Netherlands are coded as contiguous with Britain, Denmark as contiguous with Sweden, and Australia as contiguous with New Zealand. All the spatial weights matrices are row-standardized. *** significant at 1%; ** significant at 5%; * significant at 10%; †† jointly significant at 5%.

spatial and spatio-temporal multipliers. The spatial multiplier, $(\mathbf{I}_N - \rho \mathbf{W})^{-1}$, captures the feedback from, say, Belgium on France and other countries, and back from France and those others on Belgium, and so on recursively. The immediate time-t effect on the vector of policy outcomes throughout the OECD, including that recursive feedback, can now be calculated with this spatial multiplier by considering certain counterfactual shocks to variables in $\mathbf{X}$ on the right-hand side of (2.1). Specifically, multiplying $(\mathbf{I}_N - \rho\mathbf{W})^{-1}$ by an $N \times 1$ column vector with 1 in row i and 0 elsewhere gives the immediate effect of a permanent unit-shock to country i on policies in the other $(N-1)$ countries j. For example, multiplying $(\mathbf{I}_N - \rho\mathbf{W})^{-1}$ by a 20×1 column vector with 0 in all rows except that corresponding to Austria, which gets a 1, will give a 20×1 column-vector containing the estimated effects of a unit-shock in Austria on both its own spending and the spending of the other nineteen countries.

In addition to these spatial dynamics, the model of government consumption includes a time-lag of the dependent variable and corresponding temporal dynamics. We could, therefore, plot the evolution of the one-period effect over time to illustrate the spatio-temporal dynamics of responses to various counterfactuals. More compactly, we can calculate the long-run steady-state effect, including the feedback effects, of permanent hypothetical shocks to one country. (See the appendix for a discussion of how to do this.) Table 2.6 reports these steady-state calculations. The off-diagonal elements of the table report the effect of a one-unit positive shock in the column country's imports on the other countries' level of government consumption. The diagonal elements of Table 2.6 report the effect of a one-unit positive import shock in the column country on its own government consumption after spatial feedback. The long-run steady-state effects are large. For example, in the long run, a 1-unit positive shock to the log of British imports increases spending in Ireland by more than 1.2% of GDP. Of course, this effect assumes a permanent increase in British imports and would take many years to materialize. In this sense, the calculation likely represents an upper bound for the spatial effects. The results for a 1-unit increase in German imports are presented graphically in figure 2.1.

Finally, I conduct a set of counterfactual experiments that compare the effects of a permanent increase in German imports on government consumption in Germany for both the industrial and post-industrial cases.[43] I set the deindustrialization variable to its sample low and high values for Germany and then calculated the effects of a 1-unit surge in imports.[44] In figure 2.2, I plot the temporal effects (with spatial feedback) on government consumption in Germany. The solid and dashed lines with markers represent the estimated effects for the post-industrial and industrial cases, respectively. The solid and dashed lines without markers provide a 95% confidence interval around these effects. The effects are larger for industrial Germany than for post-industrial Germany—.78% vs. .5% of GDP to begin and then 5.36% vs. 3.4% after ten years—and the first differences in these effects are statistically significant for up to ten years after the initial surge in German imports.

Why do my empirical results differ from those previously reported, particularly by Iversen and Cusack? I provide a reanalysis of the Iversen and Cusack

Table 2.6 Steady-State Spatio-Temporal Effects from a One-Unit Increase in Imports on Government Consumption in Europe (Intermediate Level of Deindustrialization)

	AUT	BEL	DNK	FIN	FRA	DEU	IRE	ITA	NTH	NOR	POR	ESP	SWE	CHE	GBR
AUT	5.897* (3.272)	.028 (.02)			.078 (.054)	.438* (.264)		.435* (.262)	.025 (.017)			.003 (.003)		.439* (.264)	.006 (.005)
BEL	.019 (.014)	5.895* (3.272)			.345* (.209)	.346* (.21)	.018 (.013)	.016 (.011)	.343* (.207)	.002 (.001)		.015 (.01)		.002 (.002)	.348 (.212)
DNK	.033 (.022)	.036 (.025)	5.864* (3.253)	.048 (.033)	.035 (.024)	.618* (.37)		.004 (.003)	.034 (.024)	.048 (.033)		.001 (.001)	.62* (.371)	.003 (.002)	.006 (.005)
FIN			.048 (.033)	5.938* (3.297)		.005 (.004)				.666* (.402)			.692* (.42)		
FRA	.032 (.022)	.276 (.168)			5.908* (3.279)	.266* (.161)	.014 (.01)	.249* (.149)	.042 (.029)		.026 (.018)	.251* (.151)		.019* (.014)	.266* (.161)
DEU	.311* (.186)	.346* (.21)			.333* (.201)	5.898* (3.273)	.003 (.002)	.037 (.025)	.328* (.197)		.001 (.001)	.014 (.01)		.024 (.017)	.055 (.038)
IRE	.001 (.001)	.072 (.051)			.069 (.048)	.011 (.009)	5.885* (3.266)	.003 (.002)	.069 (.048)		.001 (.001)	.003 (.002)			1.236* (.739)
ITA	.435* (.262)	.024 (.017)			.439* (.265)	.073 (.051)	.001 (.001)	5.892* (3.27)	.006 (.005)		.002 (.002)	.019 (.013)		.439 (.264)	.02 (.014)
NTH	.023 (.016)	.457* (.276)			.07 (.049)	.437* (.263)	.023 (.016)	.005 (.004)	5.89* (3.269)			.003 (.002)		.002 (.002)	.44* (.265)
NOR			.048 (.033)	.666* (.402)		.005 (.004)				5.938* (3.297)			.692* (.42)		
POR	.001 (.001)	.006 (.005)			.131 (.09)	.006 (.005)		.006 (.004)	.001 (.001)		5.95* (3.304)	1.243* (.744)			.006 (.005)

(*Continued*)

Table 2.6 (*Continued*)

	AUT	BEL	DNK	FIN	FRA	DEU	IRE	ITA	NTH	NOR	POR	ESP	SWE	CHE	GBR
ESP	.003	.029			.628*	.028	.001	.026	.004		.622*	5.976*		.002	.028
	(.003)	(.021)			(.377)	(.02)	(.001)	(.018)	(.004)		(.372)	(3.319)		(.002)	(.02)
SWE	.002*	.003	.413*	.461*	.002	.044			.002	.461*			5.96*		
	(.002)	(.002)	(.247)	(.28)	(.002)	(.03)			(.002)	(.28)			(3.31)		
CHE	.347	.035			.351	.347*	.001	.344*	.021		.002	.015		5.869*	.018
	(.21)	(.025)			(.214)	(.211)	(.001)	(.208)	(.015)		(.001)	(.011)		(3.256)	(.013)
GBR	.004	.348			.332*	.055	.309*	.014	.33*		.001	.014		.001	5.94*
	(.003)	(.212)			(.201)	(.038)	(.185)	(.01)	(.199)		(.001)	(.01)		(.001)	(3.298)

Notes: The off-diagonal elements of the table report the effect of a one-unit increase in the column country's imports on government consumption in its European counterparts. The diagonal elements give the total effect of an exogenous one-unit increase in the column country's imports on its own government consumption. These numbers are calculated using the spatio-temporal multiplier and thus reflect all feedback effects. Parentheses contain standard errors calculated by the delta method.

*** significant at 1%; ** significant at 5%; * significant at 10%

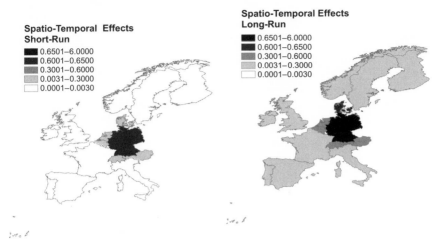

Figure 2.1 Spatio-Temporal Effects from a One-Unit Increase in German Imports on Government Consumption in Europe (Intermediate Level of Deindustrialization)

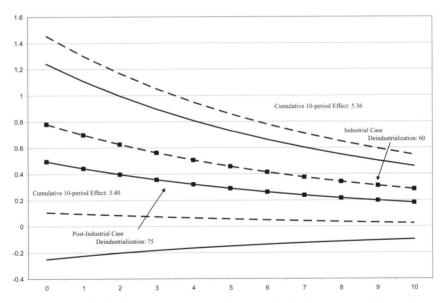

Figure 2.2 Marginal Effects on Government Consumption in Germany over Time and with Spatial Feedback from a Positive One-Unit Increase in Imports under Both Industrial and Post-Industrial Economic Structures (95% Confident Intervals)

regressions in table 2.7.[45] The short answer to this question is that my results differ from theirs because I distinguish between exports and imports. The trade openness variable used by Iversen and Cusack constrains the effects of imports and exports on government spending to have the same magnitude

Table 2.7 Reanalysis of Iversen and Cusack (2000)

	Transfers (Social Benefits)			Government Consumption	
	I&C (2000)	Reanalysis	Reanalysis	I&C (2000)	Reanalysis
Lagged Spending Level (Y_{t-1})	−.067*** (.021)	−.067*** (.026)	−.094*** (.027)	−.051*** (.013)	−.050*** (.015)
Trade Openness	−.005 (.004)			−.004* (.002)	
Δ Trade Openness	.018** (.009)			−.005 (.005)	
Imports		1.223* (.708)	1.659** (.769)		.687** (.291)
Exports		−.051 (.451)	−.550 (.482)		−.513** (.201)
Imports × Deindustrialization		−.015** (.006)	−.012* (.006)		−.002 (.003)
Deindustrialization	.044*** (.014)	.161** (.070)	.140* (.077)	.031*** (.010)	.044 (.030)
Δ Deindustrialization	.142*** (.038)	.361*** (.061)	.492*** (.068)	.090*** (.022)	.101*** (.028)
Leftist Gov. CoG	−.062 (.050)	−.082 (.059)	−.095 (.062)	.090*** (.034)	.095*** (.036)
Δ Leftist Gov. CoG	.041 (.066)	−.006 (.076)	−.017 (.081)	.049 (.041)	.031 (.042)
Electoral Participation	−.005 (.007)	−.001 (.010)	−.003 (.010)	.012*** (.004)	.011*** (.005)
Strength of Labor	.078 (.867)	.003 (.011)	−.001 (.012)	.898*** (.312)	.752** (.331)
Unexpected Growth	−.077*** (.012)	−.110*** (.016)		−.092*** (.006)	−.093*** (.007)
Automatic Transfers	.845*** (.089)				
Old Age		.100* (.053)	.096* (.053)		
Unemployment		.079** (.031)	.025 (.032)		
Automatic Consumption				.971*** (.061)	.977*** (.064)
Fixed Effects Country / Year	Yes/No	Yes/No	Yes/No	Yes/No	Yes/No
Observations	495	442	442	495	442
R-squared	.470	.353	.259	.630	.638

Notes: The fixed effect coefficient-estimates are suppressed to conserve space. Standard errors are in parentheses. *** significant at 1%; ** significant at 5%; * significant at 10%.

and sign. This is problematic because theory (as well as intuition) tells us that increasing imports and exports should have different effects on government spending. Rising imports create losers that may have to be compensated, while rising exports do not.

Other than the key change made by replacing the trade openness variables in their analysis with separate import and export variables in my reanalysis, I follow the original specifications closely with two exceptions: in the transfers regressions, I experiment with removing the automatic transfers and unexpected growth variables. I replace the automatic-transfers variable with old-age and unemployed percentages of the total population, the original controls for automatic transfers in Garrett (1998). I substitute these for Iversen and Cusack's variable because their measure of automatic transfers is calculated as the sum of the products of several ratios, and it is extremely difficult to isolate which changes (spending, demographic, or GDP) are driving the correlation with the dependent variable. Moreover, the unexpected growth variable is clearly endogenous since the dependent variable has the change in GDP (i.e., growth) in the denominator. Including this variable is likely to bias the coefficient estimates on the trade variables since rising exports are a cause of growth and growth is a cause of imports. From the table, it is clear that the main macro-level empirical results of this chapter—that imports cause increased spending both on transfers and government consumption, and that the effect is conditioned by deindustrialization—are robust and evident even when I use Iversen and Cusack's error-correction model, their sample, and most of their control variables.

To sum, the macro results presented in this section demonstrate the significance of the individual-level findings for the trade / welfare state debate. Previous research has concluded that the short-term relationship between trade and governments spending is an artifact that disappears when fixed country effects and deindustrialization are taken into account. My results show that this is not the case. The relationship between trade and government spending is robust when imports and exports are distinguished, the interactive effects of trade and deindustrialization are recognized, and the spatial interdependence in the data is modeled.

CONCLUSION

Ruggie's embedded liberalism involves a political compromise in which leaders commit their countries to freer trade while managing the dislocations that follow. My empirical tests demonstrate that this compromise is a politically feasible one. Citizens' attitudes toward trade are well informed by their self-interest according to the predictions of trade theory. At the same time, their policy preferences are malleable. Workers who compete against imports tend to oppose free trade, but their opposition can be reduced with policies designed to protect them, such as unemployment insurance.

Interestingly, the macro-level results in this chapter also suggest that governments are less responsive to imports today than in the past. As OECD countries have moved more toward service economies, the effect of import surges on spending has declined because fewer citizens work in import-competing sectors. Does this mean that the political significance of the bargain of embedded liberalism is on the decline? Probably not. The current situation with respect to trade and services is unlikely to last long. Those employed in services sectors of the economy will become increasingly exposed to international competition over time.

With respect to the U.S. economy, trade in services is growing rapidly and the balance between exports and imports is shrinking (relative to the value of these flows). According to data from the Bureau of Economic Analysis, exports of private services were worth $197 billion and imports $130 billion in 1995. By 2005, these numbers were $360 billion and $281 billion, respectively. Using measures of geographic industrial concentration, Jensen and Kletzer (2005) estimate that 13.7% of total U.S. employment is in *tradable service industries* and therefore, at least potentially, subject to international competition. Thus, it is likely that the bargain of embedded liberalism will remain politically significant well into the twenty-first century.

Appendix

In this appendix, I discuss how to estimate regression models with endogenous spatial lags on the right-hand side, show how to calculate spatio-temporal effects, and provide the STATA code I used to estimate the regressions in table 2.5.

I. ESTIMATING SPATIAL LAG MODELS

A. Least Squares Estimation

OLS estimation of model (2.1), sometimes called spatial OLS or S-OLS, is inconsistent because the regressor $\mathbf{Wy}$, the spatial lag, covaries with the residual, ε. The reason is simple; the spatial lag, $\mathbf{Wy}$, is a weighted average of the outcome in other units, thus placing the left-hand side (LHS) of some observations on the right-hand side (RHS) of others. This is textbook simultaneity. To see the implications of this endogeneity, first rewrite the spatial-lag model as

$$\mathbf{y} = \mathbf{Q\delta} + \mathbf{\varepsilon}, \tag{2.1}$$

where

$$\mathbf{Q} = [\mathbf{Wy} \quad \mathbf{My} \quad \mathbf{X}] \quad \text{and} \quad \mathbf{\delta} = [\rho \quad \phi \quad \mathbf{\beta}]'. \tag{2.2}$$

The matrices $\mathbf{Q}$ and $\mathbf{\delta}$ have dimensions $N \times (k+2)$ and $(k+2) \times 1$ respectively. The asymptotic simultaneity bias for the S-OLS estimator is given by

$$\text{plim } \hat{\mathbf{\delta}} = \mathbf{\delta} + \text{plim}\left[\left(\frac{\mathbf{Q'Q}}{n}\right)^{-1}\frac{\mathbf{Q'}\varepsilon}{n}\right]. \tag{2.3}$$

In the case where $\mathbf{Q}$ contains a single exogenous regressor $\mathbf{x}$ (i.e., $k=1$, $\text{cov}(\varepsilon, \mathbf{x}) = 0$) and the error term retains no serial dependence controlling for time-lagged $\mathbf{y}$ (i.e., $\text{cov}(\mathbf{My}, \varepsilon) = 0$), we can rewrite equation (2.3) as

$$\text{plim } \hat{\mathbf{\delta}} = \begin{bmatrix} \rho \\ \phi \\ \beta \end{bmatrix} + \frac{1}{|\mathbf{\Psi}|}\begin{bmatrix} \text{cov}(\mathbf{Wy}, \varepsilon) \times \text{var}(\mathbf{My}) \times \text{var}(\mathbf{x}) \\ -\text{cov}(\mathbf{Wy}, \varepsilon) \times \text{cov}(\mathbf{Wy}, \mathbf{My}) \times \text{var}(\mathbf{x}) \\ -\text{cov}(\mathbf{Wy}, \varepsilon) \times \text{cov}(\mathbf{Wy}, \mathbf{x}) \times \text{var}(\mathbf{My}) \end{bmatrix}, \tag{2.4}$$

where $\Psi = \text{plim}\left(\dfrac{Q'Q}{n}\right)$.

Since Ψ is a variance-covariance matrix, its determinant is strictly positive. Thus, when the data exhibit positive (negative) spatial and temporal dependence, the covariances in equation (2.4) will be positive (negative), and so S-OLS will over- (under-) estimate ρ and under- (over-) estimate ϕ and β. To elaborate, assuming $\mathbf{W}$ positive definite, $\text{cov}(\mathbf{W}y, \varepsilon)$ and $\text{cov}(\mathbf{W}y, \mathbf{M}y)$ have the same signs as ρ and ϕ, respectively, and $\text{cov}(\mathbf{W}y, \mathbf{x})$ is non-zero if $\mathbf{x}$ exhibits spatial interdependence, say $\mathbf{x} = \theta\mathbf{W}_x\mathbf{u}$, and, assuming both $\mathbf{W}$ are positive definite, has the same sign as $\rho\theta$.

In short, assuming positive spatial and temporal dependence, the most common case in practice, S-OLS estimation of spatial-lag models tends to overestimate the strength of spatial interdependence at the expense of unit-level and exogenous-external explanatory factors, including the temporal dynamics, all of which will tend consequently to be underestimated in proportion to their relative correlation with the spatial lag.

B. Maximum-Likelihood Estimation

The conditional likelihood function for the spatio-temporal-lag model, which assumes the first observation non-stochastic, is a straightforward extension of the standard spatial-lag likelihood function, which, in turn, adds only one mathematically and conceptually small complication (albeit a computationally intense one) to the likelihood function for the standard linear-normal model. To see this, start by rewriting the spatial-lag model with the stochastic component on the left:

$$y = \rho\mathbf{W}y + \mathbf{X}\beta + \varepsilon \Rightarrow \varepsilon = (\mathbf{I} - \rho\mathbf{W})y - \mathbf{X}\beta \equiv \mathbf{A}y - \mathbf{X}\beta. \qquad (2.5)$$

Assuming *i.i.d.* normality, the likelihood function for ε is then the typical linear one:

$$L(\varepsilon) = \left(\frac{1}{\sigma^2 2\pi}\right)^{\frac{NT}{2}} \exp\left(-\frac{\varepsilon'\varepsilon}{2\sigma^2}\right), \qquad (2.6)$$

which, in this case, will produce a likelihood in terms of y as follows:

$$L(y) = |\mathbf{A}|\left(\frac{1}{\sigma^2 2\pi}\right)^{\frac{NT}{2}} \exp\left(-\frac{1}{2\sigma^2}(\mathbf{A}y - \mathbf{X}\beta)'(\mathbf{A}y - \mathbf{X}\beta)\right). \qquad (2.7)$$

This still resembles the typical linear-normal likelihood, except that the transformation from ε to y is not by the usual factor, 1, but by $|\mathbf{A}| = |\mathbf{I} - \rho\mathbf{W}|$.

Note that since $|\mathbf{A}|$ depends on ρ, each time the maximum-likelihood routine recalculates the likelihood with updated estimates of ρ, it has to recalculate the determinant at these new ρ-values. Ord (1975) redressed this computational-intensity issue by using the approximation $\Pi_i \lambda_i$ for $|\mathbf{W}|$ because the vector of eigenvalues λ does not depend on ρ. Using $|\mathbf{I} - \rho\mathbf{W}| = \Pi_i(1 - \rho\lambda_i)$ for $|\mathbf{A}|$ requires the estimation routine only to recalculate a product, not a determinant, as it updates. The estimated variance-covariances of parameter estimates follow the usual ML formula (negative the inverse of Hessian of the likelihood) and so are also functions of $|\mathbf{A}|$. The analogous strategies may serve there.

II. CALCULATING AND PRESENTING SPATIO-TEMPORAL EFFECTS

Calculation, interpretation, and presentation of effects in empirical models with spatio-temporal interdependence involve more than simply considering coefficient estimates. *Coefficients* do *not* generally equate to *effects* beyond that simplest strictly linear-additive world. In empirical models containing spatio-temporal dynamics, as in those with only temporal dynamics, for example, coefficients on explanatory variables give only the pre-dynamic impetuses to the outcome variable from changes in those variables. The coefficients represent only the (often inherently unobservable) pre-interdependence impetus to outcomes associated with each RHS variable.

This section discusses the calculation of spatio-temporal multipliers, which allow expression of the effects of counterfactual shocks of various kinds to some unit(s) on itself (themselves) and other units over time, accounting both the temporal and spatial dynamics. These multipliers also allow expression the long-run, steady-state, or equilibrium impact of such permanent shocks. In this section, I also apply the delta-method to derive analytically the asymptotic approximate standard errors for these response-path and long-run effect estimates.[46]

Calculating the cumulative, steady-state spatio-temporal effects is most convenient working with the spatio-temporal-lag model in (N x 1) vector form:

$$\mathbf{y}_t = \rho\mathbf{W}\mathbf{y}_t + \phi\mathbf{y}_{t-1} + \mathbf{X}_t\beta + \varepsilon_t. \tag{2.8}$$

To find the long-run, steady-state, equilibrium (cumulative) level of $\mathbf{y}$, simply set $\mathbf{y}_{t-1}$ equal to $\mathbf{y}_t$ in (2.8) and solve. This gives the steady-state effect, assuming stationarity and that the exogenous RHS terms, $\mathbf{X}$ and ε, remain permanently fixed to their hypothetical/counterfactual levels:[47]

$$
\begin{aligned}
\mathbf{y}_t &= \rho \mathbf{W}\mathbf{y}_t + \phi \mathbf{y}_t + \mathbf{X}_t\boldsymbol{\beta} + \varepsilon_t \\
&= (\rho\mathbf{W} + \phi\mathbf{I})\mathbf{y}_t + \mathbf{X}_t\boldsymbol{\beta} + \varepsilon_t \\
&= [\mathbf{I}_N - \rho\mathbf{W} - \phi\mathbf{I}_N]^{-1}(\mathbf{X}_t\boldsymbol{\beta} + \varepsilon_t) \\
&=
\begin{bmatrix}
1-\phi & -\rho w_{1,2} & \cdots & & \cdots & -\rho w_{1,N} \\
-\rho w_{2,1} & 1-\phi & & & & \vdots \\
\vdots & & \ddots & & & \vdots \\
\vdots & & & 1-\phi & & -\rho w_{(N-1),N} \\
-\rho w_{N,1} & \cdots & & \cdots & -\rho w_{N(N-1)} & 1-\phi
\end{bmatrix}^{-1}
(\mathbf{X}_t\boldsymbol{\beta} + \varepsilon_t). \\
&\equiv \mathbf{S}(\mathbf{X}_t\boldsymbol{\beta} + \varepsilon_t)
\end{aligned}
\tag{2.9}
$$

To offer standard-error estimates for these steady-state estimates, one could use the delta method, that is, give a first-order Taylor-series linear-approximation to nonlinear (2.9) around the estimated parameter-values and determine the asymptotic variance of that linear approximation. To find the key elements needed for this, begin by denoting the ith column of $\mathbf{S}$ as $\mathbf{s}_i$ and its estimate as $\hat{\mathbf{s}}_i$. The steady-state spatio-temporal effects of a one-unit increase in explanatory variable k in country i are $\mathbf{s}_i\beta_k$ giving delta-method standard-errors of

$$
\widehat{\mathbf{V}(\hat{\mathbf{s}}_i\hat{\beta}_k)} = \left[\frac{\partial\hat{\mathbf{s}}_i\hat{\beta}_k}{\partial\hat{\boldsymbol{\theta}}}\right]\widehat{\mathbf{V}(\hat{\boldsymbol{\theta}})}\left[\frac{\partial\hat{\mathbf{s}}_i\hat{\beta}_k}{\partial\hat{\boldsymbol{\theta}}}\right]',
\tag{2.10}
$$

where $\hat{\boldsymbol{\theta}} \equiv [\rho\,\hat{\theta}\,\hat{\beta}_k]'$, $\left[\dfrac{\partial\hat{\mathbf{s}}_i\hat{\beta}_k}{\partial\hat{\boldsymbol{\theta}}}\right] \equiv \left[\dfrac{\partial\hat{\mathbf{s}}_i\hat{\beta}_k}{\partial\hat{\rho}}\ \dfrac{\partial\hat{\mathbf{s}}_i\hat{\beta}_k}{\partial\hat{\phi}}\ \hat{\mathbf{s}}_i\right]$, and the vectors $\left[\dfrac{\partial\mathbf{s}_i\beta_k}{\partial\rho}\right]$

and $\left[\dfrac{\partial\hat{\mathbf{s}}_i\hat{\beta}_k}{\partial\hat{\phi}}\right]$ are the ith columns of $\hat{\beta}_k\hat{\mathbf{S}}\mathbf{W}\hat{\mathbf{S}}$ and $\hat{\beta}_k\hat{\mathbf{S}}\hat{\mathbf{S}}$ respectively.

The spatio-temporal response path of the $N \times 1$ vector of unit outcomes, $\mathbf{y}_t$, to the exogenous RHS terms, $\mathbf{X}$ and ε, could also emerge by rearranging (2.8) to isolate $\mathbf{y}_t$ on the LHS:

$$
\mathbf{y}_t = [\mathbf{I}_N - \rho\mathbf{W}_N]^{-1}\{\phi\mathbf{y}_{t-1} + \mathbf{X}_t\boldsymbol{\beta} + \varepsilon_t\}.
\tag{2.11}
$$

This formula gives the response-paths of all unit(s) $\{i\}$ to hypothetical shocks to $\mathbf{X}$ or ε in any unit(s) $\{j\}$, including a shock in $\{i\}$ itself/themselves, just by setting $(\mathbf{X}_t\boldsymbol{\beta} + \varepsilon_t)$ to one in the row(s) corresponding to $\{j\}$. To calculate marginal spatio-temporal effects (non-cumulative) or plot the over-time path of the effect of a permanent one-unit change in an explanatory variable (cumulative), and their standard errors, working with the entire $NT \times NT$ matrix is easier. Simply redefine $\mathbf{S}$ in the (2.9) as $\mathbf{S} \equiv [\mathbf{I}_{NT} - \rho\mathbf{W} - \phi\mathbf{M}]^{-1}$ and follow the steps outlined above.

III. STATA CODE FOR IMPLEMENTING THE S-ML ESTIMATOR

```
clear
pr drop _all
set more off
************************
* Likelihood Evaluator
************************
program define splag_11
args lnf mu rho sigma
tempvar A rSL
gen 'A' = ones—'rho'*EIGS1
gen 'rSL'='rho'*SL1
qui replace 'lnf' = ln('A') + ln(normden($ML_y1−'rSL'−'mu,' 0, 'sigma'))
end
*Number of Observations in the Dataset
global nobs = ???
************************
* Open Data For Weights
************************
clear
use "C:\PATH_HERE\weights_matrix_data_file.dta," clear
* This file should contain the ful NT x NT spatial weights matrix
************************
mkmat var1-var ???, matrix(W)
matrix eigenvalues eig1 imaginaryv = W
matrix eig2 = eig1'
matrix ones=J($nobs,1,1)
**************************
* Open Data for Regression
**************************
drop _all
use "C:\PATH_HERE\data_file.dta," clear
**************************
global Y dependent_variable
global X iv_1 iv_2 iv_3
mkmat $Y, matrix(Y)
matrix SL = W*Y
svmat SL, n(SL)
svmat eig2, n(EIGS)
svmat ones, n(ones)
************************
*Produce starting values
************************
qui regress $Y $X
matrix OLSb=e(b)
```

```
local OLSsigma=e(rmse)
****************************
*Estimate spatial lag model
****************************
ml model lf splag_11 (mu: $Y=$X) (rho:) (sigma:), vce(opg)
ml init OLSb
ml init rho:_cons=0
ml init sigma:_cons='OLSsigma'
ml max
predict yhat
mkmat yhat, matrix(yhat)
matrix eye = I($nobs)
matrix mult = eye—_b[rho:_cons]*W
matrix yhat_m = ((yhat')*inv(mult))'
matrix e2 = (Y—yhat_m)'*(Y—yhat_m)
scalar e2 = e2[1,1]
qui summarize $Y
matrix ym = r(mean)*J($nobs,1,1)
matrix ym2 = (Y—ym)'*(Y—ym)
scalar ym2 = ym2[1,1]
scalar r2 = 1—(e2/ym2)
scalar list r2
```

3

Trade and Employment Volatility in Corporatist and Competitive Labor Markets

The politics of international economic openness has both a *demand* and *supply* side to it. Workers exposed to international competition *demand* protection, which governments *supply* in a number of different forms, including tariffs, insurance, and various kinds of adjustment assistance. Governments committed to economic openness prefer to supply policies like insurance and adjustment assistance (rather than tariffs) in return for public support for trade. This is the essence of embedded liberalism. In the previous chapter, I established the empirical validity of the embedded liberalism thesis. At the individual level, workers employed in import-competing industries are less likely to support free trade than those working in export-oriented sectors of the economy. The strength of their opposition to free trade, however, depends on how well they are protected from or compensated for income loss due to trade-related dislocations. At the macro-level, the evidence from the OECD countries suggests that government spending depends, in part, on how exposed the domestic workforce is to international competition.

Starting with Ruggie's notion of embedded liberalism, Rodrik (1997) identifies a significant globalization dilemma: growing international economic integration increases the *demand* on governments for protection and compensation at the same time that it undermines their ability to *supply* policies that require significant government spending. More workers are exposed to international competition through trade, and increased international capital mobility makes it difficult for governments to finance spending. Thanks to this dilemma, countries are politically vulnerable to a backlash against globalization. The unfortunate possibility is that constrained governments will abandon their commitment to economic openness by adopting restrictions on international trade and capital flows. In this way, Rodrik's globalization dilemma can be viewed as a crisis of embedded liberalism (Keohane 1984; Garrett 1998).

The purpose of this chapter and the next is to argue that, because of important cross-national differences in domestic political and economic institutions, the severity of Rodrik's globalization dilemma varies across countries. In particular, the degree to which globalization increases demands for protection depends on how, and the extent to which, shocks in international commercial markets are transmitted to domestic labor markets. This depends greatly on a country's labor market institutions (Blanchard and Wolfers 2000; Blau and Kahn 2002). I focus on the differences between corporatist (coordinated) and competitive (liberal) labor markets, arguing that trade generates more risk for those who operate in the latter. The economic insecurity leads workers to pressure their governments for protection.

In my analysis, trade generates employment volatility in countries with competitive labor markets for two reasons. First, in competitive markets, trade-related shocks to the economy (e.g., shocks to foreign demand or the competitiveness of foreign firms) are passed to workers in terms of employment levels. Second, trade makes the demand for labor more elastic in these countries, which, in turn, makes market outcomes more sensitive to all shocks, both international and domestic. The mechanisms in the competitive case, discussed below, are straightforward market mechanisms that are well-known to political economists (e.g., Rodrik 1997, chapter 2). With respect to the corporatist case, I argue that the role of unions in a system of consensual and coordinated wage bargaining generates stability. Under corporatism, workers delegate authority to negotiate employment contracts to an agent (the union) with stronger preferences for work (employment) over leisure (unemployment) than they, the principals, hold. This delegation within a system of industrial relations that encourages a consensual cost-sharing approach to economic adjustment generates employment stability. The empirical evidence strongly supports my claim that competitive labor markets experience more employment volatility than their corporatist counterparts, and trade amplifies this difference. There is support for the two causal mechanisms highlighted for the competitive case as well.

It is important to be clear about the kind of labor market volatility and employment risk that I have in mind. I focus primarily on the risk that someone will become unemployed over a given span of time. This is largely distinct from the probability that an individual remains unemployed for an extended period. In fact, these two risks seem to be inversely related. I take the position that the risk of becoming unemployed in competitive labor markets is more politically problematic, when compared with the risk of long-term unemployment, because it affects a larger portion of the citizenry. I also argue that citizens hold politicians responsible for predictable and sustained levels of labor market volatility, risk that is driven by trade-related and other factors over which politicians may have some control, and not for unexpectedly large random shocks to employment, especially when there is no volatility clustering.

In the next section, I discuss some of the new challenges to corporatism and how corporatist institutions have evolved in response to them. In the second section, I theoretically examine how trade affects labor market *volatility* in both competitive and corporatist systems, a topic that gets relatively little attention in the literature. I then turn to the empirical relationships between trade, employment, and labor market volatility. In the final section, I review the broader literature on the comparative economic performance of national labor markets throughout the OECD, focusing primarily on the issue of wage inequality. Unfortunately, the same workers who are experiencing greater employment uncertainty and risk are also seeing their real wages decline, at least relative to individuals in the top income brackets. Thus, the trends in wage inequality only exacerbate the political problems caused by higher levels of employment volatility in the Anglo-American democracies.

CORPORATISM YESTERDAY AND TODAY

In chapter 1, I discussed how globalization *pessimists* argue that corporatism is under significant pressure as a result of the internationalization of markets for goods, services, and capital and is therefore unlikely to survive over the long term. I believe the *optimists* have made a strong case, both theoretically and empirically, that this fear is exaggerated and that corporatism is not in a state of terminal decline. This is not to say that corporatist institutions have remained static in the face of global economic change. In this section, I start by defining the central features of corporatism for my purposes and then briefly discuss how corporatist institutions have evolved over the last two to three decades. In the end, I conclude that corporatism *qua* coordinated and consensual wage bargaining continues to shape how workers experience the pressures of global economic integration, particularly in the Nordic countries and Austria.

Maier (1984, 40) defines corporatism as a system of "broad concertation between employer and employee representatives across industries, which is usually established and sometimes continually supervised under state auspices." This concertation, which operates through consensual wage bargaining, perhaps the defining corporatist institution, responds "to criteria of a broader public interest, transcending the short-term profits or pay increases that a given labour market might allow."[1] According to Maier, the national will for strongly consensual industrial relations emerged from an extreme sense of economic vulnerability and a need to fairly distribute the costs of economic austerity after World War II, and, in some cases, a desire to move beyond destabilizing internal confessional and (or) class divisions. Similarly, Katzenstein (1985) argues that democratic corporatism is distinguished by an ideology of social partnership, centralized systems of interest intermediation, and continuous bargaining. He emphasizes that historically the "corporatist bargain" was built on an "electoral bargain," which was institutionalized by the adoption of proportional representation electoral systems in the small countries of western Europe. Proportional representation, by encouraging political opponents to share power, "generated its own political predictability, enhanced the prospects for consensus, and thus facilitated the corporatist compromise of the 1930s" (Katzenstein 1985, 156).

For my purposes, corporatism is defined by three central features. First and foremost, employment relations are governed by collective contracts that are negotiated by unions. Second, the relationship between employers and unions is cooperative rather than adversarial, as emphasized by both Maier and Katzenstein. This cooperation is typically encouraged and facilitated by political cooperation among left and right-wing parties, and it remains an important feature of twenty-first century corporatism (e.g., Rhodes 2001). And finally, there is economy-wide coordination with respect to wages. I do not emphasize centralization as being critical to successful wage and employment coordination, and this differs somewhat from the older conventional view, including Katzenstein's. Corporatist countries have the institutional capacity to promote coordinated economy-wide wage restraint, but centralization, as typically defined in the literature, is not the only way to achieve that end (e.g., Soskice 1990).

In its heyday, corporatism was celebrated for the flexible adaptability that it promoted. During the 1970s, the small western European countries weathered the turbulent storm that was the international economy better than their large economy counterparts, and most observers attributed this success to corporatism. However, the corporatist economies fared less well in the post-Keynesian 1980s and 1990s. Corporatist institutions were strained by changing production processes and welfare state maturation. Many scholars have pointed to the decentralization of collective bargaining in Sweden and elsewhere and the decline of unionism around the world as incontrovertible evidence of corporatism's decline. This inference is probably incorrect. Strong incentives remain for countries to pursue coordinated adjustment to economic shocks and structural change. In fact, there has been an increase in the number of "social pacts"—in countries like the Netherlands, Italy, Ireland, Portugal and Spain—designed precisely for this purpose (Rhodes 2001; Mares 2006; Hamann and Kelly 2007).

Those who see corporatism in decline have focused their attention on wage-bargaining decentralization in Sweden, the paragon country of corporatism, where for many decades centralized wage bargains were negotiated between the SAF, the Swedish peak association of private employers, and the LO, the peak association for blue-collar workers.[2] Decentralization in

Sweden began in 1983 when the Association of Engineering Employers (VF), an influential affiliate within the SAF, and the Metalworkers' union (Metall) left the system of peak-level bargaining to negotiate separate employment contracts. Seven years later the system suffered a serious blow when the SAF announced that it would not participate in centralized collective bargaining. There were unsuccessful attempts to revitalize peak-level bargaining between the mid-1980s and early 1990s, but the system had been irreversibly transformed by that point (Pontusson and Swenson 1996).

Sweden is certainly one of the most visible cases of labor market reform, but it is not the only corporatist country to have undergone significant wage bargaining decentralization over the last few decades. In Denmark, decentralization began in the early 1980s after several failures to reach national-level wage agreements (Iversen 1996). The Finnish system became more decentralized in 1993 when the peak-level confederations began negotiating "opening clauses" to industry-level collective agreements. Since the early 1990s national agreements have been used to determine the issue areas open to bargaining, typically wages and work-time related issues, at the industry and firm levels and to set minimum requirements in these and other areas for all agreements (Niemela 1999).[3] Interestingly, the trend toward decentralized bargaining has not affected industrial relations in either Austria or Norway. If anything, in Norway, there was increased centralization during the 1980s and 1990s, in large part because of the need to contain the inflationary pressure generated by the oil industry (Iversen 1996, 1999; Bowman 2002). In Austria, the level of centralization has remained remarkably stable both in the level of centralization and in the mode of corporatist coordination (Traxler 2004). Iversen (1996, 1999) attributes the stability of the Austrian system to the fact that it did not lead to the same level of wage compression as in the Scandinavian cases.

What explains wage-bargaining decentralization, and does this trend imply a general movement away from coordinated labor markets to competitive uncoordinated ones? While corporatism was celebrated for the flexibility that it promoted in 1970s, there seems to be a consensus among scholars that, by the 1980s, in some countries, centralized bargaining undermined the ability of firms to compete in global markets. Wage solidarity and interoccupational leveling of wages within industries was relatively unproblematic for employers during the age of Fordist mass production.[4] With the shift to flexible specialization, however, wage compression prevented employers from rewarding productive and creative employees and reduced incentives for workers to make investments in firm specific skills (Iverson 1996' Eichengreen and Iversen 1999). In Sweden, for example, the bargaining power of low-wage employees in the LO and the commitment of Social Democratic employers to wage solidarity in government employment led to extreme interoccupational leveling in both the private and public sectors, which, in turn, produced distributional conflicts and inflationary wage rivalries among labor groups (Pontusson and Swenson 1996).

Most scholars now agree that wage bargaining decentralization does not necessarily imply a movement to liberal uncoordinated labor markets (Traxler 1995). For Soskice (1990), informal networks can help promote coordination with respect to wage setting across economic sectors. Traxler and Kittel (2000) argue that institutions that facilitate trust between employers and workers are crucial to decentralized coordination. They emphasize the legal enforceability of collective bargaining agreements and binding prohibitions on industrial action while agreements are in force. When both conditions are present—as they are in the Nordic countries and Austria—the wage bargaining system is "highly governable." Traxler (2004) finds that decentralization has no effect on wage restraint for highly governable systems. For Iversen (1999), the move to non-accommodating monetary policy also may improve the capacity for decentralized coordination and wage restraint. He argues that a new "monetarist decentralization" equilibrium has replaced the old "Keynesian centralization" equilibrium (cf. Hall and Franzese 1998). In short, the move to more decentralized wage bargaining systems in many of the corporatist economies of western Europe does not represent a move to competitive and uncoordinated labor markets. In fact, most of these systems have the same or even greater capacity to deliver wage restraint and promote employment than previously.

In the end, I largely agree with Pontusson's (2005, 113) assessment of the future for coordinated wage bargaining:

> The wage-bargaining arrangements characteristic of northern Europe's social market economies have traditionally facilitated coordinated wage restraint by enabling national union and employer organizations to manage their internal conflicts more effectively. The macro-economic benefits of coordinated wage bargaining do not appear to have diminished over time: quite the contrary, they have probably increased as globalization has progressed. To the extent that the capacity of unions and employers to coordinate their wage-bargaining behavior has diminished, this trend has been more pronounced in liberal than social market economies...coordinated bargaining remains possible and desirable for the social market economies.

EMPLOYMENT VOLATILITY IN COMPETITIVE AND CORPORATIST SYSTEMS

The formal theoretical literature on corporatism in both economics and political science is large and sophisticated (for example, Calmfors and Driffill 1988; Summers et al. 1993; Hall and Franzese 1998; Iversen 1999; Mares 2006).

Scholars are now focusing on complex interactive relationships between corporatism and central banking institutions, welfare state regimes, and tax systems, to name just a few of the topics at the research frontier. In this section, I focus on the role of consensual wage bargaining. The theoretical models suggest that trade will affect employment volatility more in competitive labor markets than in corporatist ones because the employment effects of demand shocks are minimized in the latter. In this way, my argument differs from Rodrik's (1997: 23–25) that globalization will have similar effects on labor markets, regardless of the particular system of industrial relations in place, because trade and the multinationalization of production undermine the bargaining power of unions, which affects wages and the distribution of economic surplus between capital and labor. I argue that the consensual nature of bargaining in most of the corporatist countries is firmly entrenched politically and unlikely to change, at least in the near future, as a result of economic globalization. However, before turning to the corporatist case, I show theoretically how trade and the globalization of production affect employment volatility in competitive labor markets. The competitive case is widely known, and the theory is well-developed. My purpose is to remind readers of the factors at work rather than to provide a new theoretical model.

Trade and Employment in Competitive Labor Markets

I rely on a partial-equilibrium model of production with three inputs: domestic (or home) labor, foreign labor, and capital, denoted L^h, L^f, and K, respectively. I present the model's basic assumptions and key results below, and describe the intuition behind the results. I save most of the math and formal proof for the appendix at the end of the chapter. With respect to notation, unless noted otherwise, I use superscripts for indexes and subscripts for partial derivates. The first step is to find the demand for domestic labor. In particular, we are interested in the slope of the labor demand curve, the change in labor demanded for a unit change in the wage. Assume a representative firm with output

$$Y = F(L^h, L^f, K). \tag{3.1}$$

Domestic and foreign labor are paid wages w^h and w^f, and capital is paid a return r. The firm is not taxed, and the competitive price of the good sold by the firm is fixed at one. Therefore, profits are

$$\Pi = F(L^h, L^f, K) - w^h L^h - w^f L^f - rK. \tag{3.2}$$

The first-order conditions for equation (3.2), the conditions under which the firm's profit is maximized, imply $F_{L^h} = w^h$ and $F_{L^f} = w^f$. In other words, wages are equal to the marginal productivity of labor. For now I assume that the supply of capital is fixed and perfectly inelastic. Consequently, investment decisions drop out of the model. In the next chapter, I make the supply of capital endogenous.

The positive cross-effects of L^f on the marginal productivity of L^h make the optimal input of domestic labor a function of both the domestic and foreign wage. To solve for $\dfrac{\partial L^{h*}}{\partial w^h}$, the slope of the labor demand curve (where L^{h*} represents the optimal input of domestic labor), we examine how the profit maximizing behavior of firms described by the first-order conditions changes with an exogenous increase in the domestic wage. The solution for $\dfrac{\partial L^{h*}}{\partial w^h}$ is

$$\frac{\partial L^{h*}}{\partial w^h} = \frac{F_{L^f L^f}}{F_{L^h L^h} F_{L^f L^f} - F_{L^h L^f}^2},\qquad (3.3)$$

where L^{h*} is the profit maximizing labor input. (See appendix for the derivation.) Equation (3.3) shows that, as the cross-effects of foreign labor on domestic labor productivity increase, the demand for domestic labor becomes more sensitive (i.e., more elastic) to changes in the domestic wage. Note that if the marginal productivity of domestic labor does not depend on the level of foreign labor, the two input decisions are made independently, and the right-hand side simplifies to the well-known result for a single factor, $\dfrac{\partial L^{h*}}{\partial w^h} = \dfrac{1}{F_{L^h L^h}}$

where the demand for domestic labor is the inverse of the change in its marginal productivity (Hamermesh 1993). Expression (3.3) generalizes this result to allow for cross-effects on productivity.

How does trade affect labor demand? In this model, trade affects the elasticity of the demand for domestic labor by increasing the size of the cross-effects on marginal labor productivity ($F_{L^h L^f}$). The most straightforward example of this kind of cross-effect is when foreign labor is used to provide intermediate inputs for production through outsourcing or foreign direct investment. As trade becomes cheaper, either as a result of changing technology or policy, the firm is able to provide more intermediate inputs using a fixed amount of foreign labor. This, in turn, raises the productivity of domestic labor. When there is an exogenous increase in the domestic wage, the firm cuts back its employment of domestic labor and expands employment of foreign labor until domestic labor productivity matches the new wage rate. The firm reduces domestic employment by more when the cross-effect on productivity is large. Of course, this is not the only way that trade can affect the elasticity of the demand for domestic labor (see, for example, Rodrik 1997, 1998; Slaughter 2001). Outside of the model presented here, trade can make it easier to substitute foreign labor directly for domestic labor. Trade can also increase the competitiveness of the goods markets, making the demand for these goods more elastic, which, in turn, makes the demand for the labor used to produce these goods more elastic.[5]

Turning next to labor supply, the standard derivation draws on consumer theory. Individuals consume levels of a market good (c) and leisure (ℓ) that maximize their utility (u),

$$u = u(c, \ell), \tag{3.4}$$

subject to a budget constraint

$$w^h t = w^h \ell + c + e, \tag{3.5}$$

where w^h is the wage paid (per-period) to labor, t is the total time available for work, and e is a non-wage income endowment. An individual's labor effort l^h is the total time available for work less the time devoted to leisure ($t - \ell$). Therefore, another way to state the budget constraint in (3.5) is: $c = w^h l^h + e$.

The first order condition, which determines the utility maximizing work effort, is

$$u_\ell(l^{h*}(w^h))/u_c(l^{h*}(w^h)) = w^h. \tag{3.6}$$

The left-hand side of equation (3.6), the ratio of the marginal utilities evaluated at (c, ℓ), is the marginal rate of substitution of consumption for leisure (i.e., the marginal utility of leisure in terms of forgone consumption), which is equal to the wage. We can find the labor supply curve by taking the derivative of (3.6) with respect to the wage rate, w^k, and solving for $\dfrac{\partial l^{h*}}{\partial w^h}$. Both leisure and the market good are assumed to be normal goods—their consumption increases with income—and therefore the sign of the labor supply curve's slope is ambiguous. Rising wages have both a substitution and an income effect on work effort. As wages rise, the cost of leisure relative to the market good increases and so individuals substitute more of the latter for the former. But the income effect implies that individuals will choose more leisure at higher wages. The substitution and income effects work in opposite directions. The slope of the supply curve, written in terms of its constituent parts, is

$$\frac{\partial l^{h*}}{\partial w^h} = \frac{\partial \bar{l}^{h*}}{\partial w^h} + (t - l^{h*})\frac{\partial l^{h*}}{\partial e} \tag{3.7}$$

where $\dfrac{\partial \bar{l}^{h*}}{\partial w^h}$, the change in labor supplied holding utility constant, represents a pure substitution effect, an increase in labor supplied due to the increased cost of leisure, and $(t - l^{h*})\dfrac{\partial l^{h*}}{\partial e}$ is a pure income effect.[6] It is generally assumed that the slope of the supply curve is positive at low wages—the substitution effect is greater than the income effect—but may bend backward at some point as wages increase. In the analysis below, I assume that the labor supply curve is upward sloping. Summing over the individual firms' and workers' schedules, which are assumed to be identical, gives the aggregate labor demand and supply curves, L^D and L^S, respectively, which are

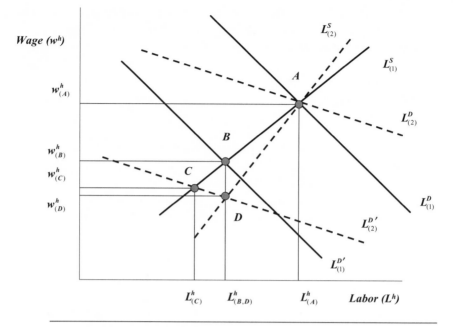

Notes: The market begins at point *A* where the inelastic (steep) labor demand curve $L^D_{(1)}$ intersects the initial labor supply curve $L^S_{(1)}$. A negative demand shock changes the equilibrium to point *B* at which both wages and employment are lower. If the demand for labor is more elastic (flatter) $L^D_{(2)}$, then the same shock (measured by vertical distance in the wage-employment space) leads to a larger decline in both equilibrium wages and employment at point *C*.

Figure 3.1 Labor Demand Shocks in a Competitive Market

graphed in figure 3.1. Note that I have dropped the *h* superscripts from the supply and demand curves (except along the axes), and the subscripts do not represent partial derivatives, but rather index alternative labor market conditions. I make these notational changes because my focus is exclusively on the domestic labor market and how changing market conditions affect equilibrium levels of employment. The curves are drawn as lines for convenience.

As the cost of trade declines, the elasticity of the demand for labor increases. This implies that a change in the domestic wage leads to relatively larger changes in the quantity of domestic labor demanded. Graphically, the demand curve becomes flatter. Figure 3.1 illustrates some of the labor market consequences from this change in demand. There are two sets of labor demand curves labeled (1) and (2), and each set contains both a high and low demand curve. The latter (low) demand curve is marked with a prime ($L^D_{(\cdot)}$) while the former (high) demand curve is not ($L^D_{(\cdot)}$). The curves in the first set are relatively inelastic compared to those in the second. There are also two supply curves with the first ($L^S_{(1)}$) being relatively elastic when compared to the second ($L^S_{(2)}$).

Figure 3.1 shows the market response to the same negative demand shock, a parallel downward shift in the labor demand curve, when demand is both elastic and inelastic. The size of the shock is measured by the vertical distance between the original and post-shock curves, the wage difference for a given level of labor demand. For example, if labor is paid the value of its marginal product and the price of the good produced by labor drops by 10%, then the wage at each level of labor demand should drop by 10% as well. In each case, the market begins at point **A**. After the shock, the market moves to point **B** when the demand for labor is relatively inelastic and point **C** when the demand for labor is elastic. In the latter case, the negative shock leads to a larger decrease in the equilibrium wage and level of employment. If we were to draw figure 3.1 with a positive demand shock, we would see that there is a larger increase in equilibrium wages and employment when the demand for labor is elastic. In short, we expect more labor market volatility.

I include the second labor supply curve (the dashed line $L^S_{(2)}$) to show that, in a competitive market, the only way to offset the employment consequences of an increase in the elasticity of labor demand is a decrease in the elasticity of labor supply. In other words, preferences would have to change such that workers value leisure relatively less compared to work (and consumption) at low wages and relatively more at high wages. With a more vertical labor supply curve, shocks to labor demand produce smaller changes in equilibrium employment. In the elastic demand case described above, the new market equilibrium is at point **D** instead of point **C**.[7] This is important because I argue below that, by delegating authority to an agent that values leisure less than they (i.e., a labor union), workers may experience less employment volatility and higher utility than they would otherwise.

Unions and Corporatist Labor Markets

As a system of industrial relations, corporatism differs from competitive market regimes in several ways. First and foremost, in corporatist labor markets, unions play an important role in determining wages and levels of employment. From the older conventional perspective (Katzenstein 1985; Calmfors and Driffill 1988), the unions are also more "encompassing"—that is, they represent a larger share of the workforce and are organizationally more centralized under corporatism. The formal theoretical models of corporatism in the literature, almost invariably, focus on "encompassment" (e.g., Summers et al. 1993; Iversen 1999; and Mares 2006). The feature of corporatism that often gets overlooked in the formal models is the consensual nature of the bargaining between unions and employers. Despite the importance of bargaining under corporatism, almost all of the models, with the exception of Summers et al. (1993), build upon the "monopoly union" framework in which bargaining is wholly absent. Unions set the wage and firms set the level of employment; both actions are taken unilaterally.

In this section, I focus on the effects that consensual bargaining has on employment outcomes in corporatist systems. I start with the "efficient contracts" framework in which firms and unions bargain over both the wage and levels of employment. The theory suggests that there is less labor market volatility when unions and employers cooperate to set wages and employment. By consensual bargaining, I mean that the negotiated contracts reflect the state of the economy in the following way. When wages and employment are high and profits are low, the negotiated terms of employment will be closer to the firm's ideal outcome. Conversely, when wages and employment are low and profits are high, the negotiated terms will be closer to those most preferred by the union. In other words, workers and employers share the costs of economic adjustment. I assume this behavior for now. In chapter 5, I argue that governments play an important role in inducing this cost-sharing behavior, and multiparty governments are more successful in doing so than their single-party counterparts. Because the recent literature (discussed above) downplays the importance of centralization, I do not focus on this aspect of corporatist systems.

To begin, we need to specify a utility function for the union. One of the simplest functions is

$$U = wL^\gamma + (N - L^\gamma)\overline{b} \qquad (3.8)$$

where N is the number of union members, assumed to be exogenous, L is the number of employed union members, and w and $\overline{b}$ are the wage paid to employed union members and the average value of leisure among the unemployed union members respectively.[8] The union's utility is an aggregate function of its members' individual-level utilities. The parameter γ determines the extent to which the union values employment relative to wages. To see the importance of γ, it is useful to write down the individual-level version of (3.8). Assuming $u(c) = wl$ and $u(\ell) = (t - l)b$, where b is an individual-specific constant value of leisure, we have

$$u = l(w - b) + tb, \qquad (3.9)$$

a specific form of the utility function (3.4) in which the individual's total utility is the sum of his or her utility from regular consumption financed by work and leisure. In this setup, the individual's optimization problem has a corner solution.[9] Those for whom the wage is higher than the value of leisure will work full time and the others will choose not to work. If $\gamma = 1$, the union's utility (3.8) is the sum of its individual members' utilities (3.9). I assume that the union values employment more and leisure less than its members do, up until the point where L^*, the competitive equilibrium level of employment, equals N. In other words, I assume γ is a function of L^*, or, more completely: if $L^* \geq N$, then $\gamma = 1$ and $\dfrac{d\gamma}{dL} = 0$, else $\gamma > 1$, $\dfrac{d\gamma}{dL} < 0$. A couple of justifications that could be given for this are, inter alia, the union collects more dues at higher levels of employment among its membership or the union sees employment promotion for the rank-and-file as its primary raison d'être. The key result is that workers collectively can achieve higher levels of employment stability at lower cost (i.e., higher wages) by delegating authority to negotiate employment contracts to an agent with stronger preferences for employment over leisure than they themselves have.[10]

The union's utility function is represented in the wage-employment space by a set of indifference curves (see figure 3.2). These curves, labeled I^1–I^4, give all combinations of wage and employment outcomes over which the union is indifferent. The indifference curves are convex to the origin, and higher indifference curves represent higher levels of utility. The labor market preferences of profit maximizing firms are represented in the wage-employment space with isoprofit curves that give the combinations of wages and levels of employment over which profits are constant. Isoprofit curves intersect the labor demand schedule at their maximum point, and lower curves imply

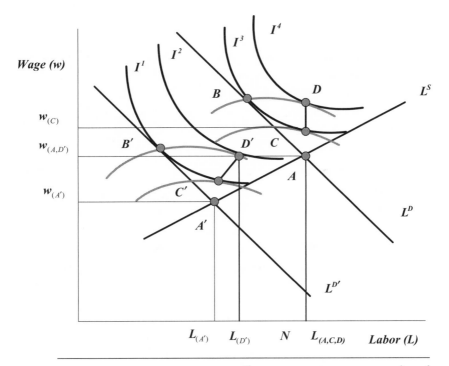

Notes: When the demand for labor is low $L^{D'}$, the union's indifference curves, I^1 and I^2, are such that the contract curve is upward sloping from point C' to D' ($\gamma > 1$). When the demand for labor is high L^D, the union's indifference curves, I^3 and I^4, are such that the contract curve is vertical from point C to D ($\gamma = 1$). The intertemporal cost-sharing approach to economic adjustment implies the firm will accept D' when the demand for labor is low and the union will accept C when the demand for labor is high.

Figure 3.2 Consensual Bargaining under Corporatism

larger profits. To simplify the analysis, I assume that there are no labor productivity cross-effects (i.e., $F_{L^h L^f} = 0$). Again, there is a high demand curve (L^D)
and a low demand curve marked with a prime ($L^{D'}$) and therefore two sets of
isoprofit curves underlying them. Finally, there is a single labor supply curve.

If the union sets the wage and the firm chooses the level of employment,
as in the "monopoly union" model, the equilibria in figure 3.2 are **B** when
demand is high and **B'** when demand is low. The union simply chooses the
point along the labor demand curve that is tangent to its highest indifference
curve. Despite the popularity of this model, its usefulness for understanding
corporatist labor markets seems limited because it fails to capture the fact that
unions and employers bargain consensually over both the wage and levels of
employment. It does not allow unions to trade lower wages for higher levels
of employment (i.e., practice wage restraint), which some consider to be the
sine qua non of successful corporatism in the Nordic countries and Austria.

If unions and employers bargain over wages and employment, it is clear
that the outcomes **B** and **B'** are not Pareto efficient. In the case of low labor
demand, for example, both the union and firm could be made better off with
lower wages and higher levels of employment. In fact, the union is much
happier with outcome **D'** while the firm is indifferent between **B'** and **D'**.
The firm, on the other hand, is much happier with **C'** while the union is
indifferent between **B'** and **C'**. Both **B'** and **C'** are points of tangency between
the union's utility curve and the firm's isoprofit curve. The line that connects
these outcomes, called the efficient-contracts curve, has the slope:

$$\frac{dL}{dw} = \frac{[1-\gamma]}{F_{LL} + [w-b]\dfrac{d\gamma}{dL}} \tag{3.10}$$

For any point off the efficient-contracts curve, there is a point on the curve
where at least one of the actors is better off and the other is indifferent. (See
appendix for the derivation of (3.10).) This curve slopes upward when $\gamma > 1$
(i.e., when $L^* < N$) and is vertical when $\gamma = 1$ ($L^* \geq N$). Again, when $\gamma = 1$ the
union's preferences are the same as its members, so the equilibrium level of
employment is set at the competitive level. When $\gamma > 1$ and the demand for
labor is low, the level of employment will be greater than or equal to the competitive level. One useful way to think about my model is that it combines the
standard "overemployment" result (e.g., Oswald 1985, 169–173) with the efficient employment outcome in Summers et al. (1993) where the union "wants
to set labor supply at the level that maximizes social surplus and then garner
its portion of that surplus by setting the wage appropriately."

The main difference between my model and the Summers et al. model
is my argument that, with consensual bargaining, market conditions and
an intertemporal cost-sharing approach to economic adjustment determine

where outcomes fall along the efficient contracts curve. When the demand for labor, wages, and employment are low, the negotiated terms of employment will be closer to the union's ideal outcome, point **D'** in figure 3.2. When the demand for labor, wages, and employment are high, the union has no interest in pushing employment even higher (i.e., beyond $L_{(A)}$). Under these conditions, consensual bargaining will produce negotiated terms of employment closer to the firms's ideal outcome, point **C** in figure 3.2. When the union has stronger preferences for employment than its rank-and-file membership, consensual bargaining implies less labor market volatility in corporatist economies. When the demand for labor is low, corporatist economies will maintain higher rates of employment than their competitive counterparts. When the demand for labor is high, corporatist economies will achieve competitive market outcomes with respect to employment. (See the appendix for a proof of this proposition.) In theory, therefore, shocks to labor demand can have different employment consequences in competitive and corporatist labor markets. More specifically, in the former case, shocks to labor demand have larger effects on employment compared to corporatist systems.

EMPIRICAL ANALYSIS

My primary objective in this section is to test the hypotheses outlined above using regression analysis. Before turning to the regressions, however, I break down the globalization trends discussed in chapter 1—deindustrialization, terms of trade volatility, import penetration, and financial openness—by country and labor market type. This data is presented in table 3.1. For the analysis in this chapter and the remainder of the book, my subset of corporatist economies includes Norway, Sweden, Finland, Denmark, (i.e., the Nordic countries) and Austria. These five corporatist economies were the initial focus of the Golden, Lange, and Wallerstein project on wage-setting practices and institutions (Lange, Wallerstein, and Golden 1995).[11] Sweden, Norway, and Austria are considered by most to be the *loci classici* of corporatism, and Denmark and Finland consistently score high on comparative scales of corporatism. The five Anglo-American democracies—the United States, Canada, the United Kingdom, Australia, and New Zealand—represent my cases of competitive labor markets.

The interesting point about table 3.1 is that the globalization trends observed from the beginning of post–Bretton Woods until the end of the century are more or less universal. All countries experienced deindustrialization and a decline in their terms of trade volatility. Import penetration and financial openness increased across the board as well. There are important differences in levels, of course. At the end of the period, the liberal market economies have the fewest workers employed in "tradable" sectors of the

Table 3.1 Exposure and Sensitivity to External Risk, 1973–1999

	Employment in Tradables			Terms of Trade Volatility			Import Penetration			Financial Openness		
	1970s	1980s	1990s	1970s	1980s	1990s	1970s	1980s	1990s	1970s	1980s	1990s
Liberal Market Economies:												
Australia	26.31	22.08	18.9	7.83	5.39	3.94	12.32	13.92	19.1	-0.09	1.09	2.51
Canada	22.19	20.62	17.85	4.48	2.34	2.17	22.89	23.34	34.02	2.54	2.54	2.54
New Zealand	29.71	26.9	23.34	13.73	4.22	2.55	19.52	22.12	30.61	-0.09	1.22	2.54
United Kingdom	30.05	24.52	20.81	5.46	1.78	1.65	15.56	17.9	23.54	-0.44	2.38	2.54
United States	20.2	19.18	17.45	5.60	3.44	1.47	6.07	7.27	10.5	2.54	2.54	2.54
Average:	25.69	22.66	19.67	7.42	3.43	2.36	15.27	16.91	23.55	0.89	1.95	2.53
Corporatist Economies:												
Austria	33.72	30.47	27.34	2.46	1.44	0.66	25.86	30.05	36.82	1.19	1.19	2.13
Denmark	29.79	25.76	23.46	4.36	1.92	1.00	23.26	26.42	34.16	-0.09	0.25	2.46
Finland	35.28	31.98	23.16	3.55	2.53	2.52	20.35	21.83	27.54	0.64	1.19	2.13
Norway	29.64	25.97	21.06	4.18	5.83	5.92	31.21	28.5	32.77	-0.09	-0.09	1.21
Sweden	31.82	27.83	21.58	4.65	2.18	1.71	23.23	24.97	32.22	1.19	1.19	1.86
Average:	32.05	28.4	23.32	3.84	2.78	2.36	24.78	26.35	32.7	0.57	0.75	1.96

Other:

Belgium	24.55	16.35	1.44	1.65	0.9	51.52	56.18	71.93	1.33	0.6	2.3
France	30.45	18.53	6.12	3.74	1.12	14.9	16.32	21.23	-0.18	-0.19	1.89
Germany	33.72	26.24	3.72	4.28	1.86	16.35	18.91	25.2	2.54	2.54	2.54
Ireland	30.77	22.22	6.2	2.92	1.63	33.25	40.42	63.96	-0.57	-0.09	1.62
Italy	29.8	21.21	5.61	4.06	3.31	15.11	17.03	22.87	-1.55	-0.43	1.89
Japan	33.59	29.22	11.22	9.12	3.28	6.29	6.13	8.14	1.22	2.38	2.4
Netherlands	21.14	17.62	2.07	1.29	0.43	37.97	41.88	52.13	0.85	2.54	2.54
Portugal	42.42	31.85	6.38	3.87	1.97	17.58	19.67	30.53	-1.13	-0.92	1.48
Spain	32.84	19.72	7.48	6.6	1.61	9.36	11.62	22.14	-0.54	-0.09	1.34
Switzerland	37.36	27.37	4.79	3.93	2.21	21.24	28.15	33.83	NA	NA	2.54
Average:	31.66	23.03	5.50	4.15	1.83	22.36	25.63	35.2	0.22	0.7	2.05

Notes: The deindustrialization, terms of trade volatility, and import penetration variables reported in this table are the same ones considered in chapter 1. I report the Chinn and Ito (2007) measure of financial openness (instead of Quinn's measure) because it is available through 2006. (See Table 6.1.) The correlation between the Quinn and Chinn and Ito measures is .84.

economy, import the fewest goods and services in relation to the size of their economies, and are, financially speaking, the most open economies in the sample. Nevertheless, all countries experienced similar changes along these four dimensions over the last quarter of the twentieth century. What I demonstrate over the next few chapters is that the labor market, public policy, and political effects of these common trends differ significantly, starting with employment.

To reiterate, the empoloyment-related hypotheses I want to evaluate are:

Shocks to labor demand have larger employment effects in countries with competitive labor markets compared to countries with corporatist systems.

Trade increases the elasticity of labor demand in countries with competitive labor markets.[12]

Trade increases employment volatility in competitive labor markets and not in corporatist systems.

There is surprisingly little quantitative empirical research examining the effects of trade on labor markets that is cross-national and comparative in nature.[13] The work that has been done largely focuses on the United States. Slaughter's (2001) research is particularly notable, and my empirical analysis largely follows his lead with a few important differences. Therefore, I briefly review Slaughter's important study before turning to my own analysis.

Trade and the Demand for Labor

Slaughter examines the effect of trade on labor demand elasticity for U.S. manufacturing industries using a two-stage estimation process. His data, which are from the Productivity Database (1997) of the National Bureau of Economic Research (NBER), include observations on 450 4-digit SIC manufacturing industries over the period 1958 to 1991. Slaughter begins by estimating the labor demand elasticity (stage one).[14] He regresses the quantity of labor employed on the relevant factor prices and output using a log-linear specification. The coefficient on wages is an estimate of the own price labor demand elasticity while the coefficients on the other factors of production gives the cross-price labor demand elasticity.

Typically, one cannot estimate the slope of the labor demand curve with a simple regression of employment on wages because market-clearing quantities and prices are determined simultaneously. Wages are endogenous, and therefore the effect of an exogenous wage change on employment is not identified. The use of industry-level data is crucial to Slaughter's identification strategy. He assumes that, at the industry level, wages are exogenous, which implies that the level of employment is determined taking the price of labor as given. This is almost certainly true at the firm level, and, in general, the more disaggregated the data, the more appropriate this assumption is for identification purposes. To identify over time variation in the elasticity of demand for labor, Slaughter assumes this elasticity is constant across all manufacturing industries or eight large sets of industries.[15]

Slaughter estimates separate regressions for production and non-production workers. The number of workers is the dependent variable. The nominal wage per employee is calculated by dividing the total nominal payroll by the number of workers. He uses price indices for capital, energy, and materials. One problem with the price indices is that the levels are not comparable across industries. Therefore, Slaughter differences the data to get the percentage change in the price indices.[16] Slaughter finds that the constant-output price elasticity for production workers increases significantly between 1960 and 1990. It does not increase for non-production workers.

In the second stage, Slaughter regresses the elasticity estimates on a full set of industry and period dummies and measures of international trade, technology, and labor market institutions. Slaughter finds limited support for the hypothesis that trade makes the demand for labor more elastic. The trade coefficient estimates for production workers typically have the correct signs, but they are not statistically significant when controls for time—deterministic trends or period dummies—are included in the regression model. The trade coefficients for non-production workers are correctly signed and marginally significant.

Some of the important differences between my empirical analysis and Slaughter's are: I use a cross-national sample of data at the industry-level; I estimate the effect of trade on labor demand elasticity in a single step using a simple interaction model; and I use a dynamic log-linear specification with variables in levels rather than long-differences. My data are from the OECD's STAN data set. At the level of industrial aggregation that gives the best cross-national coverage, there are thirteen industries per country, giving 260 units (country-industries) in the sample.[17] The observations span from 1970 to 2000. I estimate three constant output labor demand regressions using the full sample of countries and the baseline specification with the corporatist and liberal subsamples.

In the first model (the baseline model), I regress logged employment at the industry level on a one-period temporal lag of logged employment, the log of labor compensation per employee (at the aggregate level: total manufacturing), the compensation variable interacted with a labor market institutions dummy variable that takes a value of 1 for the liberal market economies, -1 for the corporatist economies, and 0 otherwise, the log of value added per worker, value added interacted with the labor market institutions dummy, the lagged ratio of exports to value added, and the lagged ratio of imports to value added. I use the last two variables as proxies for trade-induced shocks to the labor demand curve. A high ratio of exports to value added signals strong global demand for the industry's products, while a high ratio of imports to value added is an indicator of an industry's domestic decline.

I use the aggregate (total manufacturing) wage as my independent variable in a way similar to Slaughter (2001) to deal with the endogeneity problem. In other words, I assume that industries face a relatively horizontal supply curve with wages determined exogenously at the aggregate level. I make this assumption on the basis that employment in each industry represents a relatively small portion of total employment in manufacturing. Note that in the corporatist countries, wages are endogenous, especially when bargaining is coordinated across sectors of the economy, and adjusted to minimize changes in employment outcomes. Therefore, the identification strategy is much more problematic for the corporatist economies, especially prior to the period of decentralization discussed above.

In the second model, I interact the log of the aggregate domestic manufacturing wage with each industry's level of trade openness (i.e., the sum of exports and imports expressed as a ratio to value added). In the third model, I include spatially lagged labor compensation variable. Theoretically, this regressor, like the export and import to value added variables, shifts the labor demand curve (see equation (3.11) in the appendix). I generated this spatial lag with a binary contiguity weighting matrix using shared territorial borders as the criterion, excepting that France, Belgium, and the Netherlands are coded as contiguous with Britain, Denmark as contiguous with Sweden, and Australia as contiguous with New Zealand. The spatial weights matrix is row-standardized. All of the regressions include fixed industry and period (year) effects.[18]

The results, which are provided in table 3.2, largely confirm my theoretical expectations. In the full sample (columns 1, 2, and 3), an exogenous increase in the manufacturing wage results in a decrease in employment, holding output constant (i.e., value added per worker). This effect is larger for liberal market economies and is magnified by an increase in trade openness. For example, using the estimates in column 2, when trade openness is at its median value for the industries in the sample (≈1.5), the effect of a 1% increase in labor compensation is to reduce employment in competitive labor markets by about 1.35% in the long run; this estimated effect is statistically significant; in the case of corporatist labor markets the estimated effect is a statistically insignificant increase of a little more than .2%. When trade openness is at the sample's 90th percentile (≈4.5), the effect from a 1% increase in labor compensation is to lower the steady state equilibrium in competitive labor markets by approximately 1.65%. In the corporatist labor markets, the estimated effect is a decrease, in the long run, of about .5%. Again, the former estimate is statistically significant and the latter is not. The size of the difference in estimated effects is about 1.15, and this difference is statistically significant. These results are confirmed when I estimate the baseline model using the corporatist and liberal market subsamples (columns 4 and 5). In short, the empirical evidence suggests that trade increases the elasticity of demand for labor in competitive markets. The results for the corporatist economies are mixed, inconclusive, and certainly consistent with the expectation of no short-run trade effects.

Trade shocks have significant direct effects on employment as well, the size of which depends on the wage level. Using the full sample estimates in column 2 of table 3.2, an increase in the export orientation of an industry has a positive and statistically significant effect on employment; a 1% increase in

Table 3.2 Trade, Labor Market Institutions, and the Demand for Labor

	(1)	(2)	(3)	(4)	(5)
Temporal Lag	.955***	.953***	.953***	.943***	.914***
(Employment)	(.004)	(.005)	(.005)	(.009)	(.013)
Labor	−.036***	−.030***	−.006	−.026	−.264***
Compensation	(.010)	(.011)	(.012)	(.027)	(.081)
per Worker					
Labor	−.023**	−.027**	−.027**		
Compensation ×	(.011)	(.012)	(.012)		
Labor Market					
Labor		−.005***	−.009***	−.003	−.036**
Compensation ×		(.002)	(.002)	(.005)	(.017)
Trade Openness					
Value Added per	.025***	.026***	.034***	.009	.061***
Worker	(.005)	(.005)	(.005)	(.010)	(.014)
Value Added ×	.033***	.033***	.039***		
Labor Market	(.007)	(.007)	(.007)		
Spatial Lag (Labor			.028**	−.022	−.175**
Compensation)			(.012)	(.034)	(.078)
Ratio of Exports	.009***	.026***	.026***	.020	.154***
to Value Added	(.002)	(.006)	(.006)	(.018)	(.056)
Ratio of Imports	−.006***	.009*	.009*	.001	.090
to Value Added	(.001)	(.005)	(.005)	(.016)	(.055)
Fixed Effects	Yes	Yes	Yes	Yes	Yes
Sample	Full	Full	Full	Corporatist	Liberal
Observations	5471	5471	5218	1653	1041
R^2 (within industry)	.938	.938	.939	.965	.894

Notes: All regressions included fixed unit (industry) and period (year) effects. These coefficient estimates are suppressed to conserve space. Standard errors are in parentheses. The spatial lags are generated with a binary contiguity weighting matrix using shared territorial borders as the criterion, excepting that France, Belgium, and the Netherlands are coded as contiguous with Britain, Denmark as contiguous with Sweden, and Australia as contiguous with New Zealand. All the spatial weights matrices are row-standardized. *** significant at 1%; ** significant at 5%; * significant at 10%.

the ratio of exports to value added leads approximately, in the long run, to a 0.336%, 0.309%, and 0.284% increase in employment when wages are low, intermediate, and high, respectively. An increase in import penetration has a negative and marginally statistically significant effect on employment when wages are high; a 1% increase in the ratio of imports to value added leads approximately, in the long run, to a 0.065% decrease in employment in the high wage case. These results, along with the same counterfactuals using the coefficient estimates from corporatist and liberal subsamples, are presented in table 3.3.

For the corporatist countries, the estimated effects of an increase in export orientation are marginally statistically significant and smaller than for the full sample. A 1% increase in the ratio of exports to value added leads to a 0.238%, 0.223%, and 0.209% increase in the equilibrium level of employment when wages are low, intermediate, and high, respectively. The estimated effects of import penetration are negative as expected but not statistically significant. The estimated effects of an increase in export orientation, for the liberal countries, are statistically significant and much larger than the size of the estimated effects for the full sample: 0.851%, 0.737%, and 0.631% for the three wage levels.

While the estimates for the liberal countries are highly significant statistically, they are also somewhat imprecise. To test whether the export effects are larger for the liberal countries than for the rest of the sample, I estimated the model-2 regression with liberal and corporatist dummies interacted with the export and import variables and calculated the difference in long-run effects

Table 3.3 Trade Shocks and Employment

	Full Sample	Corporatist	Liberal
Exports (Low Wage)	.336***	.238*	.851***
	(.074)	(.143)	(.277)
Exports (Median Wage)	.309***	.223*	.737***
	(.068)	(.125)	(.228)
Exports (High Wage)	.284***	.209*	.631***
	(.062)	(.109)	(.186)
Imports (Low Wage)	−.017	−.097	.178
	(.048)	(.124)	(.251)
Imports (Median Wage)	−.041	−.110	.073
	(.042)	(.105)	(.201)
Imports (High Wage)	−.065*	−.123	−.025
	(.036)	(.087)	(.157)

Notes: Calculations assume sample median levels of import and export shares. Low and high wages are at the 10th and 90th percentiles. Standard errors are in parentheses. *** significant at 1%; ** significant at 5%; * significant at 10%.

and the standard error for the difference in long-run effects. The estimated difference for a 1% increase in export orientation (liberal effect less the corporatist effect) is .491% and the estimated standard error for this difference is .20%; hence, the difference is statistically significant. The estimated difference from a counterfactual increase in import penetration is not statistically significant.

Trade and Employment Volatility

Rodrik argues that the well-known empirical relationship between trade openness and government spending is explained by the fact that trade increases labor market volatility. There are at least three reasons that this might be the case. First, it could be that trade leads countries to specialize in the production of a small number of goods. If this occurs, these countries might be more vulnerable to product-specific shocks (Rodrik 1998). Second, it could be that industries in countries that trade extensively experience larger price and quantity shocks for the goods that they produce than countries that do not trade (Rodrik 1998). These shocks are then passed on to the labor market. Finally, if trade increases the elasticity of labor demand, as discussed above, the same size shocks will produce more market volatility (Rodrik 1997). In other words, even if countries that trade do not experience larger shocks than countries that do not trade, it is still possible that the former will experience more labor market volatility than the latter because the same shocks (or even smaller shocks) have larger effects on employment and wages when the elasticity of the demand for labor is high.

The most significant challenge to this line of thinking comes from Iversen and Cusack (2000). They argue that trade is just as likely to reduce the amount of risk that workers face because trade diversifies the set of economies to which a country sells its products.[19] Moreover, Iversen and Cusack claim there is no theoretical reason to expect industries that produce for foreign markets to experience more price volatility than industries that produce for domestic markets.[20] They criticize Rodrik's empirics because he does not show a direct connection between trade and labor market volatility. To support their argument, Iversen and Cusack show there is no simple bivariate relationship between a country's level of export dependence and its employment, wage, and output volatility in manufacturing sectors of the economy.

The relationship between trade and labor market risk in liberal market economies is critical to the overall argument that I make in this book, so I take Iversen and Cusack's challenge seriously. With respect to theory, Iversen and Cusack largely ignore the third (and most plausible) mechanism highlighted by Rodrik and emphasized throughout this chapter: trade increases the elasticity of the demand for labor. Empirically, their bivariate null results are not very compelling, especially given that they lump all the OECD countries together without regard for labor market institutions. It is true that there is no simple bivariate relationship that shows up in a scatter plot, but that is hardly surprising. In the remainder of this section, I reexamine the empirical relationship between trade and employment volatility.

I take a different approach from Iversen and Cusack to examine whether a country's exposure to trade affects its overall labor market volatility. First, I examine economy-wide employment data. This allows me to evaluate the interactive effects of trade openness and deindustrialization on employment volatility and test some of the underlying causal mechanisms assumed in chapter 2. Second, and most importantly, instead of trying to explain differ- ences in average or fixed levels of labor market volatility across countries, I focus on within-country variation. It is difficult to identify causal relation- ships in data that are so highly aggregated temporally. Iversen and Cusack calculate a single standard deviation in annual manufacturing employment growth for each country in their sample over the period 1970 to 1993. OECD labor markets experienced periods of both instability and tranquility. If we are willing to accept that labor market volatility is heteroscedastic in this sense—that is, periods of high and low volatility cluster temporally in a non- random way—it is clear from the economy-wide employment data that there is much over-time variation in this volatility. In figure 3.3, I plot the average

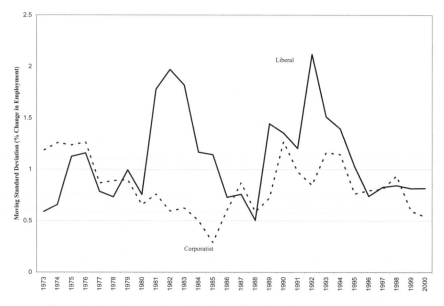

Figure 3.3 Employment Volatility in the Liberal and Corporatist Economies

moving (3-period) standard deviation in employment growth for the liberal and corporatist subsamples.

Several things are notable about this chart. First, when measured this way, the over-time variation in employment volatility in the liberal economies seems to correspond with known periods of price instability in international markets (early 1970s and early 1980s), rapid structural change in domestic labor markets—i.e., deindustrialization in the early 1980s and early 1990s, and global recession. Since theoretically the effects of all these factors on labor markets should depend in part on levels of economic openness, this pattern is consistent with an important role for trade. Second, employment volatility, again, measured in this way, rises to much higher levels on average in the liberal competitive markets when compared to the corporatist economies. Third, the corporatist economies weather the terms-of-trade volatility much better than their liberal counterparts. Finally, the employment volatility spikes in the liberal economies during the economic recessions of the early 1970s, 1980s, and 1990s suggest that negative labor demand shocks produce more employment volatility in countries with competitive labor markets, which confirms the theoretical differences highlighted earlier about how corporatist and competitive labor markets respond to falling labor demand. It is also interesting to note that the volatility observed in the liberal market economies across these three recessionary periods rises over time. This is consistent with the idea that, due to expanding trade, the labor markets in these economies are growing more sensitive to demand shocks. The preliminary evidence in figure 3.3 suggests the importance of both trade and labor market institutions. To evaluate this possibility more rigorously, I estimate several multiplicative heteroscedasticity models (Harvey 1976; Tsebelis 2002). This model has two equations, one for the mean level of the dependent variable and one for its variance, which, in this context, allows me to examine the determinants of employment volatility.

In the regressions, I use employment growth (i.e., the log difference in levels of employment) for my dependent variable. I focus on three variables that condition the effect of trade on labor markets: labor market institutions, deindustrialization, and terms of trade volatility. The key interaction is between a country's labor market institutions and its level of trade openness. Based on the theory presented above, I expect trade to lead to more volatility in the liberal competitive market economies. I measure labor market exposure to trade by interacting a country's level of trade openness (the ratio of imports and exports to GDP) with its deindustrialization score, the latter being, roughly, the size of the non-traded sector of the aggregate economy. As countries experience deindustrialization, the percentage of the aggregate labor market exposed to foreign competition declines.[21] I measure shock intensity by interacting a country's terms of trade volatility with its level of trade openness.

The results are reported in table 3.4. In the first regression, I include trade openness, a trichotomous labor market dummy variable, and the interaction term in the variance equation. The trichotomous labor market dummy variable takes a 1 for the liberal competitive labor markets, –1 for the corporatist coordinated labor markets, and 0 for all the intermediate cases. A positive coefficient on the interaction term implies that trade has the largest effect on labor market volatility in the liberal market economies and the smallest effect in the corporatist case. In this regression, the mean equation contains country dummy variables.

The results in the first regression imply that labor market volatility starts low in the liberal countries and rises with trade. The opposite pattern holds for the corporatist cases. In the second regression, I add the deindustrialization variable, terms of trade volatility, and the respective interactions with trade openness. In this specification, trade increases employment volatility in both liberal and corporatist economies, but the effect is larger in the former case. Deindustrialization reduces the size of the trade effect in all countries. In this regression, the coefficient on the interaction of terms of trade volatility and trade openness has the wrong sign. In the third regression, I keep the same specification for the variance equation, but add a temporal lag of the dependent variable and period (year) dummies to the mean equation. In this regression, all of the interaction terms are correctly signed and statistically significant. In the last two regressions, I substitute two dichotomous labor market dummy variables for the single trichotomous dummy. This relaxes the constraint that the trade effects on liberal and corporatist labor markets be the same size with opposite signs. The difference between these two specifications is the last one includes decade period dummies in the variance equation. These results imply, with respect to trade's effect on the labor market volatility, that it is the corporatist economies that are distinct from the rest of the sample: the trade effect, while positive, is smaller for corporatist economies. The main consequence of adding decade period dummies is that the terms of trade volatility effect disappears.

In figures 3.4 and 3.5, I plot the estimated standard deviation in employment growth for the liberal and corporatist economies, respectively, using the final model (model 5) from table 3.4. The volatility that we observe in labor markets has both a systematic and stochastic component to it. The estimates in figure 3.3 do not distinguish between the two sources of volatility, while the estimates in figures 3.4 and 3.5 do, giving only the systematic component. One way to think about the difference is in terms of controllable and uncontrollable risk. The volatility that can be explained by observable changes in the economy, for example a country's level of trade openness, is relatively controllable compared to the truly stochastic volatility. I argue that politicians are more likely to be held accountable for "predictable"

Table 3.4 Trade, Labor Market Institutions, and Employment Volatility

	(1)	(2)	(3)	(4)	(5)
Trade Openness	-.001	.179***	.185***	.201***	.218***
	(.002)	(.067)	(.070)	(.070)	(.069)
Deindustrialization		.119***	.059	.096*	.038
		(.048)	(.053)	(.056)	(.055)
Terms of Trade Volatility		.026	-.238***	-.347***	.103
		(.064)	(.078)	(.083)	(.092)
Labor Market	-1.278***	-1.406***	-1.015**		
	(.255)	(.364)	(.515)		
Liberal Market				-.231	-.786
				(.617)	(.767)
Corporatist Market				2.736***	1.835*
				(1.010)	(1.101)
Trade Openness × Deindustrialization		-.002***	-.003***	-.003***	-.003***
		(.001)	(.001)	(.001)	(.001)
Trade Openness × Terms of Trade Volatility		-.002**	.003*	.005***	.000
		(.001)	(.001)	(.002)	(.002)
Trade Openness × Labor Market	.026***	.027***	.026***		
	(.005)	(.007)	(.009)		

(*Continued*)

Table 3.4 (*Continued*)

	(1)	(2)	(3)	(4)	(5)
Trade Openness × Liberal Market					.000
					(.013)
Trade Openness × Corporatist				−.059***	−.049***
				(.016)	(.107)
Constant	1.331***	−7.678***	−2.738	−5.123	−1.753
	(.112)	(3.761)	(4.126)	(4.279)	(4.257)
Mean Equation:					
Fixed Effects (Country/Year)	Yes / No	Yes / No	Yes / Yes	Yes / Yes	Yes / Yes
Lagged Dependent Variable	No	No	Yes	Yes	Yes
Variance Equation:					
LM Dummy Variable	Trichotomous	Trichotomous	Trichotomous	Dichotomous	Dichotomous
Decade Dummies	No	No	No	No	Yes
Observations	537	506	503	503	503
Log-Likelihood	−1064.15	−1001.32	−848.05	−838.60	−790.28

Notes: Results are for multiplicative heteroscedasticity models. The dependent variable is the logged difference in national employment. The coefficient estimates in the equation for the mean are suppressed to conserve space. The independent variables in the variance equation are lagged temporally by one period (year). The trichotomous labor market dummy variable takes a 1 for the liberal competitive labor markets, −1 for the corporatist coordinated labor markets, and 0 for all the intermediate cases. Standard errors are in parentheses. *** significant at 1%; **significant at 5%; *significant at 10%.

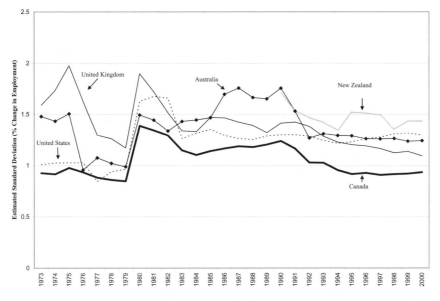

Figure 3.4 Estimated Employment Volatility in the Liberal Market Economies

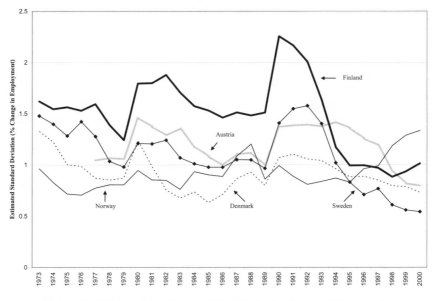

Figure 3.5 Estimated Employment Volatility in the Corporatist Economies

volatility, and therefore these estimates are important for understanding political responses to expanded trade (e.g., Hellwig 2001). Put in a slightly different way, politicians will be held responsible for the structural conditions that magnify the employment effects of uncontrollable shocks. I use these estimates below in chapter 5 to evaluate the effects of labor market volatility on government spending.

There are some important differences when compared with figure 3.3. For example, a good bit of the over-time variation in employment volatility for the liberal market economies seems to be random, including the precipitous decline in the late 1990s. The estimates in figures 3.4 and 3.5 suggest that significant differences remain between the liberal and corporatist markets in terms of the underlying potential for volatility. By the end of the series, all but one of the liberal market economies (Canada) fell in the range of 1% to 1.5% standard deviations (average: 1.2%). For the corporatist countries, all but one (Norway) fell in the .5% to 1% range (average: .93%).

OTHER DIMENSIONS OF LABOR MARKETS PERFORMANCE

There are many ways to evaluate and measure the performance of labor markets. In this chapter I focus primarily on the risk that someone will lose his or her job over a given span of time, which is different from the probably that an individual remains unemployed for an extended period. It is difficult to say whether an economy in which the risk of becoming unemployed is high but the risk of staying unemployed is low is more or less desirable for workers than an economy where the risk of becoming unemployed is low but, if it should happen, the probability of long-term unemployment is high. To a large extent, this difference represents a trade-off in competing risks faced by workers employed in competitive labor markets versus those employed in more densely institutionalized ones. The same institutions and policies that protect workers—wage-setting institutions, employment regulations, benefits systems—may make the labor market more rigid. The evidence is clear that turnover is higher in competitive labor markets, but the duration of unemployment spells is shorter on average. This largely explains why, for example, the problem of long-term unemployment in the United States is relatively small in comparison to Europe. In 1999, for example, only 7.4% of the unemployed workers in the United States had been without a job for more than a year compared with an average of 46.2% in the European Union (EU) member countries. And while high in comparison with the United States, the United Kingdom (34.8%), Australia (31.8%), New Zealand (23.0%), and Canada (12.8%) all had long-term unemployed percentages under the EU average (Blau and Kahn 2002).

Therefore, it is important to keep in mind that the negative welfare consequences associated with the risk of becoming unemployed are at least partially offset in the liberal market economies by the relative ease with which those without jobs can (re)enter the workforce. Nevertheless, I take the position that the kind of risk faced by workers in competitive labor markets is more politically problematic because it affects a larger portion of the citizenry, and it is especially problematic for political parties and elected politicians who operate in majoritarian democracies.[22] Along these lines, Quinn and Woolley (2001) argue that there is a strong public preference for economic stability among the mass electorate and that this preference affects the electoral fortunes of politicians.[23] They find robust evidence that economic volatility leads to declining vote shares for incumbent parties, and that democracies, *ceteris paribus*, enjoy lower volatility than non-democracies. Thus, it is quite likely that policy makers, particularly those in majoritarian democracies, will be sensitive to economic anxiety generated by competitive labor markets that are closely linked to the global economy.

Clearly, unemployment risk is not the only concern that workers face today. Wages and salaries are equally if not more concerning. Interestingly, the evidence is clear here too. In liberal market economies, workers at the lower end of the income scale have experienced relative declines in their real wages. Blau and Kahn explore changes in wage levels and inequality in a sample of OECD countries including Australia, Austria, Canada, Finland, France, Germany, Japan, New Zealand, Sweden, the United Kingdom, and the United States. Among this group of countries, the largest percentage increases in the 50–10 earnings ratios from the beginning of the 1980s to the mid-1990s were in the United States (13%), New Zealand (11.8%), and the United Kingdom (10.5%), and Canada was above the group average with a 7% increase (Blau and Kahn Table 2.12). Notably, in Australia, the 50–10 earnings ratio remained at the same level over this period. As for the 90–50 ratios, these numbers, starting with the highest, were the United Kingdom (19%), New Zealand (17.1%), the United States (16.7%), and Australia (11.2%). In this case, Canada performed relatively well with a below average increase of 1.3%.

The data are particularly bleak for the United States where, according to Blau and Kahn's calculations, men experienced an absolute decline in their median real weekly earnings over the 1980 to mid-1990s period, down from $608.98 to $575.75 (1998 $). Scheve and Slaguhter (2007) also emphasize large changes in wage and salary inequality in the United States. Between 1966 and 2001 the median pre-tax real earnings rose by only 11%, compared with 58% and 121% with those at the 90th and 99th percentiles, respectively. They also highlight a disturbing change in the return to education: between 2000 and 2005 the real weekly earnings of those with bachelor's degrees and non-professional master's degrees declined for the first time in recent decades.

What role does trade play in these developments? Economists have been debating this question for some time. For the 1980s, in the United States, the answer was "not much." Paul Krugman pointed out that trade flows with developing countries were too small to account for a large fraction of the growing inequality. Another highly influential trade economist, Jagdish Bhagwati, argued that trade's effects on wages derive from changing prices in the market for products and that the necessary price changes for implicating trade were absent. In his review of the literature, Cline (1997) attributes 20% of wage inequality of the 1980s to international forces. For Collins (1998, 34), the "bottom line" is that globalization may explain "1 to 2 percentage points of the 18 percentage point overall change in wages for high school-educated workers relative to those who are college educated." That was then. Interestingly, opinions may have begun to change. For example, in a recent *New York Times* Op-Ed piece, Krugman argued that we may have to reconsider the lessons learned during the 1980s because trade with low wage countries has increased from 2.5% in 1990 to 6% in 2006.[24]

I neither theorize about nor examine empirically the issue of wage inequality, but this does not mean that I find it unimportant or unrelated to my argument. Most of the time, the developments outlined above complement and reinforce the points I make about employment volatility. The same workers who are experiencing greater employment uncertainty and risk are also seeing their real wages decline, at least relative to individuals in the top income brackets.

CONCLUSION

In this chapter I have demonstrated that the effects of trade on employment outcomes depend crucially on a country's labor market institutions. Trade and wage shocks have employment consequences in countries with relatively competitive labor markets. These results should not come as a complete surprise. The varieties of capitalism literature (e.g., Hall and Soskice 2001) has shown convincingly that firms in liberal market economies are quick to hire and fire in response to changing economic conditions. The volatility results should not come as a complete surprise either. One of the reasons the corporatist countries created their labor market institutions in the first place was to buffer their workers from unexpected shocks in international markets (Katzenstein 1985).

The political significance of these largely economic findings is seen in the context of my broader argument about globalization and domestic politics. As a result of globalization, democratically elected leaders, especially leaders from parties of the Left, face a dilemma. Workers are more likely to pressure their governments for protection from the ill effects of foreign competition. Governments will find it more difficult to supply income support and other forms of adjustment assistance as a means to compensate trade losers. Starting with the demand side of this dilemma, I have argued that governments in countries with relatively competitive labor markets will face the strongest pressures for protection. There are two separate reasons. First, trade and wage shocks have employment consequences in these economies. Second, trade, by increasing the elasticity of the demand for labor, makes employment outcomes in these countries more sensitive to economic shocks of all kinds. Both of these imply that competitive labor markets will become more volatile as globalization proceeds.

My argument differs from Rodrik's (1997) point that globalization will have similar effects on labor markets, regardless of the particular system of industrial relations in place, because trade and the multinationalization of production undermine the bargaining power of unions, which, in turn, affects wages and the distribution of economic surplus between capital and labor. I argue that the consensual nature of bargaining in most of the corporatist countries is firmly entrenched and is not likely to be undermined by globalization. In part, this is because the consensual nature of industrial relations in these countries is driven by their political institutions. Political institutions are the focus of the next chapter.

More specifically, in the next chapter I argue that countries with majoritarian political institutions face the strongest revenue constraints as a result of globalization because they are more dependent on capital taxes to finance government spending. The countries with majoritarian polities are also the ones with competitive labor markets. Given my argument, these countries are the most vulnerable to a political backlash against globalization. The disturbing reality is that they are also the most powerful and important actors when it comes to governing the international economy. A backlash in any one of them would have seriously negative consequences for the global economy.

Appendix

LABOR DEMAND

The conditions $F_{L^i} = \dfrac{\partial F}{\partial L^i} > 0$, $F_{L^i L^i} = \dfrac{\partial^2 F}{\partial L^i \partial L^i} < 0$, $F_{L^i L^j} = \dfrac{\partial^2 F}{\partial L^i \partial L^j} > 0$, and $F_{L^i L^i} F_{L^j L^j} - F_{L^i L^j}^2 > 0$ are sufficient to guarantee a finite profit maximum. The labor demand functions are

$$L^h = L^{h*}(w^h, w^f)$$
$$L^f = L^{f*}(w^h, w^f), \tag{3.11}$$

where L^{i*} is the profit maximizing labor input. Substitute the right-hand side of the equations in (3.11) into the first-order conditions:

$$F_{L^h}\left(L^{h*}(w^h, w^f)\right) = w^h$$
$$F_{L^f}\left(L^{f*}(w^h, w^f)\right) = w^f. \tag{3.12}$$

To get the demand curve for domestic labor, take the derivative of the profit maximizing labor input with respect to the domestic wage w^h:

$$F_{L^h L^h} \frac{\partial L^{h*}}{\partial w^h} + F_{L^h L^f} \frac{\partial L^{f*}}{\partial w^h} = 1$$
$$F_{L^h L^f} \frac{\partial L^{h*}}{\partial w^h} + F_{L^f L^f} \frac{\partial L^{f*}}{\partial w^h} = 0. \tag{3.13}$$

Substitute for $\dfrac{\partial L^{f*}}{\partial w^h}$ in equation (3.13) and solve for $\dfrac{\partial L^{h*}}{\partial w^h}$. This gives

$$\frac{\partial L^{h*}}{\partial w^h} = \frac{F_{L^f L^f}}{F_{L^h L^h} F_{L^f L^f} - F_{L^h L^f}^2} \tag{3.14}$$

Efficient-Contracts Curve

The union's indifference curves give all combinations of wage and employment outcomes over which its utility is constant. That is, they satisfy the condition

$$\frac{\partial U}{\partial w^h} + \frac{\partial U}{\partial L^h}\frac{dL^h}{dw^h} = 0. \qquad (3.15)$$

The isoprofit curves give the combinations of wage and employment outcomes for which profits are constant, which implies

$$\frac{\partial \pi}{\partial w^h} + \frac{\partial \pi}{\partial L^h}\frac{dL^h}{dw^h} = 0. \qquad (3.16)$$

The points of tangency must satisfy the condition

$$\frac{\partial U}{\partial w^h}\bigg/\frac{\partial U}{\partial L^h} = \frac{\partial \pi}{\partial w^h}\bigg/\frac{\partial \pi}{\partial L^h}, \qquad (3.17)$$

Substituting for the partial derivatives in (3.17)

$$\frac{L}{\gamma[w-b]} = \frac{-L}{F_L - w} \qquad (3.18)$$

or

$$F_L - \gamma b = w[1-\gamma]$$

Taking the derivative of both sides of (3.18) with respect to L

$$F_{LL} - \frac{d\gamma}{dL}b = -\frac{d\gamma}{dL}w - \frac{dw}{dL}[1-\gamma]. \qquad (3.19)$$

After rearranging terms, we have

$$\frac{dw}{dL} = \frac{F_{LL} + [w-b]\dfrac{d\gamma}{dL}}{[1-\gamma]} \qquad (3.20)$$

Employment Stability

To see that employment with efficient bargaining is at least as high as the competitive level, add b and subtract w from both sides of (3.18), and rewrite as

$$\gamma[w-b] - [w-b] = b - F_L \qquad (3.21)$$

For $\gamma > 1$, the left-hand side of (3.21) must be positive and therefore $b > F_L$. At the competitive level, people work until the point where the marginal productivity of labor equals the marginal utility of leisure ($b = F_L$), which, given $F_{LL} < 0$, implies higher employment under efficient bargaining when compared to the competitive equilibrium. Whenever $L \geq N$, $\gamma = 1$ and the competitive and efficient bargain equilibrium levels of employment are equivalent.

4

Globalization and Capital Taxation in Consensus and Majoritarian Democracies

After surveying the research on international capital mobility and capital taxation in his influential book on globalization, Duane Swank (2002a, 47) concludes, "the weight of the evidence leads to the unanticipated impression that international capital mobility may be unrelated (or even positively related) to capital taxation." This is arguably one of the most important and, as Swank notes, unexpected findings to come out of the literature on globalization. The debate over capital taxation, perhaps more than any other, clearly divides those who are pessimistic about the domestic political consequences of globalization and those who believe governments still have substantial room-to-maneuver in the global economy.

While it may be reassuring to think that the tax constraints associated with globalization are weak, this conclusion is often based on one of two problematic assumptions: (1) that globalization implies a race to the bottom in capital taxes or (2) that the tax systems of the social democratic corporatist countries are undermined the most by international capital mobility. In other words, most of the empirical research either starts with the assumption that globalization causes capital tax revenues to decline in all OECD countries, or, if a subset of countries is singled out as having tax systems that are particularly vulnerable to globalization pressures, it is the social democratic corporatist countries. Scholars who design their research on one of these assumptions are either looking for the wrong thing (a race to the bottom in capital taxes) or searching in the wrong places (the capital tax policies of social democratic corporatist countries). I argue in this chapter that globalization will lead to (partial) capital tax convergence—not to the bottom, but to somewhere near the center of the existing distribution of capital tax rates. Moreover, the countries that are the most dependent on capital taxes are the ones that will feel the revenue pinch. These are the majoritarian democracies with liberal market economies, not the social democratic corporatist countries. I concluded, in the last chapter, that the conventional wisdom with respect to corporatism and unemployment volatility is largely correct. In this chapter, I argue that the conventional wisdom about corporatism and capital taxation in political science is not.

This chapter is organized into six sections. In the first, I review the debate over globalization and capital taxation, placing particular emphasis on the theoretical case against tax policy convergence. I present some data that challenge this position and then argue that consensus democracy can help account for the puzzling empirical patterns we observe. In the second section I build a game-theoretic model of a small open-economy democracy that incorporates the distinction between consensus and majoritarian polities in order to theorize about how political institutions might mediate globalization pressures. The model predicts that globalization—specifically increased international capital mobility—will have the greatest negative impact on capital tax rates in relatively closed and capital-rich countries with majoritarian political institutions.[1] I test this and related hypotheses quantitatively with regression analysis in the third section. I discuss possible causal mechanisms that link consensus democracy to low capital taxes in the fourth and, in the fifth section, explore the plausibility of various causal mechanisms through a comparative case study of capital taxation, focusing primarily on Britain and the Netherlands. I conclude in section six.

THE DEBATE OVER GLOBALIZATION AND CAPITAL TAXATION

While some scholars, for example Dani Rodrik, have argued that increased international capital mobility undermines the ability of governments to finance spending on social insurance and other public goods, many are skeptical of this argument.[2] The first line of attack for the skeptics has always been to point out that capital tax rates in the OECD have not declined over the past four decades or so (see figure 4.1). Admittedly, this is evidence against a race to the bottom in capital taxation, but it should not lead to the conclusion that globalization does not constrain the capital tax policies of any countries.[3] The budgets of governments that are highly dependent on capital taxes for revenue are likely to be adversely affected by globalization. On the other hand, if some governments "under tax" capital—for whatever reasons—capital inflows resulting from globalization might strengthen the incentives these countries have to raise taxes by increasing the associated marginal revenue gains. Given that there is no reason to expect a priori a race to the bottom, a much more reasonable hypothesis is tax convergence somewhere in the middle, an outcome that produces both revenue winners and revenue losers. It is also consistent with the facts.

A more sophisticated version of the argument is that international economic integration leads to tax convergence on terms that are more (less)

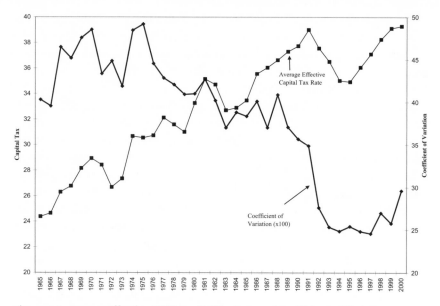

Figure 4.1 Average Effective OECD Capital Tax Rate and Coefficient of Variation.
Data Source: OECD Revenue Statistics

favorable to capital (labor). This thesis is much easier to defend empirically. Figures 4.1 and 4.2 show why. Figure 4.1 plots the average effective capital tax rate for twenty OECD countries and the coefficient of variation in these rates.[4] While it is true that effective capital tax rates have not declined on average, the (standardized) variance in these rates has. Moreover, figure 4.2, which plots the labor-capital tax rate differential (i.e., the average effective labor tax rate less the average effective capital tax rate), shows that effective tax rates on labor income have increased at a faster rate than capital tax rates. Thus, tax systems are becoming regressive in the sense that the more of the burden is being shifted from capital income to labor income.[5] If it is true that capital taxes are converging to the middle, countries that are revenue losers will face dramatic changes in the relative tax burden across capital and labor income. For countries that are revenue winners, the changes will be far less significant.

As discussed in chapter 1, the theoretical case against policy convergence has been made persuasively in the "varieties of capitalism" literature. This research claims that domestic institutions strongly condition national responses to globalization: "institutional divergence has a tendency to persist and to reconstitute itself."[6] According to this line of thinking, globalization has ushered in a new era of "divergent reconfiguration" in the varieties of national capitalism. Geoffrey Garrett's (1998a) coherency thesis, a variant

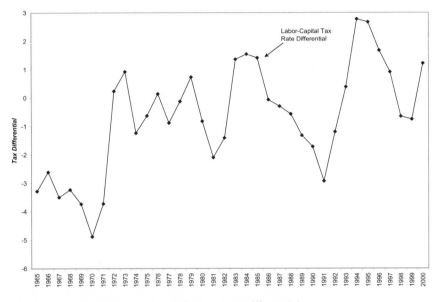

Figure 4.2 Average OECD Labor-Capital Tax Rate Differential.
Data Source: OECD Revenue Statistics

of the divergent paths argument, is particularly relevant to capital taxation. Garrett argues that there are two distinct paths to strong macroeconomic performance in the global economy.[7] One path combines free markets with minimalist government. This combination is found in countries like the United States, the United Kingdom, and Japan. The other path—taken by countries like Austria, Denmark, and Finland—combines coordinated markets with interventionist government. There is no reason to expect these paths to converge; if anything, globalization reinforces the differences between them.

Social Democratic Corporatism and Taxation

According to Garrett, the combination of left-wing governments and corporatist labor market institutions leads to high levels of capital taxation. Governments want to redistribute wealth to their core constituencies, but their willingness to do so is limited by the possibility that such transfers will have negative effects on the economy. Incumbent governments give priority to being reelected, and electoral success requires that they preside over a healthy macroeconomy. Therefore, the highest levels of redistribution will occur where it is the least distorting, that is, in those cases where redistribution has the least burdensome impact on the economy as a whole. Garrett refers to these cases as "coherent" political economies. There are two types of coherent systems—social democratic corporatism and market liberalism.

In the former, the Left can successfully pursue its redistributive agenda while in office. In the latter, the Right can pursue its redistributive agenda without serious macroeconomic consequences. When there is political-economic coherence, the economic constraints on partisan redistribution are weak.

Generally speaking, the political Left has an interest in redistributing wealth from capital to labor but is prevented from doing so to the extent that such transfers negatively affect the economy. Taxing capital income to subsidize wage earners negatively affects the economy by reducing both levels of investment and the number of hours worked. Any reduction in the supply of labor puts upward pressure on wages. In theory, these distortions should be smaller in corporatist political economies where there are encompassing labor organizations that bear part of the excess burden of socially inefficient behavior by their members. Encompassing unions have an incentive to pursue wage moderation. Thus, left-wing governments are able to pursue social democratic policy agendas in corporatist political economies because encompassing unions help minimize the negative macroeconomic consequences of redistribution and other Keynesian welfare state policies. The moderating influence of encompassing unions creates an investment friendly economic environment. At least some of the direct cost of taxation is offset by these indirect benefits. In theory, business does not bear the full burden of capital taxation and therefore is less averse to it.

Supposedly, globalization does nothing to undermine this political-economic logic. Garrett (1998b, 823) summarized what has become the conventional wisdom on this topic in the fiftieth anniversary edition of *International Organization:*

> Governments wishing to expand the public economy for political reasons may do so (*including increasing taxes on capital to pay for new spending*) without adversely affecting their trade competitiveness or prompting multinational producers to exit. The reason is that governments provide economically important collective goods . . . that are undersupplied by markets and valued by actors who are interested in productivity. *This is particularly the case in corporatist political economies where the potential costs of interventionist government are mitigated by coordination among business, government, and labor* (emphasis added).

Is this view supported by the data? Are high levels of government spending financed with relatively high rates of capital taxation in the corporatist countries? Have these countries been able to buck the trend toward more regressive tax systems? The average effective labor-capital tax rate differentials are provided for the coherent cases of social democratic corporatism and market liberalism in table 4.1.[8] While it is true that governments in countries with corporatist labor market institutions have maintained relatively high levels of public spending, comparing the tax structures of the countries that Garrett classifies as cases of coherent social democratic corporatism with

Table 4.1 Political-Economic Coherence and Tax Structures, 1966–1990.

Social Democratic Corporatism (Garrett 1998a)	Labor-Capital / Capital Tax Rate (Mendoza et al. 1997)	Market Liberalism (Garrett 1998a)	Labor-Capital Tax / Capital Tax Rate (Mendoza et al. 1997)
Austria	16.195 / 20.912	United States	–17.360 / 42.719
Denmark	7.172 / 34.976	United Kingdom	–31.802 / 57.290
Finland	–3.873 / 32.942	Japan	–12.820 / 34.147
Norway	–0.034 / 38.950	France	15.611 / 23.741
Sweden	–4.712 / 50.683	Canada	–17.623 / 40.896
Average	2.950 / 35.693		–12.799 / 39.759

the countries he classifies as cases of coherent market liberalism reveals an unexpected pattern: the social democratic corporatist countries have higher average effective labor-capital tax rate differentials than their liberal market counterparts. In other words, labor tax rates are high relative to capital tax rates in the social democratic corporatist countries. This contrasts starkly with the liberal market countries, where labor tax rates tend to be lower than capital tax rates. This puzzling pattern holds for capital tax rates as well. The average capital tax rate for the social democratic corporatist countries is 35.69, whereas the average capital tax rate for the liberal market countries is 39.76.[9] If the Left's redistributive agenda is less distorting in corporatist political economies, why are their capital tax rates lower than in countries with liberal market economies? Clearly the labor market constraints that Garrett emphasizes can provide, at best, only part of the explanation.

Consensus Democracy and Taxation

Looking at the list of social democratic corporatist countries, it is clear that they share more than just the combination of left-wing governments and centralized wage bargaining. In addition, they all have proportional representation electoral institutions, are examples of multiparty systems, and are typically governed by oversized coalitions. By contrast, most of the liberal market countries have plurality electoral systems; they all have a smaller number of parties that effectively compete in national elections; and they are all more likely to have single-party bare-majority governments than the social democratic corporatist countries. In short, the social democratic corporatist countries are all cases of what Arend Lijphart (1999) has called consensus democracy, and the liberal market countries are, for the most part, cases of majoritarian democracy.[10] How strong is the empirical relationship between consensus democracy and capital taxes?

Figure 4.3 shows the bivariate relationship between a country's consensus democracy score (1971–1996) and its average labor-capital tax rate differential (1965–2000). The relationship is positive—consensus democracies tax labor income at a high rate relative to capital income—and strong; Lijphart's consensus democracy measure accounts for about 22% of the sample variance in cross-national labor-capital tax differentials.[11] While this simple correlation does not prove a causal relationship exists, it is certainly suggestive. Theoretically, is there any reason to believe there is a causal link between consensus democracy and capital tax rates?

The simple answer to this question is yes. As Persson and Tabellini (2000, 305) note: "Capital income is more concentrated than labor income. Hence a majority of the voters gain from shifting a larger share of the tax burden to capital, despite the efficiency losses." In any society a majority earns its income in wages while a minority earns its income from capital investments. Because consensus democracy combines institutions that are designed to constrain majority power and influence, it is not surprising that wage earners are constrained in these countries from pushing a disproportionately high level of the tax burden onto capital. This intuition can be sharpened using the median voter construct. In theory, policy making in majoritarian democracies will be more responsive than in consensual democracies to the demands of the median voter. If the median voter is a wage earner, she or he will prefer the revenue (i.e., transfer) maximizing capital tax rate. The tax systems in majoritarian democracies will reflect this preference and therefore, all else being equal, should have higher capital taxes.[12] Thus, capital taxes could be

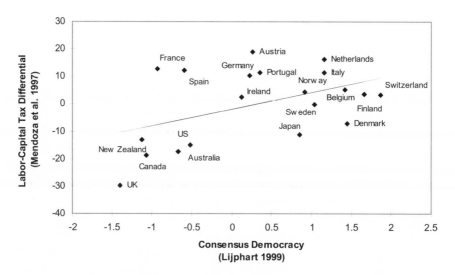

Figure 4.3 Consensus Democracy and Labor-Capital Tax Differentials, 1965–2000

lower in consensus democracies because the political institutions constrain political majorities from choosing transfer maximizing capital tax rates. As a minority interest, capital has more and better opportunities to influence tax policy in these countries.

To sum, Garrett's argument about the importance of political-economic coherence is an important one. Labor market institutions partly determine the macroeconomic consequences of redistribution and therefore shape the nature of partisan politics within countries. But political institutions also affect how left- and right-wing parties will govern in office by determining the distribution of power across the multiple actors within each state and by shaping the influence of different interest groups and political constituencies in society. The research on the politics of redistribution suggests that these institutions will have a significant impact on capital taxes. For the countries in table 4.1, the constraints that their political institutions place on partisan redistribution through capital taxes seem to overwhelm the enabling effects that their labor market institutions might have.

While the connection between consensus democracy and corporatism provides an intuitive explanation for why capital tax rates are lower in corporatist countries, this intuition needs to be more strongly grounded in theory. Furthermore, the discussion to this point has not provided any insight into the likely impact of globalization on tax structures in countries with different political-economic institutions. In the next section, therefore, I develop a theoretical model to address these concerns. The model improves upon those found in earlier research by examining the influence of both domestic political institutions and the size of a country's capital endowment on its tax policy. The political setup in the model is based on the assumption that consensus democracy constrains the influence of political majorities. I do this rather than modeling the specific nature of the constraint (e.g., proportional representation electoral institutions, coalition bargaining, multiple issue dimensions) since it is not yet clear which of the elements of consensus democracy is most important when it comes to capital taxation. Despite the fact that the model has a highly stylized polity, it serves to elucidate the nature of the relationship between consensus democracy and capital taxation as well as the role these institutions play in mediating globalization pressures.

A GAME-THEORETIC MODEL OF CAPITAL TAXATION IN AN OPEN-ECONOMY DEMOCRACY

The standard tax competition model in economics shows that welfare-maximizing governments in small countries with multiple tax instruments will not tax internationally mobile capital (Gordon 1986). The reason is that the net return to capital is fixed at the global rate, and, therefore, labor bears the full burden of any capital tax. Since labor pays the tax on capital, it is more efficient to tax labor directly because capital taxes distort investment deci- sions while labor taxes do not. The optimal small-country source-based tax on perfectly mobile capital is zero. Empirically, however, governments raise substantial revenue from internationally mobile capital. One explanation for why the standard competition model fails as a positive theory of capital taxa- tion is that it ignores politics.[13]

A couple of recently developed models explore the politics of international tax competition. Persson and Tabellini (2000) have a stylized model of tax competition, which I discuss in the appendix to this chapter. Dehejia and Genschel (1999) argue that the lack of international tax cooperation in the European Union can be attributed to the fact that large and small countries do not have a mutual interest in limiting tax competition. Small countries that are poorly endowed with capital benefit from tax competition, while large states that are richly endowed are harmed by it. Basinger and Hallerberg (2004) correctly stress the role that domestic political institutions play in influencing the degree to which countries will lower capital taxes to compete for revenue, but their model ignores the importance of size. Clearly, however, both size and political institutions are important, yet no one has put the two factors together in a single theoretical framework.

My model begins with the production function from chapter 3, and I fol- low the same notational rules as in that chapter. I incorporate a slightly modi- fied version of the international economy in Rodrik (1997, 89–95). The capital endowment (K^h) is allocated between domestic and foreign production. Labor (L^h, L^f) is fixed and supplied inelastically at wage 1. The net return to capital (r) is equal to its marginal product less the domestic capital tax (τ). The amount of capital invested in domestic production is denoted by K. This gives

$$r = \rho^* - \rho K - \tau. \tag{4.1}$$

International arbitrage guarantees that the net domestic return to capital equals the net foreign return (r^*) less the cost of producing abroad. There are increasing costs to foreign production captured by the capital mobility parameter λ.[14] This arbitrage condition can be written as

$$r = r^* - \lambda(K^h - K), \qquad \lambda \geq 0. \tag{4.2}$$

Following Rodrik, increased globalization (i.e., increased capital mobility) is captured in the model by reducing λ. The equilibrium level of investment in domestic production is found by substituting (4.1) into (4.2):

$$K = \frac{(\lambda K^h + \rho^* - r^* - \tau_k)}{\lambda + \rho} \tag{4.3}$$

The polity is loosely based on Becker's (1983) model of interest group competition. There are two politically active groups: wage earners (or workers), who collectively make up a majority of society; and shareholders (or capitalists), who are a minority. Both groups choose levels of political expenditures to influence the rate of capital taxation. Capital taxes finance an income transfer to wage earners.[15] Political expenditures are the resources spent "maintaining a lobby, attracting favorable votes, issuing pamphlets, contributing to political campaign expenditures, [and] cultivating bureaucrats and politicians."[16] At a minimum level of political participation—that is, when political expenditures are close to zero—wage earners and shareholders vote collectively. The main difference between my polity and Becker's is that I assume collective action is unproblematic. Although this assumption simplifies the model, it does not drive the key result, as I explain below.[17] Conceptually, democracy is thought of as a function that maps the political expenditures of wage earners and shareholders into political pressure and influence. The political pressure of wage earners (p^w) is assumed to be a linear function of expenditures (e^w)

$$p^w = \alpha e^w, \alpha > 0. \tag{4.4}$$

Democracy empowers political majorities, but their political strength varies across types of democracies. Following Lijphart, majority power is constrained in consensus democracies. The scaling parameter (α), therefore, takes large values in majoritarian democracies and relatively low values in consensus democracies. This specification is also consistent with the idea that proportional representation (PR) electoral systems constrain labor power.[18] Similarly, the political pressure generated by shareholders is a function of their political expenditures $p^s(e^s)$. The conditions $p^s_{e^w} > 0, p^s_{e^w e^w} < 0$ are assumed to hold. As in Becker, political influence is zero-sum. The per unit capital tax rate is set equal to the political pressure differential:

$$\tau = p^w - p^s. \tag{4.5}$$

Wage earners choose political expenditures that maximize their utility, given the parameters of the model and political expenditures by shareholders. Their utility is simply wages plus the income transfer less political expenditures. Shareholders also choose political expenditures to maximize their utility, given the parameters of the model and political expenditures by workers. Their utility is the net of tax return to capital times the capital stock less their political expenditures. The utility functions of wage earners and shareholders are

$$U^w = L^h + \tau K - e^w \quad \text{and} \quad U^s = rK_0 - e^s \tag{4.6}$$

respectively.

Solving for the first-order condition, we find that the best response for wage earners to the political pressure generated by shareholders is

$$e_w = \frac{1}{2\alpha}\left[\lambda K^h - \frac{\lambda+\rho}{\alpha} + \rho^* - r^*\right] + \frac{p_s}{\alpha}, \qquad (4.7)$$

subject to the constraint that $e_w < \tau_k k$. The best response function reveals an interesting relationship between majoritarian democracy and the cost of collective action for workers. As $\alpha \to \infty$, political expenditures by wage earners and the collective action cost per worker go to zero. Thus, in majoritarian democracies, there is less incentive to "free ride" off the efforts of others because the cost of collective action is relatively low. At the majoritarian extreme, workers only have to vote collectively to exercise their influence. Political participation in consensus democracies is more intensive, which makes free riding more likely. In short, collective action is treated as unproblematic in the model, but making it endogenous would only reinforce the result that workers exercise more political influence in majoritarian democracies.

From the first-order condition it is clear that wage earners will match the political pressure generated by shareholders, and the Nash equilibrium capital tax, found by substituting (4.7) into (4.5), will be

$$\tau = \frac{1}{2}\left[\lambda K^h - \frac{\lambda+\rho}{\alpha} + \rho^* - r^*\right] \qquad (4.8)$$

Interestingly, as $\alpha \to \infty$, the equilibrium capital tax rate converges to the revenue-maximizing tax rate, which implies that at the majoritarian extreme, workers face only an economic constraint on their ability to redistribute income.

Comparative statics can be used to show the impact of globalization or capital mobility for countries with different institutions and capital endowments. The change in the equilibrium per unit capital tax rate with respect to λ is

$$\frac{d\tau}{d\lambda} = \frac{1}{2}\left(K^h - \frac{1}{\alpha}\right). \qquad (4.9)$$

In words, the impact of greater capital mobility on a country's capital tax rate is proportional to its capital endowment and inversely proportional to the degree to which its political institutions are consensual. Thus, globalization has the largest negative impact on the capital tax rates of majoritarian democracies with large capital endowments.

The intuition for why political institutions and capital endowments mediate globalization pressures is straightforward. Globalization affects the capital tax rate in two ways. First, it shifts the revenue-maximizing tax rate downward. And second, by making the supply of capital more elastic, it increases the marginal gain from increasing (decreasing) the capital tax rate when it is below (above) the revenue-maximizing level. The degree to which globalization shifts the revenue-maximizing tax rate downward is a function of a country's capital endowment: the drop will be large for rich countries and small for poor countries. In figure 4.4 the thick Laffer curve represents the revenue possibilities for a capital-poor consensus democracy after a decrease in λ (post-globalization). The impact of increasing the elasticity of the supply of capital on tax rates is a function of a country's political institutions because these institutions determine the marginal cost of increasing the tax rate. This cost is represented in figure 4.4 by the lines tangent to the Laffer curves. Wage earners will choose political expenditures that equate the marginal gain from increasing the tax rate (a function of the elasticity of the supply of capital) with the marginal cost of increasing the tax (a function of political institutions). Thus, the impact of globalization on a country's capital tax rate will depend on that country's institutions. In the case illustrated in figure 4.4, globalization raises the marginal gain from climbing the revenue curve— that is, a one-point increase in the capital tax rate generates more revenue post-globalization. In response, wage earners increase political pressure and the tax rate creeps upward.[19]

Why does my model's (partial) equilibrium differ so starkly from that found in the standard model of tax competition? Politics is not the only reason. Since the labor supply and wages are fixed, capital pays the full tax. One

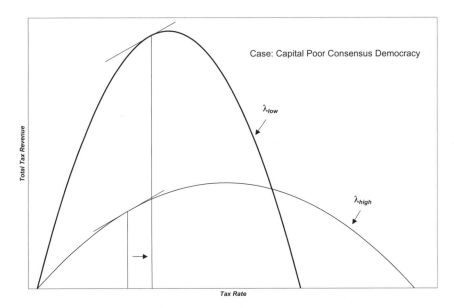

Figure 4.4 Globalization and Capital Taxation: Two Laffer Curves

way to interpret my theoretical results is that under economic conditions most favorable for redistribution from capital to labor, majoritarian democracies will redistribute more than consensus democracies. My model produces very clear tax policy predictions that are easily tested. I do this below using my macro-level panel of twenty OECD countries.

QUANTITATIVE EMPIRICAL EVALUATIONS OF THE MODEL'S POLICY PREDICTIONS

The quantitative empirical research has produced mixed results about the consequences of economic globalization for capital taxation. For example, Rodrik (1997) finds that the relationships between both trade and financial openness and capital taxation are negative and statistically significant. Bretschger and Hettich (2002) and Winner (2005) produce similar empirical findings. Both Mutti (2003) and Slemrod (2004) find evidence of corporate tax convergence. Mutti attributes this to international tax competition, but Slemrod does not.[20] Swank (1998) finds that levels of trade are negatively associated with capital taxation but that financial openness is positively related to capital taxes. Quinn (1997) also finds that financial openness and capital taxation are positively associated. Garrett and Mitchell (2001), on the other hand, find no relationship between financial openness and capital taxes, but they do find that foreign direct investment is positively and significantly associated with higher levels of capital taxation. The inconclusive nature of these empirical results has been used to support the conclusion that globalization's constraints on capital taxation are weak (e.g., Swank and Steinmo 2002). However, if a country's capital endowment and political institutions mediate the impact of increased capital mobility on its capital taxes, it should not be surprising that the previously published research has not found a robust, negative relationship between the two. Moreover, despite the connection between globalization and strategic interdependence in fiscal policy making (see Persson and Tabellini 2000 and the appendix to this chapter), very few empirical studies incorporate this interdependence into their analyses, let alone recognize its importance for the debate over globalization and capital taxation.

In my analysis I estimate a set of fixed-effects linear regression models in which a country's capital mobility at a particular point in time is interacted with both its initial capital endowment and its political institutions. Note that a country's endowment and its political institutions are time-invariant, so their independent effects on taxation are absorbed into the regression model's fixed effects. When it is possible, I include period dummies in the analysis as well.

The dependent variable in the regressions is the Mendoza et al. capital tax rate. These tax estimates are constructed in two steps. First, to calculate individual capital income tax revenue, an average household income tax rate is computed. This is equal to the proportion of total taxes collected on the income, profits, and capital gains of individuals out of the total individual tax base, which is defined as the sum of (1) wages, (2) property and entrepreneurial income, and (3) the operating surplus of private unincorporated enterprises. This average household tax is multiplied by the sum of the operating surplus of private unincorporated enterprises and property and entrepreneurial income to estimate the capital income taxes on individuals. The capital tax rate is equal to the total revenues from capital income—the sum of capital income taxes on individuals, taxes on corporations, taxes on immovable property, and taxes on financial and capital transactions—over the capital tax base, which is the total operating surplus of the economy.[21]

It is generally agreed that capital is more mobile today than at any time since the end of World War II for two reasons: technological advances have made it less costly to invest capital abroad, and most countries over time have removed their legal restrictions on capital flows. It is reasonable to assume that technological advances have led to a monotonic decline in costs for all countries over time, and therefore, at a minimum, the evidence should be consistent with the notion that capital taxes have fallen in the capital-rich majoritarian democracies and risen in the capital-poor consensus democracies. However, it is also important to examine the effects of government policy. This is especially true given that the path to financial liberalization has varied substantially across countries. Some countries like the United States have had relatively liberal policies with regard to financial flows for most of the post–World War II period. Other countries have gradually liberalized the extent to which they limit financial flows over time. Still other countries, like Australia, tightened restrictions in the 1970s, only to reverse these policies in the 1980s.[22] Therefore, the evidence should also show that capital tax rates are the highest for majoritarian capital-rich countries and lowest for the capital-poor democracies during periods when they have more stringent legal restrictions on financial flows.

I estimate the regression models using three separate measures of capital mobility: a deterministic time trend, which can be viewed as a proxy for technological development, and Quinn's (1997) measures of capital account and financial openness.[23] I use Lijphart's consensus democracy scores and each country's per worker capital stock in 1965 as a measure of its initial capital endowment.[24] I also interact the capital mobility measures with several control variables highlighted in the literature that might mediate the impact of globalization on capital taxation. Since Garrett stresses the importance of partisanship and labor market institutions (union density), variables that are correlated with the consensus democracy scores, I control for these. I also control for membership in the European Union during the post-1986 period, when we would expect tax competition to be the strongest.[25] In the British case, for instance, the drop in capital tax rates may have more to do with its membership in the European Union than with its majoritarian political institutions. Finally, I include a temporal lag, a spatial lag, and country and year dummies in the regressions to control for persistence in tax rates, spatial interdependence, and fixed unit and period heterogeneity, respectively.[26] The temporal lag is a one-period lag of the dependent variable. The spatial lag is calculated using a row-standardized *binary contiguity-weights matrix*, which gives the average of capital taxes in neighboring countries.

I use a binary contiguity-weights matrix because a number of recent papers have concluded that geographic location is important for determining which countries compete for capital.[27] The main reason is that multinational enterprises (MNEs) use host countries as "export platforms" to nearby markets. A good example of this is Ireland, where a large percentage of the foreign direct investment is used to produce goods that are then exported to the European continent. The implication is that Ireland and Britain compete not only for each other's capital but also for the capital of third countries. American MNEs may see Ireland and Britain as substitutable production bases for export to the nearby Benelux, French, and German markets. Portugal and Spain may compete in the same way. Canada attracts foreign direct investment (FDI) from firms intending to service the American market, and therefore, because of its proximity, competes with the United States for foreign capital from third countries in a way that Germany, for example, does not.

The regression estimates are reported in table 4.2. It is clear from the results that the spatiotemporal specification is the right one. The coefficients on both the temporal and spatial lags are large and statistically significant in each of the models. The fact that the coefficient on the spatial lag is positive and statistically significant suggests that globalization constrains the capital tax autonomy of governments through the strategic policy interdependence it creates. This result is robust to the inclusion of fixed period effects in the model and therefore does not reflect a common trend in tax policy.

Moreover, in all three of the regressions, the relationship between capital mobility and capital tax rates depends on a country's capital endowment, and the relationship has the predicted negative sign. Greater capital mobility has a larger negative impact (and, in some cases, a smaller positive impact) on capital tax rates in countries that are richly endowed with capital. I also find evidence that the relationship between capital mobility and capital tax rates depends on a country's political institutions. The estimated coefficients have the predicted positive signs. Increased capital mobility has a larger positive effect (or smaller negative effect) on capital tax rates in consensus

Table 4.2 Capital Tax Rates and International Capital Mobility

Independent Variables	Deterministic Time Trend	Capital Account Openness	Financial Openness	Financial Openness
Temporal Lag	.768***	.778***	.763***	.773***
	(.026)	(.024)	(.025)	(.025)
Spatial Lag	.069***	.043***	.049***	.052***
	(.013)	(.007)	(.012)	(.010)
Capital Mobility	.193***	.093**	.119***	.079***
	(.067)	(.038)	(.042)	(.022)
Capital Mobility ×	−.006**	−.004***	−.005***	−.004***
Capital Endowment	(.003)	(.001)	(.001)	(.001)
Capital Mobility ×	.047**	.017*	.030**	.023**
Consensus Democracy	(.019)	(.010)	(.012)	(.011)
Capital Mobility ×	−.211*	−.047	−.075	
Union Density	(.112)	(.064)	(.070)	
Capital Mobility ×	.058	.040*	.052*	
Left Government	(.053)	(.024)	(.028)	
Capital Mobility ×	−.025	−.071**	−.062**	
European Union	(.081)	(.029)	(.030)	
Observations	581	581	581	581
R²	.919	.932	.932	.929
Log-Likelihood	−1519.8	−1488.9	−1487.5	−1494.4

Notes: The regressions were estimated with fixed unit and period (i.e., country and year) effects and union density, leftist government, and European Union membership variables, with the exception of the deterministic time trend model, which does not include period dummies. The coefficients for these variables are not shown. Parentheses contain standard errors. *** significant at 1%, ** significant at 5%, * significant at 10%.

democracies. By contrast, the coefficients on the union density interaction terms are always negative. This finding undermines the conventional wisdom about corporatism, globalization and taxes, but it is consistent with the observed cross-national pattern of capital taxation (see table 4.1). As for the other control variables, the coefficients on the partisanship and EU interactions terms have the expected signs. Both are statistically significant in the capital account openness and financial openness regressions. The effect of removing policy barriers to capital flows on capital taxation is magnified for European Union countries in the post-1986 period and lessened under left-wing governments.

To help demonstrate the implications of the regression results reported in table 4.2, I conduct two counterfactual globalization "experiments." The counterfactuals examine the effect of financial liberalization on capital tax rates in majoritarian democracies with capital-rich economies and consensus

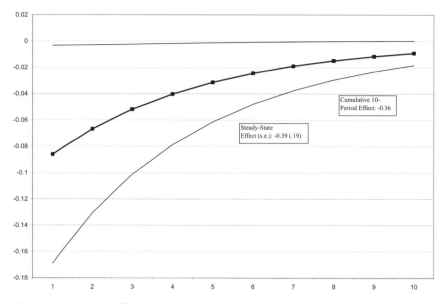

Figure 4.5 Temporal Effects with Spatial Feedback on Capital Taxation from a Positive 1% Increase in Financial Openness with 95% Confidence Interval (Majoritarian Democracy and Capital-Rich Economy with UK Spatial Weights)

democracies with capital-poor economies. To represent each case I use the minimum and maximum sample values for the consensus democracy and capital endowment variables. For convenience, I use Britain's spatial weights for the majoritarian-rich case and the Netherland's spatial weights for the consensus-poor case. The results are based on the fourth and final regression presented in table 4.2, which omits the control-interaction terms. This does not change the results but simplifies greatly the calculations, which are done using the steps outlined in the methodological appendix to chapter 2.

In the case of capital-rich majoritarian democracies, the experimental 1% increase in financial openness is expected to produce a 0.39% drop in the capital tax rate in the long run (i.e., the steady-state effect). Figure 4.5 plots the temporal response path to this exogenous change in financial openness. The steady-state effect in this experiment is statistically significant at the .05 level. Most of the effect is felt within the first few years. The same increase in financial openness is expected to produce a 0.49% rise in the tax rate in capital poor consensus democracies. This effect is statistically significant at the .01 level. Figure 4.6 plots the response path over time. Overall, the quantitative results strongly support the theoretical prediction: convergence in the capital tax rate with capital rich majoritarian democracies converging from above and capital poor consensus democracies converging from below.

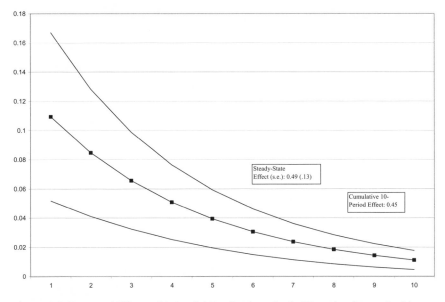

Figure 4.6 Temporal Effects with Spatial Feedback on Capital Taxation from a Positive 1% Increase in Financial Openness with 95% Confidence Interval (Consensus Democracy and Capital-Poor Economy with Dutch Spatial Weights)

To get a better sense of the model's explanatory power, consider that New Zealand's capital tax rate was 49.3% in 1988, the last year that it restricted international financial transactions. By 1996, the year that New Zealand adopted its proportional representation electoral system, the capital tax rate was 37.7%. I estimate that approximately 3.6% of this 11.6% drop in capital taxes, nearly one-third of the reduction, can be explained by New Zealand's removal of capital controls.

CAUSAL MECHANISMS

Which of the many elements of consensus democracy identified by Lijphart is (are) likely to be the most important when it comes to the politics of capital taxation? The research on the politics of redistribution has identified several mechanisms that could account for why capital taxes are low in consensus democracies. First, Roemer (1998) argues that leftist parties will propose lower taxes and redistribution when there are multiple salient issues in election campaigns. In his formal model, there are two issues that divide the electorate—redistribution and religion. The left-wing party is anti-clerical, as are most (but not all) of the poor voters whom it represents. Likewise, the right-wing party is pro-clerical, as are most (but not all) of the rich voters. Even when median income is less than the mean, if the left-wing party stays true to its anti-clerical position, it will propose a low tax rate in equilibrium in order to attract some of the rich anti-clerical voters. In other words, multiple-issue dimensions create incentives for parties that want to win elections to moderate their policy positions on one dimension as a means of attracting voters who agree with the party's position on other dimensions. Multiple-issue dimensions characterize consensus democracies (Lijphart 1999, 78–87), and tend to be associated with proportional representation (PR) electoral systems, but this logic applies to single-member-district-plurality (SMDP) systems as well.

A second line of thinking focuses on the distinct electoral institutions and party systems in consensus democracies.[28] First, Crepaz (1996) has argued that encompassing governments, because they represent a larger portion of the total population and therefore internalize much of the social cost of economic policy, are more sensitive, for political reasons, to the distortions caused by redistribution. He contends that this explains why the consensus democracies have outperformed their majoritarian counterparts in terms of unemployment and inflation. To the extent that they reduce investment and labor productivity and lead to underemployment, this logic extends to capital taxes. Second, fiscal policy is broadly redistributive, as opposed to narrowly targeted, in consensus democracies (Persson and Tabellini 2000; Milesi-Ferretti et al. 2002). In other words, fiscal policy is not a tool to transfer income from political losers to political winners as it is in the majoritarian context. Along these lines, Crepaz writes: "There is strong evidence that, the more encompassing institutional structures are, the more responsibly governments behave, in the sense that policies do not bluntly redistribute from members supporting opposition parties to members of the ruling government coalition" (1998, 66). The logic that drives this inclusive behavior, beyond the possibility of economy-wide distortions or consensual decision-making norms, is unclear, however. What prevents governments from taxing capital heavily?

One possibility is that consensus democracy, PR electoral systems in particular, may increase the likelihood that the policy preferences of shareholders are reflected in tax policy. PR electoral systems create incentives for parties to adopt platforms that reflect the tax preferences of shareholders by increasing the likelihood that these small parties will be included in the government and their preferences will be disproportionately influential when it comes to policy making. Austen-Smith and Banks (1988) show in their model that with three parties the equilibrium coalition will include the largest and smallest party and that the policy outcome will reflect the policy position of the small party. Hence, in PR systems legislative influence is not monotonic in vote share. Similarly, Persson, Roland, and Tabellini (2000) show formally that the vote of confidence in parliamentary systems gives enhanced bargaining power over policy proposals to junior partners in coalition governments.

But what about center-left governments? If Crepaz's observation about transfers, or lack thereof, from political losers to winners is correct, we might expect shareholders' interests to be protected even when right-wing parties are outside the government. McGann (2006) provides a political explanation for why we might observe this kind of inclusive behavior. He argues that the combination of PR electoral institutions and majority rule in parliamentary decision making protects minority parties even when they are excluded from government. The reason is that the combination of multiple parties and issue dimensions with majority rule makes all governing coalitions inherently unstable. To use Roemer's language and issue dimensions, if a pro-clerical center party is governing with an anti-clerical left-wing party that wants to raise capital taxes, and an anti-clerical right-wing party wants to prevent this tax increase, the right-wing party can moderate its position on the religion dimension to make itself a more attractive coalition partner for the center party, thus either breaking up the ruling coalition or moderating the government's behavior.

The idea that consensus democracy prevents wage earners and the politicians who represent them from setting transfer-maximizing capital tax rates may seem counterintuitive, especially in the light of recent debates about the partisan bias of PR electoral institutions. Labor power and influence in consensus democracies like Austria and the Nordic countries are typically inferred from the strength of the Social Democratic parties and the frequency with which the Left governs in these countries. In fact, Iversen and Soskice (2006) point out that empirically the Left governs in PR systems about three-fourths of the time, whereas the Right governs in majoritarian systems at the same frequency. How could it be that the political institutions in consensus democracies disadvantage labor?

In these cases (i.e., the Austro-Nordic democracies) it helps to think about the relevant counterfactual. If these countries had majoritarian systems instead, it is likely that the Left would dominate national politics even more than it does today. Imagine how strongly the Social Democrats would dominate political life in Sweden, if there were a first-past-the-post electoral system there. The traditional view is that PR constrains the Left (Rokkan 1970; Boix 1999), and the reason that countries like Sweden switched from plurality to proportional representation electoral systems after granting universal suffrage was precisely to limit the political power of rising socialist parties and to protect the influence of ruling liberal and conservative parties.

This view has been challenged over the last few years by a number of scholars (Blais et al. 2005; Andrews and Jackman 2005; Cusack, Iversen, and Soskice 2007). Iversen and Soskice (2006) argue that PR benefits left-wing parties because center parties, representing the middle classes, will choose to form coalitions with them in order to tax and redistribute the income of the rich. Under majoritarianism, two centrist parties emerge, a center-left and center-right party. Tax policies depend on the party leadership. If the leader of the center-left party is a member of the lower class, the party will tax both middle- and high-income individuals and redistribute the income. If the leader of the center-right party is a member of the upper class, the party will not tax and redistribute any income. In the end, under majoritarian electoral systems, the middle classes have more to fear from a center-left party led by a member of the lower class than a center-right party led by a member of the upper class and therefore vote for center-right parties. According to Iversen and Soskice, this logic explains the leftist bias of PR and the rightist bias of majoritarianism.[29]

The views that PR constrains the Left (e.g., Boix), on the one hand, and enables it (e.g., Iversen and Soskice) on the other, are not mutually exclusive. In fact, they can be complementary. Iversen and Soskice's argument suggests that the Left is safe to govern under PR, from the perspective of the median voter, precisely because it is constrained by its coalition partners. Left-led coalition governments are able to make commitments, particularly business-friendly commitments, that would not be credible if made by single party leftist governments.

This possibility is clearer when viewed in light of the capital-tax time-inconsistency problem (Fischer 1980). Let us assume for a moment that the median voter wants to set low capital taxes in order to attract internationally mobile capital. It is typically future profits that provide the necessary incentive for firms to make employment-generating investment, and once it is made, this kind of investment is relatively fixed. This creates an incentive for short-sighted politicians to promise low capital taxes *ex ante*—i.e., before the investment is made—and renege *ex post*. One liability of majoritarian democracy is that governments may find it difficult to make credible policy commitments. Moe and Caldwell note the political uncertainty that majoritarianism—what they call the classic parliamentary model, which has single-party majority governments at its core—creates for social actors: "The classic parliamentary model, therefore, drastically heightens the dangers of political uncertainty: if the other side comes to power, it can pass whatever laws it wants. *Worse, the governing party itself has full authority to renege at any time on any political deals it has second thoughts about*" (1994, 177, emphasis added). By contrast, coalition governments differ from single-party governments in that they contain multiple veto players (Tsebelis 2002), which, in turn, leads to more policy stability. *Ex ante* agreements are enforced *ex post* by the vote of no confidence. Bawn (1999) and Tsebelis and Chang (2004) find support for this stability hypothesis with respect to budgetary policy specifically.

QUALITATIVE EMPIRICAL EVALUATIONS OF THE
CAUSAL MECHANISMS

In this section, I compare capital tax changes in the United Kingdom and Netherlands during the 1980s and 1990s, a period of significant reform, in order to check the plausibility of the causal relationships highlighted by the theoretical model presented above (small open-economy democracy) and to identify more specifically the mechanisms through which consensus democracy shapes capital tax policy and tax reform. The reasoning behind the choice of countries is simple. Since I am interested in how institutions interact with globalization to affect tax policy, I want to examine countries with tax systems that have been significantly affected by international economic integration. Using this criterion, the countries of the European Union immediately come to mind as potential cases. The removal of all internal barriers to the free movement of capital (as well as labor and goods) has put pressure on high-tax EU member countries to reform their systems in order to maintain their tax bases.[30] From this group, the United Kingdom and the Netherlands are natural selections because they are, in many ways, the exemplars of majoritarian and consensus democracy, respectively.[31] Moreover, the United Kingdom is a large low capital return (or richly endowed) country, while the Netherlands is a small high capital return (or poorly endowed) country; and both countries have undertaken significant capital tax reforms since the 1980s. [32]

According to the theoretical model, globalization is the main impetus for tax reform, but its consequences are strongly conditioned by a country's political institutions. More specifically, the model suggests that globalization will lead to lower capital tax rates in majoritarian democracies—particularly capital-rich ones—and higher capital tax rates in capital-poor consensus democracies. It is not easy to take a parsimonious theoretical model and use it to understand tax reform in the real world. The main difficulty with using my model for this purpose is that it has no parties in it. This is problematic because political parties are important actors when it comes to tax policy, and we largely observe the politics of tax reform through the prism of party politics. I am not saying that the model cannot help us understand British and Dutch tax reform, but we first need to draw out the implications of the model for partisan politics.

If we are willing to accept that labor is the core constituency of the Left and capital is the core constituency of the Right and that therefore, all else being equal, the Left will try to shift the tax burden from labor to capital and the Right will try to do the reverse (simple partisan prediction), the implications of globalization for party politics are straightforward:[33] in majoritarian democracies the Right will be much more successful than the Left in achieving tax reforms that benefit its core constituency. This is because capital taxes in majoritarian democracies will be at or near their revenue-maximizing levels. Globalization will push the revenue-maximizing capital tax rate down, particularly in capital-rich majoritarian democracies, empowering the political Right to cut capital taxes.

In consensus democracies the Left will be more successful than the Right in achieving tax changes that benefit its core constituency. This is because capital tax rates are theorized to be below their revenue-maximizing levels. When capital is immobile the revenue cost of being below the revenue-maximizing tax rate is small, especially for capital-poor countries. With globalization the opportunity cost of low capital taxes increases. This prediction is counterintuitive in an era of economic globalization. It implies that globalization constrains right-wing parties from shifting the relative tax burden onto labor and empowers left-wing governments to shift the burden onto capital. Empirical support for this prediction should be viewed as strong evidence in favor of the theoretical model.

These are the "within-country" predictions. Across countries it is clear that the Right in majoritarian democracies should be more successful at cutting tax rates than the Right in consensual democracies. In majoritarian democracies, globalization provides the impetus for right-wing governments to pursue capital tax reform and there are few if any political constraints on their ability to enact these reforms. In consensus democracies, the Right is constrained both economically and politically. With respect to the Left, the predictions are ambiguous. In majoritarian democracies, the Left, when it comes to power, is less constrained politically, but leftist governments are constrained by globalization. The Left in consensus democracies faces less of an economic constraint on its ability to redistribute income, but Left-led governments are constrained by the nature of consensus democracy. Whether the economic or political constraints are more binding is largely an empirical question.

In Britain the simple partisan predictions are borne out. Successive right-wing governments under Margaret Thatcher and John Major lowered capital taxes, and more recently, Labour has raised them (slightly). While the tax reforms under Thatcher are well-known, those under Labour are not.[34] Tony Blair's Labour government enacted several important reforms after taking office in 1997. Like its Conservative predecessors, the Labour government has cut the main corporate tax rate, but steps have also been taken to increase the revenue generated from capital taxation. Specifically, the government replaced the system of indexation for capital gains taxation with a capital gains tax taper—which is intended to preserve incentives for holding assets over the long term while taxing short-term capital gains at high rates—and the imputation system has been scrapped.[35] Under the new system, pension funds, which hold approximately 50% of corporate stock in Britain, do not receive a tax credit on their dividend income. Together these changes will significantly increase the capital tax base and should offset the losses from a lower corporate income tax rate.[36]

Despite these reforms, the Labour government has not reversed the capital tax rate cuts under Thatcher and Major. Figure 4.7 shows the capital tax rate in Britain using the Mendoza et al. data over the period 1965–2000. At the beginning of the 1980s, the average effective capital tax rate in the United Kingdom was as high as 70%. By the mid-1990s, Conservative reform had dropped the tax rate to the mid-40% range.[37] Under Labour, the tax rate has rebounded to about 50%, but there is little chance that the government will be able to push it much higher. Labour increased the average effective capital tax by raising tariffs on capital gains. Also, the stamp tax, a 0.5% surcharge paid by those who buy shares, has generated significant capital tax revenue recently, but Labour is not responsible for this tax. The ratio of taxes levied on capital gains and financial transactions to total taxes on individuals rose for the first three years of Blair's Labour government. By contrast, the ratio of taxes paid by corporations to taxes paid by individuals has actually decreased under Labour (Hays 2003). In sum, the British case is certainly consistent with the theory. One way to understand the Labour government's behavior in the area of taxation recently is to view it as a partisan government, highly constrained by globalization but trying nonetheless to raise capital taxes wherever possible.

During the same period right-wing and left-wing governments also carried out major tax reforms in the Netherlands. The Christian Democratic

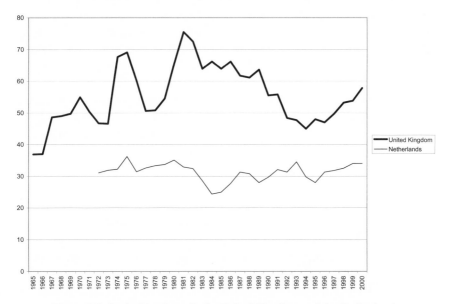

Figure 4.7 Capital Tax Rates in the United Kingdom and the Netherlands

Party (CDA) simplified the Dutch tax system, lowered statutory tax rates, and broadened the tax base during the 1980s and early 1990s. More specifically, the statutory corporate tax rate was lowered to 35%; the investment tax credit system was eliminated; and the personal income and social security tax systems were integrated. Because the tax rate reductions were combined with significant base-broadening measures, the reforms were largely revenue neutral with respect to capital taxation. In other words, the right-center government did not reduce the tax burden on capital (see figure 4.7).

In the 1994 and 1998 elections, the Social Democrats (PvdA) won a plurality of parliamentary seats and became the senior party in a coalition with the Free Market Liberals (VVD) and the Democrats '66 (D66). As expected, the Social Democrats put capital tax reform on the political agenda in the 1990s. For example, in the 1998 election campaign, the PvdA placed capital tax reform at the center of its manifesto and called for a new tax system in which "work costs less and... large stock-exchange profits (a lot) more" and "all capital gains are taxed." [38] Before 1997 capital gains were exempt from taxation except when a "substantial interest" in a corporation, defined as 33.3% ownership, was sold. After 1997 the capital tax base was expanded by redefining a "substantial interest" from 33.33% to 5% ownership (a very significant change) and by setting a fictitious wage for director-shareholders, who previously were able to reduce their taxes by labeling their income as profit. Furthermore, the tax rate on the sale of a substantial interest was raised from 20% to 25%.

The coalition agreement reached after the 1998 election included a comprehensive set of proposed income tax reforms, of which the most important involve moving to a "box" approach to taxing income. For the most part, these reforms were adopted in the 2001 Income Tax Act.[39] Under the new system, income is separated into one of three boxes according to how it is earned. These boxes include labor income (Box I), income from substantial business interests (Box II), and imputed income from wealth (Box III). The top tax rate on labor income was lowered from 60% to 52%; the tax on income from the sale of a substantial business interest was kept at 25% (despite a push from the PvdA to raise it to 30%); and it was agreed that imputed income from wealth would be taxed at 30%. The presumptive return on individually held assets is 4%, making the tax on imputed income equivalent to a net assets tax of 1.2% (30% of 4%). The basic exemption on this income is 17,000 euros, which is much smaller than the previous net wealth tax exemption of 90,756 euros. A dividend tax of 25% is used as an advanced levy for the tax on imputed wealth even though individuals are not responsible for paying taxes on their actual dividends. For foreign investors, this dividend tax is a final tax. The tax on imputed income replaces both the progressive tax on actual capital income and the existing net wealth tax.[40]

Changes in the personal income tax that took effect in 2001 should increase capital tax revenues by expanding the tax base (reduced basic exemption) and closing a loophole that allowed investors to avoid tax through the capital gains exemption.[41] If so, these reforms will push up the average effective capital tax rate. The most noteworthy point about the capital tax reforms prior to 2001 is that they took place against a backdrop of significant tax cuts. Therefore, their impact is most evident when looking at the relative tax burden. Both the ratio of taxes levied on corporate profits to taxes levied on wages and the ratio of dividends taxes to taxes on wages increase sharply beginning in 1994, the first year with a PvdA-led government.

Was European economic integration the impetus for British and Dutch capital tax reforms? In Britain, the idea that reform was spurred by capital outflows is consistent with the basic facts. During this period the value of British portfolio and direct investment abroad always exceeded the value of foreign portfolio and direct investment in Britain (Hays 2003). In the early 1980s it was not very profitable for firms to produce in the United Kingdom; given the multinational nature of production, this had severe economic consequences. Firms simply produced elsewhere. Tory reforms offered an effective solution to the problem. Young (1999), for example, finds that Tory tax reform substantially improved the tax competitiveness of the United Kingdom and therefore raised levels of investment in Britain, both domestic and foreign.[42] He estimates that a 1% increase in the British capital tax rate reduces investment in Britain in the long run by 1.76% and concludes that a large part of the growth in investment between 1983 and 1990 can be attributed to the reduction in corporate tax rates. These investment distortions are very large and suggest that tax rates may have been above their revenue-maximizing levels. Tory spending and tax cuts increased the return on investment and, at least initially, increased the revenue from capital taxes and improved economic performance in Britain.

What about the Dutch case? There is evidence to suggest that the opportunity costs in lost revenue from forgoing capital tax reform in the late 1990s would have been high. By the time the PvdA came to power in 1994, the value of foreign direct and portfolio investment in the Netherlands was greater than the value of Dutch direct and portfolio investment abroad. Moreover, capital inflows grew substantially during the 1990s. In 1995 the size of capital inflows into the Netherlands relative to GDP was close to the OECD average (4.5%). By 2000 this ratio was approximately 33% of GDP, almost twice the OECD average.[43] In the late 1990s there was a large increase in the capital tax base, and the PvdA-led government took advantage of the revenue opportunities this created. Thus, it seems globalization did in fact constrain the Right and empower the Left in the Netherlands.

At the same time it was not easy for the PvdA to achieve these revenue gains. The Dutch case is a clear example of politically constrained change in tax policy. It is therefore suggestive about why consensus democracies typically tax capital at low rates. One does not have to look hard to find the source of the constraint in the Netherlands: Dutch budgetary policy is the product of coalition bargaining, and this acts as a political constraint on taxation.[44] It should not be surprising that the actual reforms enacted fell short of what the Social Democrats would have preferred ideally—in other words, fell short of what the PvdA would have done had Wim Kok led a single-party government. The PvdA failed to significantly increase the taxes on large stock exchange returns (beyond the changes made in 1997) despite its campaign promises in 1998. The tax rate on capital gains from a substantial interest remains at 25% despite the initially proposed increase to 30%.[45] Moreover, the Social Democrats failed to extend the capital gains tax to all capital gains, and the new broad imputed tax on capital income replaces a progressive tax on actual interest, dividend, and rental income. In short, the recent tax reforms implemented in the Netherlands are likely to increase capital tax revenues, but they also reflect the fact that the PvdA had to bargain and compromise with the VVD, its partner to the right.

One final comparison provides a check on this interpretation of the evidence. If it is true that the constraints associated with governing by coalition are the key to explaining the differences in capital tax policies between majoritarian and consensus democracies, then we should observe that the capital tax policies of any countries typically classified as consensual that have single-party governments should look more like Britain than the Netherlands, and any countries typically classified as majoritarian that govern by coalition should look more like the Dutch case than the British case. Sweden and the United States are natural choices for this comparison.

Sweden is considered by most to be a consensual democracy. It has a PR electoral system with a low degree of disproportionality, a large number of effective parliamentary parties, and a corporatist system of interest intermediation. At the same time, Sweden is unique among the consensual democracies in that single-party Social Democratic governments are the norm. These are frequently minority governments, but minority governments are more similar on many dimensions to majority-party governments than they are to coalition governments (Strom 1984, 1990). Moreover, the median legislator is almost always from the Social Democratic Party, making it extremely difficult to form a majority coalition around the Social Democrats. The United States, on the other hand, is a majoritarian democracy. It has a plurality-rule-based electoral system, two major adversarial parties, and a pluralistic system of interest intermediation. The executive is held by a single party, and yet, because its system is presidential, the United States is unique among the majoritarian democracies. When the U.S. government is divided—one party controls the presidency and the other party controls the Congress—it is, in effect, a coalition government, especially when it comes to taxation (Sundquist 1988; Alesina and Rosenthal 1995).

Again, if it is true that the constraints associated with governing by coalition are the key to explaining the differences in capital tax policies between majoritarian and consensus democracies, then we should observe that Swedish capital tax rates look more like British capital tax rates than Dutch rates, and American capital taxes should look more like the Dutch than British taxes. Empirically, this is the case. All four tax rates are plotted in figure 4.8. The British and Swedish tax rates are much more volatile and higher than the U.S. and Dutch rates, though the British rate is higher than the Swedish rate on average over the entire period. The American capital tax rate starts higher than the Dutch rate and declines slowly throughout the period and, even after two consecutive Democratic administrations, never returns to its pre-Reagan era levels. Dutch rates are cut moderately under center-right coalitions during the 1980s, but by 2000, after two PvdA-led governments, are back to pre-Lubbers levels. To sum, majoritarian democracy, to the extent that it produces politically unconstrained single-party governments, leads to higher capital taxes and greater capital tax volatility than consensus democracy, which tends to produce more politically constrained coalition governments.

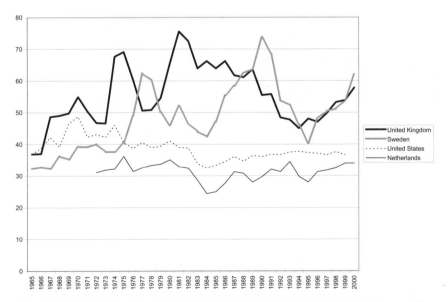

Figure 4.8 Capital Tax Rates in the United Kingdom, Sweden, the United States, and the Netherlands

CONCLUSION

I began this chapter by revisiting the debate over whether globalization limits the ability of governments to tax capital. Empirically speaking, it is clear that there is no race to the bottom in capital taxes, but there is evidence that effective rates are converging somewhere in the middle. Convergence of this kind implies that there will be revenue winners and losers. Countries that tax capital at high rates will face pressure to lower them. The theoretical case against tax convergence is strong, however. Corporatist institutions should allow some countries to compete for internationally mobile capital despite high rates of taxation. The problem with this argument is that the countries that depend most heavily on capital taxes are majoritarian democracies with liberal market economies.

It seems that political institutions are more important than labor market institutions in determining a country's tax mix. Much of the cross-national variance in capital taxation can be explained by the degree to which a country's polity is majoritarian or consensual in nature: in majoritarian democracies, the influence of the median voter through elections pushes the capital tax rate to its revenue maximizing level, while in consensus democracies the constraints that come with governing in a coalition keep capital taxes below this rate. But globalization is eroding these differences by simultaneously lowering the revenue-maximizing capital tax rate and increasing the opportunity costs of staying below it.

Past research has focused on the consequences of globalization for corporatism (e.g., Lange et al. 1995; Western 1995), predicted that consensus democracies will be the most financially constrained by increased capital mobility (Hallerberg and Basinger 1998; Basinger and Hallerberg 2004), and addressed such questions as whether the welfare state can survive in social democratic countries (Garrett 1998a). I have argued, in essence, that the globalization literature has emphasized the wrong set of countries. The Social Democratic corporatist countries are likely to do quite well in the increasingly connected global economy. These are the countries that, for the most part, have had very open economies since the end of World War II. They have developed large welfare states to cushion their citizens from the vagaries of the international economy and financed this spending with taxes on consumption and labor. It is surprising that so little research has focused on globalization's impact on the majoritarian democracies. Countries with majoritarian polities are the ones that face the globalization dilemma described throughout this book. And in the event of a serious backlash, these are the same countries that are vulnerable to radical changes in their foreign economic policies.

In the next chapter, I argue that the best guarantee against a return to autarky is a new bargain of embedded liberalism, one based on carefully crafted insurance and compensatory programs. During the early postwar period, Keynesian policies of demand management were crucial to the bargain of embedded liberalism in the liberal market economies. Today, there are no clear alternatives to these policies. A number of recommendations have been made—labor market reform, retraining, and insurance—but very little attention has been paid to the political sustainability of these policies. They all have political and economic costs that make them potentially problematic. Thus, the design of these programs is critical to their long-term success. I discuss the nature of these costs and potential strategies for minimizing them.

Appendix

A STYLIZED THEORETICAL MODEL OF CAPITAL-TAX COMPETITION

In this appendix, I leverage Persson and Tabellini's (2000, chapter 12) for-mal-theoretical model to show that tax competition implies spatial interde-pendence in capital tax policy. The model's essential elements are as follows. In two jurisdictions (i.e., countries), denote the domestic and foreign cap-ital-tax rates τ_k and τ_k^*. Individuals can invest in either country, but foreign investment incurs *mobility costs*. Taxation follows the source (not the resi-dence) principle. Governments use revenues from taxes levied on capital and labor to fund a fixed amount of spending. Individuals differ in their relative labor-to-capital endowment, denoted e^i, and make labor-leisure, l and x, and savings-investment, $s = k + f$ (k = domestic; f = foreign), decisions to max-imize quasi-linear utility, $\omega = U(c_1) + c_2 + V(x)$, over leisure and consump-tion and in the model's two periods, c_1 and c_2, subject to a time constraint, $1 + e^i = l + x$, and budget constraints in each period, $1 - e^i = c_1 + k + f + \equiv c_1 + s$ and $c_2 = (l - \tau_k)k + (l - \tau_k^*)f - M(f) + (l - \tau_l)l$.

The equilibrium economic choices of citizens i in this model are as follows:

$$s = S(\tau_k) = 1 - U_c^{-1}(1 - \tau_k) \tag{4.10}$$
$$f = F(\tau_k, \tau_k^*) = M_f^{-1}(\tau_k - \tau_k^*) \tag{4.11}$$
$$k = K(\tau_k, \tau_k^*) = S(\tau_k) - F(\tau_k, \tau_k^*) \tag{4.12}$$

With labor, $L(\tau_l)$, leisure, x, and consumption, c_1, c_2, implicitly given by these conditions, this leaves individuals with indirect utility, W, defined over the policy variables, tax rates, of:

$$W(\tau_l, \tau_k) = U\{1 - S(\tau_k)\} + (1 - \tau_k)S(\tau_k) + (\tau_k - \tau_k^*)F(\tau_k, \tau_k^*)$$
$$- M\{F(\tau_k, \tau_k^*)\} + (1 - \tau_l)L(\tau_l) + V\{1 - L(\tau_l)\} \tag{4.13}$$

Facing an electorate with these preferences over taxes, using a Besley-Coate (1997) citizen-candidate model wherein running for office is costly and citi-zens choose whether to enter the race by an expected-utility calculation, some citizen candidate will win and set tax rates to maximize his or her own wel-fare. The model's stages are: (1) elections occur in both countries, (2) elected citizen-candidates set their respective countries' tax rates, and (3) all private economic decisions are made. In this case, the candidate who enters and wins will be the one with endowment e^p such that she or he desires to implement the following *Modified Ramsey Rule:*

$$\frac{S(\tau_k^p) - e^p}{S(\tau_k^p)} \left[1 + \varepsilon_l(\tau_k^p)\right] = \frac{L(\tau_l^p) + e^p}{L(\tau_l^p)} \left[1 + \frac{S_\tau(\tau_k^p) + 2F_\tau^*(\tau_k^{p*}, \tau_k^p)\tau_k}{S_\tau(\tau_k^p)}\right] \quad (4.14)$$

Equation (4.14) gives the optimal capital-tax-rate policy for the domestic policy maker to choose, which, as one can see, is a function of the capital tax-rate chosen abroad. The game is symmetric, so the optimal capital tax rate for the foreign policy maker to choose looks identical from his or her point of view and, importantly, depends on the capital tax rate chosen domestically. That is, equation (4.14) gives best-response functions $\tau_k = T(e^p, \tau_k^*)$ and $\tau_k^* = T^*$ (e^{p*}, τ_k), the foreign and domestic policy maker, respectively. In other words, the domestic (foreign) capital tax rate depends on the domestic (foreign) policy maker's labor-capital endowment and the foreign (domestic) capital tax rate—that is, capital taxes are strategically interdependent. The slope of these functions, $\partial T/\partial \tau_k^*$ and $\partial T^*/\partial \tau_k$, can be either positive or negative. An increase in foreign tax rates induces capital flow into the domestic economy, but the domestic policy maker may use the increased tax base to lower tax rates or to raise them (the latter to seize the greater revenue opportunities created by the decreased elasticity of this base).

5

Saving Embedded Liberalism in the Anglo-American Democracies

To this point my argument has been much more explanatory in nature than prescriptive. I have tried to explain how and to estimate the extent to which domestic economic and political institutions shape the globalization forces that press upon OECD governments. Clearly, for those who want their governments to respond positively to these pressures with policies that help stabilize and grow the liberal international economy, the preceding analysis has important implications. In this chapter, I examine the possibility of building a new bargain of embedded liberalism that can effectively maintain or even generate public support for policies of economic openness in majoritarian democracies with competitive labor markets. This new bargain must be crafted with the economic constraints of twenty-first century globalization in mind, and it must be built on a set of policies that are robust and compatible with the incentives of office-seeking politicians, particularly those from the Left, since these politicians tend to be more sensitive than their counterparts on the Right to anti-trade political pressure.

Others have made similar calls, most notably John Ruggie, Ethan Kapstein, and Kenneth Scheve and Matthew Slaughter. John Ruggie (2002, 2007) has argued that it is time to consider embedded liberalism on a global scale. In his view, globalization has made it impossible to reconstitute a social bargain of this type at a national level. The policy tools that governments previously used to redistribute the benefits and share the costs of economic openness no longer work. The new bargain of embedded liberalism should be rooted in multilateralism and engage global non-governmental (civil society and corporate) actors. Like Ruggie, I believe this is a desirable long-term objective, but "taking embedded liberalism global," even if it were politically feasible, would not generate much support for free trade in the near future.[1] Moreover, Ruggie takes the argument that national governments are impotent and incapable of compensating globalization's losers a bit too far. Kapstein (1996, 1999), who sees many of the policy constraints that Ruggie attributes to globalization as politically self-imposed, argues for a more traditional Keynesian macroeconomic response at the national level, while Scheve and Slaughter (2007) have called for broad-based redistributive policies to build support among Americans for international trade and investment.[2] More specifically, Scheve and Slaughter call for the elimination of payroll taxes for workers who earn below the national median, financed with an increase in the payroll taxes paid by workers above the median.

Like Kapstein and Scheve and Slaughter, I argue that it is possible to build a new and politically robust bargain of embedded liberalism at the national level, but my focus is primarily on targeted programs aimed at compensating and insuring globalization's biggest losers. While it may seem necessary to have policy change on a larger scale, there is considerable evidence to suggest that the political benefits from targeted programs (e.g., Trade Adjustment Assistance in the United States) are far greater than their economic costs, which makes them attractive to policy makers in an era of fiscal retrenchment. I begin, in the next section, by quantifying the severity of the globalization dilemma for governments in majoritarian-liberal political economies. Then I examine the political feasibility of corporatist-style labor market reform, active labor market policies, and insurance and compensation policies as responses to economic globalization. Based on this analysis, I argue that governments should focus on providing insurance and compensation rather than structural reform and/or retraining.

The purpose of this chapter is to emphasize and preliminarily evaluate the political feasibility and sustainability of policies that are being offered as solutions to the globalization dilemma. Governments must strike a balance between economic efficiency and political feasibility in a way that maintains support for trade among its core proponents (i.e., highly skilled labor and individuals employed in export-oriented industries). For the Left, I argue that this balance requires intermediate levels of labor mobility across sectors of the economy. Domestic economic adjustment to globalization is necessary, but the costs should be spread over time, and the process should be largely determined by market forces. There is a "natural" rate of structural change, and, in the absence of significant market failures—for example, the failure of economic agents to correctly anticipate future prices or wage rigidities—it is not evident that speeding up the process is welfare enhancing, even from a purely economic standpoint (e.g., see Steigum 1984), and the political calculus unambiguously favors gradual adjustment. What governments can and should do is minimize the extent to which their insurance and compensatory programs distort market-driven adjustment. The challenge is to increase the levels of protection provided to those who are vulnerable and, at the same time, decrease the extent to which these protective policies distort market-driven behavior.

HOW SERIOUS IS THE GLOBALIZATION DILEMMA FOR
ANGLO-AMERICAN DEMOCRACIES?

Globalization creates a dilemma for governments because it increases the political demands on them to provide social insurance and other public goods at the same time that it undermines their ability to finance additional spending. I have argued that countries with majoritarian polities and competitive labor markets, the Anglo-American democracies, are uniquely vulnerable to this dilemma because trade and the multinationalization of production simultaneously increase employment volatility and constrain capital taxation in these countries.

To quantify the severity of the globalization dilemma for governments in the Anglo-American democracies, I return to the macro-level regressions presented in table 2.5. In the chapter 2 analysis, I regressed government consumption and social benefits spending on a set of trade, labor market structure, and labor market performance variables. Here I regress government consumption and social benefit spending on the capital tax rate and employment volatility. For my measure of employment volatility, I use the estimated variances from the multiplicative heteroscedasticity models in chapter 3 (table 3.4). The capital tax variable is the same one I used in chapter 4. Both variables are lagged one year in the regressions. Note that I do not include the original independent variables from the earlier analysis because most of their impacts on spending were theorized to be a consequence of labor market effects, which are captured now in the employment volatility variable.[3]

The results from two sets of regressions for government consumption and social benefits spending are reported in table 5.1. One of the regressions includes country (unit) dummies and the other includes both country and year (period) dummies. All of the regressions include a temporal and spatial lag of the dependent variable. In both sets of regressions, the coefficients are correctly signed (positive) and statistically significant. All else being equal, an increase in employment volatility leads to an increase in government spending, and a decrease in capital taxes leads to a decrease in government spending. To this analysis, I add a third dependent variable: budget balance as a percentage of GDP. This regression gives us a better sense of the budgetary pressures attributable to globalization. I also add an employment volatility capital tax interaction term to the regressions since Rodrik's globalization dilemma is a conditional hypothesis.[4] I expect countries that experience increases in employment volatility when capital taxes are high to experience the most budgetary pressure—that is, deficits should increase the most under these conditions because the governments face stronger revenue constraints. The estimates support this argument.

Table 5.1 Employment Volatility, Capital Taxes, and Government Spending

	Govcon		Socben		Deficits	
	(1)	(2)	(3)	(4)	(5)	(6)
Temporal Lag	.793***	.875***	.851***	.921***	.786***	.833***
	(.021)	(.021)	(.015)	(.017)	(.028)	(.027)
Spatial Lag	.013***	.010***	.009***	.021***	.125***	.045
	(.000)	(.000)	(.001)	(.002)	(.029)	(.028)
Employment	.040***	.022**	.032***	.009	.339***	.319***
Volatility	(.012)	(.011)	(.012)	(.010)	(.108)	(.100)
Capital Tax	.013**	.014***	.022***	.022***	−.006	−.024
	(.005)	(.005)	(.005)	(.004)	(.018)	(.017)
Employment					−.014***	−.012***
Volatility ×					(.004)	(.004)
Capital Tax						
Fixed Effects						
Country / Year	Yes/No	Yes/Yes	Yes/No	Yes/Yes	Yes/No	Yes/Yes
Observations	494	494	482	482	471	471
R^2	.973	.982	.975	.981	.766	.819
Log-Likelihood	−451.3	−355.9	−449.9	−359.1	−869.9	−823.3

Notes: The fixed effects coefficient-estimates are suppressed to conserve space. Standard errors are in parentheses. The spatial lags are generated with a binary contiguity weighting matrix using shared territorial borders as the criterion, excepting that France, Belgium, and the Netherlands are coded as contiguous with Britain, Denmark as contiguous with Sweden, and Australia as contiguous with New Zealand. All the spatial weights matrices are row-standardized. The deficits models include an EU dummy variable, and model (5) includes decade dummies. Govcon = government consumption; Socben = social benefits. *** significant at 1%; ** significant at 5%; * significant at 10%.

For the Anglo-American democracies, as well as other countries that rely heavily on capital taxation, the combination of increased trade exposure and capital mobility, to the extent that the former increases employment volatility and the latter decreases revenues, could lead to significant budgetary pressures. By my estimates, a permanent one-unit increase in employment volatility for a country with Britain's 2000 capital tax rate leads to an increase in the steady-state deficit by 2.8% of GDP. For comparison, this effect is larger than both the size of the U.S. deficit in 2006 (1.9%) and close to the maximum annual budget deficit that EMU members are allowed under the Maastricht Treaty (3.0%).[5] Of course, this effect assumes a permanent increase in employment volatility, would take many years to materialize, and is best viewed as an upper bound, but it is sizable nonetheless. The estimated effect is close to 1% of GDP after two years. The over-time response path to this counterfactual increase in employment volatility is presented in figure 5.1.

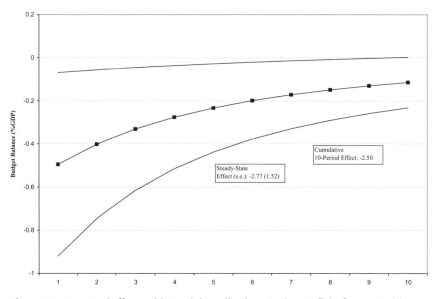

Figure 5.1 Temporal Effects with Spatial Feedback on Budget Deficits from a Positive One-Unit Increase in Employment Volatility (UK Capital Tax Rate 2000)

A New Bargain of Embedded Liberalism

The bottom line is that it will be difficult and costly for politicians in the Anglo-American democracies, particularly politicians on the Left, to maintain public support for policies of economic openness among their core constituencies. This will require an updated version of the bargain of embedded liberalism, one that effectively protects workers in the liberal market economies from the new risks they face at minimal cost and is, at the same time, compatible with the political incentives of left-wing parties and politicians. This is what the old bargain of embedded liberalism did so well, and it is one important reason the Left was able to maintain its commitment to policies of economic openness throughout the last half of the twentieth century. My focus is on the Left because globalization losers are generally thought to be a more important political constituency for the left-wing parties, and, generally speaking, left-wing parties are less supportive of free trade policies (Milner and Judkins 2004). If the unraveling of embedded liberalism undermines one of the major parties' commitments to free trade, it is generally thought to be the party on the Left rather than the Right.

A number of policy recommendations have been made. Unfortunately, very little attention has been paid to the political feasibility and sustainability of these recommendations. Ruggie would like to see a multilateral version of the classic bargain, but this is almost certainly a long-term possibility at best.

With respect to national-level policies, political constraints have been ignored as well. Are the policies robust to partisan changes in government? Do they provide lasting justification for more than minimalist governments?

One possible globalization strategy for leftist governments in the liberal market countries is labor market reform. These governments could "import" corporatism (Garrett 1998, 155–157). Corporatism helped the small states of western Europe adjust to the rapid expansion of international trade in the post–World War II period (Katzenstein 1985). Another strategy that is frequently discussed and debated is the use of training programs and other (active) policies to improve the supply side of the labor market. If they work, active labor market programs keep unemployment low and generate income growth, which makes them cost effective. This strategy is the hallmark of "third way" social democracy. Finally, countries with competitive labor markets could simply redesign (and boost) their unemployment insurance and compensation programs.

During the early postwar period, Keynesian policies of demand management were crucial to the bargain of embedded liberalism in the Anglo-American democracies (Blyth 2002, 126). Today, there is not yet a clear alternative to these policies. Labor market reform, retraining, and insurance all have political and economic costs that make them potentially problematic. Thus, the design of these programs is critical to their long-term success. Often the policies that are economically efficient are not politically feasible and vice versa. The key is finding the right balance between efficiency and feasibility. I argue that the goal should be to achieve intermediate levels of labor mobility across sectors of the economy. More specifically, governments should increase the speed of economic adjustment (i.e., intersectoral transfers of labor) by removing disincentives generated by their compensatory programs, but they should not push the pace too far above the "natural" rate.

STRUCTURAL REFORM: "IMPORTING" CORPORATISM

More than fifteen years ago, Garrett and Lange (1991) asked "What's 'left' for the Left?" They answered this important question by arguing that leftist governments can continue to pursue partisan supply-side policies in countries with densely and centrally organized labor unions. The policies they had in mind are public employment, retraining and relocation programs, industrial subsidies, tax codes that encourage private investment, and public investment. It follows from their analysis that one possible response for leftist governments in the liberal market countries to economic globalization is labor market reform. These countries could "import" corporatism (Garrett 1998a, 155–157). This, in turn, would allow leftist governments to pursue the kind of supply side policies identified by Garrett and Lange. The basic idea, which has since been developed by Hall and Soskice and others in the varieties of capitalism tradition, is that having the right social market institutions is the key to progressive policy reform.[6]

In this section, I focus primarily on the political feasibility of restructuring labor markets rather than the economic consequences of structural reform. The economic consequences of corporatism were discussed in chapter 3. The most important among these are wage restraint, wage compression, and employment stability.[7] With respect to feasibility, historically, it seems that this kind of labor market reform is not politically sustainable in the majoritarian democracies. The Left has tried to build lasting corporatist institutions in two majoritarian democracies—Britain during the 1970s and Australia during the 1980s—and in both cases the experiment failed.[8]

Simply put, these reforms are not robust to partisan changes in government. The first major structural change made by both Margaret Thatcher and Australian prime minister John Howard after taking office was to decentralize and deregulate their respective labor markets. Unless corporatist reforms follow a major political realignment of New Deal proportions (America in the 1930s), they are unlikely to provide a solid foundation upon which a new bargain of embedded liberalism can be built.[9] The short duration of these institutions contrasts sharply with their long survival in consensus democracies. After a brief discussion of Britain's and Australia's experiments with corporatism, I explain why this might be the case.

Corporatism in Britain and Australia

The United Kingdom has always had a more decentralized labor market when compared with other European countries, but the post-Thatcher system of industrial relations is markedly liberal. Britain experimented briefly with an incomes policy under the Wilson and Callaghan governments between 1974 and 1979. During this period, Labour attempted to reconstruct relations with the Trade Union Congress, and, in 1973, the two sides agreed to what became known in Britain as the "social contract." If Labour returned to power, according to the agreement, it would repeal the Industrial Relations Act, pass a "shop stewards' charter" that would improve mediation mechanisms and job protection during strikes, create new work safety regulations, and increase pensions and family allowances. Labour would use price controls to keep inflation down. In exchange, the TUC would push for wage moderation in collective bargaining.

This agreement failed to achieve the desired levels of union-government cooperation. Only in 1976 did the unions actually pursue wage moderation. The TUC had passed a six-pound upper-limit guideline for wage increases, and for the most part these guidelines were respected. The following year, the TUC backed a 5% limit, but this limit was not respected in collective bargaining agreements. In 1978 the unions rejected the notion of a guided wage policy altogether. The Callaghan government asked that the unions adhere to the 5% guideline for another year, but this request was largely ignored. That year British Ford settled a strike by offering the equivalent of a 17% pay increase. The government lost a vote in the House of Commons attempting to exclude Ford from public contracts. That winter, known as the "winter of discontent," the public unions went on strike. It is widely believed that these strikes cost Labour the election in May of 1979 (Scharpf 1991, 70–88).

Thatcher's labor market reforms are well-known. Under her leadership, the Tory government passed legislation that restricted both the scope and likelihood of industrial action by making secondary action illegal and requiring secret ballot authorization of strikes. The closed shop was outlawed. The relationship between union rank-and-file and leadership was altered by requiring that union leaders be elected. Many of the legal supports for collective bargaining and statutory wage setting, including Wage Councils and the Fair Wages Resolution, were abolished (Robinson 1996, 43–44). After more than a decade in power, the Labour government has done little to reverse these changes.

For most of the last century, Australia's labor market institutions were somewhat unique among the advanced industrial democracies. One of the Australian system's most distinguishing features was its use of compulsory arbitration to determine wages and employment conditions. These employment regulations, contained in legally binding decisions called "awards," were made by special labor tribunals and courts (Brennan and Pincus 2002, Wooden 2005). The most important of these tribunals was the Australian Industrial Relations Commission (AIRC), which, in addition to creating awards, was responsible for certifying enterprise bargaining agreements and adjudicating unfair dismissal claims. Another unique feature of the Australian system is the important role played by State governments, which are given primary responsibility by the constitution to regulate industrial relations. The role of the Commonwealth is, according to Section 51(35), "conciliation and arbitration for the prevention and settlement of industrial disputes extending beyond the limits of any one State." Two waves of extensive labor market reforms under the leadership of John Howard have mainly eliminated the distinctive aspects of the Australian system of industrial relations.

Interestingly, the Australian system, established in the early decades of the twentieth century, was explicitly tied to trade protectionism in what is referred to as "Deakin's New Protection" regime. The government provided industry with trade protection, and, in exchange, industry agreed to compensate labor with "fair and reasonable" terms and conditions.[10] Australia's labor market institutions came under pressure from the inflationary shocks of the 1970s. The Liberal/National government (1975–1983) was ineffective in managing the crisis, and this brought the Australian Labor Party (ALP) to power. The initial response by the Labor government was corporatist. The government centralized industrial relations under the Accords Policy and began to negotiate with the Australian Council of Trade Unions (ACTU), the peak labor association, over wages and social policy (Wooden 2005, 2–3; Hampson and Morgan 1998). Corporatism was more successful and lasting in Australia than in the United Kingdom, but it did not survive the partisan change in government. In fact, decentralization began under the ALP. The height of centralized wage bargaining in Australia was between 1983 and 1986. After 1986, reforms were made to introduce flexibility in Australian labor markets.[11]

At the federal level, Labor promoted significant decentralization during its record fifth term in office with the passage of the Industrial Relations Reform Act (1993). These reforms accelerated under the Liberal/National coalition with Howard at the helm. The first wave of Howard's labor market reforms, contained in the Workplace Relations Act of 1996, amended the Industrial Relations Act of 1988, replaced award terms with Australian Workplace Agreements, allowed for certified collective agreements with non-union employees, restricted the authority of the AIRC, and strengthened the sanctions that employers can use against unions engaged in industrial action.[12]

The second wave of reforms came in the Workplace Relations Amendment (Work Choices) Act of 2005, which took effect in March 2006. This legislation, based on the "corporations power" given to the Commonwealth under the Australian constitution, forces all corporations into a single federal system of industrial relations. The Act also exempted small businesses with 100 employees or less from unfair dismissal laws. Workers are still protected from unlawful dismissal, but the scope of protection is significantly narrowed and claims require adjudication in the court system, whereas unfair dismissals were handled by the AIRC. The Act simplifies the agreement certification process by removing the "no disadvantage" test and requiring only that the agreement be lodged with the Office of the Employment Advocate. (See Howe et al. 2005 for a discussion of these reforms.) These changes reduce the role of the AIRC significantly. In sum, the Howard reforms are among the most sweeping changes in Australia's system of industrial relations over the last century.

Why Did Corporatism Fail in Australia and Britain?

The factors leading to the demise of corporatism in Australia and Britain are both numerous and complex, but the same political forces that help account for capital tax differences across the OECD (discussed in chapter 4) also contribute significantly to explaining the failures of centralized wage bargaining in these two cases—namely, the policy preferences of the median voter and the inability of single-party governments to commit to time-inconsistent policies over the long term. Moreover, it is likely that consensual bargaining in industrial relations (discussed in chapter 3) is facilitated by consensus politics in government.

There is much empirical evidence showing that corporatism causes wage compression (Wallerstein 1999; Rueda and Pontusson 2000), and there are conditions under which the median citizen does not benefit from compression. These are highlighted nicely by Lee and Roemer (2005), who provide a theoretical model of endogenous labor market regimes in which the electorate chooses between unionized and competitive systems. Wage compression under corporatism leads the median citizen to prefer a unionized regime when income inequality is either very low or very high. When inequality falls in the intermediate range, the median citizen prefers a competitive regime. This implies that the success of corporatism could ultimately undermine its own political support.

This story about the median citizen is largely consistent with the observed patterns of change in both the Australian and British income distributions. The bulk of available evidence suggests either that the middle classes suffered losses during the periods of corporatist experimentation or did relatively well afterward. Peetz (1998, 147), for example, calculates that real average weekly earnings in Australia dropped by approximately 7% between the spring of 1984 and the fall of 1989. Harding (1997, 353) finds that Australians in the middle 40% of the income distribution lost $12 a week in equivalent household disposable income between 1982 and 1993. Goodman and Webb (1994) find that in the United Kingdom individuals at the middle of the income distribution fared well after Thatcher's reforms, especially relative to those at the lower end of the income distribution.

Given these facts, perhaps it is not too surprising that the parties in power in Australia and the United Kingdom adopted policies of labor market reform. However, we also know from chapter 3 that corporatism can produce employment stability. Wage restraint itself is a source of both wage compression and employment stability, so the median voter must always weigh the costs of wage compression, if there are any, alongside the benefits of employment stability. Is there any reason to believe that majoritarianism tips the balance in favor of competitive labor markets?

One possibility is that the employment benefits of corporatism require a consensual political environment. I noted the empirical connection between corporatism and consensus democracy in chapter 4 (Lijphart and Crepaz 1991). Both Katzenstein (1985, 156) and Maire (1984) stress the importance of this complementary relationship in their discussions of the origins of corporatism. Our understanding of the theoretical connections between proportional representation (majoritarian) electoral institutions and corporatist (competitive) market institutions has advanced significantly over the last few years (see Cusack et al. 2007, Martin and Swank 2008).[13] For my purposes, the critical links are that proportional representation imposes political constraints that stabilize economic policy commitments that, in turn, help foster cooperative relations between labor and capital. These constraints are mostly absent in majoritarian democracies.

Consider again Garrett's (1998a) argument about coherent social democratic corporatism where there are no political constraints on the Left. In countries with strong left-wing governments and centralized labor markets, union leaders will recognize that the government's policies create slack in the labor market that could be used to push up wages. The unions internalize the costs of wage push inflation, which would raise interest rates, generate unemployment, and decrease the incentive for left-wing governments to manage the economy and provide social insurance and services. Encompassing unions recognize this problem and therefore pursue wage moderation. They do this in part because the government is able to credibly commit to generous welfare state policies over the long term. And if union leaders happen to forget that wage moderation is in their enlightened self-interest, party leaders have strong political incentives to remind them.

This explains why labor behaves cooperatively, but what about capital? Why should capital behave cooperatively with respect to investment and employment when the Left is strong and unconstrained? In this way, Garrett's argument leaves capital out of the model. Yet we know that capital's cooperation is essential to successful corporatism (Swenson 2002). To the extent that the exchange of low capital taxes for high rates of investment is an important part of the corporatist bargain, the theoretical argument put forth in chapter 4 suggests that corporatism cannot perform as well under majoritarianism as under consensus democracy. Some have even argued that the lack of consensual politics—that is, the political hegemony of the Social Democrats—explains the collapse of centralized bargaining in Sweden (Thörnqvist 1999). At the same time, right-wing governments need to commit credibly to maintaining corporatist institutions. In short, the employment benefits of corporatism depend on the ability of right-wing and left-wing governments to commit credibly to maintain wage-bargaining institutions and low capital taxes, respectively, and these commitments are not credible in majoritarian polities.

The importance of consensus democracy to the functioning of corporatism almost certainly extends beyond its role in facilitating political commitments by governing parties to a particular set of economic policies. In chapter 3, I argued that employment stability in corporatist systems depends on consensual bargaining, which entails cost (and surplus) sharing between workers and employers. This cooperation in industrial relations can only be enhanced by a political environment in which the major left-wing and right-wing parties are mutually dependent and necessarily cooperative when it comes to governing. The need for political consensus helps to ensure that the parties will pressure the "social partners" to bargain cooperatively. When leftist parties are willing and able to pressure unions to accept wage restraint during inflationary periods (accept a point on the contract curve close to the firm's ideal point) and right-wing parties are willing and able to pressure employers to expand employment and pay higher wages during recessionary ones (accept a point on the contract curve close to union's ideal point), corporatism is much more likely to produce employment stability. And the political incentives for the parties to do this are stronger the more consensual the polity is.

These arguments and the historical evidence suggest that a corporatist economy cannot flourish alongside a majoritarian polity. Consequently, labor market reform—specifically, building corporatist institutions—is not a viable policy solution to the globalization dilemma faced by politicians in the Anglo-American democracies. In addition to structural labor market reform, there are two major kinds of labor market policies that could be used by politicians to build support for trade and economic openness: active and passive labor market policies. The former are designed to improve job seekers' prospects of finding employment and increase the earning potential of workers. They include spending on public employment, labor market training, and other policies that promote employment among the unemployed. These policies are intended to improve the supply side of the labor market. Passive labor market policies simply provide income support during bouts of unemployment. Economists have focused on the welfare and economic consequences of these policies, but very little attention has been paid to their political consequences.[14] After a brief survey of the literature, I consider the political feasibility of active and passive labor market policies in turn.

ACTIVE LABOR MARKET POLICIES: EDUCATION AND RETRAINING

The conventional wisdom is that active labor market policies can help workers adjust to trade-related labor market pressures. Moreover, if these policies work, they keep unemployment low and generate income growth, which makes them cost effective. Active labor market policies are the hallmark of "third way" social democracy (e.g., Boix 1997) with Tony Blair's and now Gordon Brown's Labour government in Britain being the most prominent example in a majoritarian political context. Much scholarly attention recently has focused on the role of active labor market policies in promoting economic adjustment, and, on balance, these programs seem to be viewed favorably despite evidence suggesting that they may not be effective. However, even if these programs work, there are reasons to suspect they might be too costly politically, especially for left-leaning governments.

The goals of ALM programs are *inter alia* to improve job search matching, market competition, worker productivity, and the allocation of labor across sectors of the economy. However, counteracting these employment-promoting effects are "lock-in," which occurs when individuals choose to complete training programs rather than take available jobs (i.e., they choose to remain unemployed), higher reservation wages that offset increased employer demand, and education-training arbitrage, which leads to more unskilled job seekers in low-productivity sectors of the economy and higher rates of unemployment.[15] There seems to be a consensus based on the micro-level empirical research that ALM program participants benefit from an increased probability of employment (Heckman, LaLonde, and Smith 1999; Martin and Grubb 2001). Using the language of this literature, the average treatment effect among the treated is an increase in the probability of employment (Heckman et al. 1999).

The problem with the micro-level research is that it tells us nothing about the effects of ALM programs on non-participants, and so it is impossible to say anything based on these studies about the net employment consequences. Net effects can only be discerned from aggregate data, and there is much less agreement among scholars about the macro-level employment effects of ALM programs implemented on a large scale. Several studies find sizable displacement rates, particularly for subsidized employment programs (e.g., Forslund and Krueger 1997; Dahlberg and Forslund 2005).[16] In their review of micro-level evaluations of Swedish active labor market programs, Calmfors et al. (2001) conclude that on balance the evidence is negative, but they also note that it suggests better performance in the 1980s than the 1990s and in the long run than the short run.

Others find much more positive direct employment effects (Layard, Nickell, and Jackman; Kraft 1998; Webster 1999; Estevao 2003). Perhaps the strongest evidence in favor of ALM policies is found in the mediating influence these programs have on negative macroeconomic shocks. In their seminal paper on the interaction of shocks and institutions in determining employment outcomes, Blanchard and Wolfers (2000) estimate that a counterfactual labor market shock that reduces employment by 1% at the sample-mean level of ALM program expenditures reduces employment by just 0.2% at the maximum level of ALM spending.[17] Franzese and Hays (2006) find evidence of positive ALM policy externalities spilling across the borders of EU member countries. Again, we would expect the aggregate long run effects to be stronger since employment levels should adjust to changes in aggregate supply, reducing the degree of displacement (Martin and Grubb 2001).

Political Consequences for the Left and Trade Policy

Even if active labor market policies achieve their employment objectives, there may be a political downside to this strategy for left-wing governments over the medium to long term. Thatcher's economic reforms were politically successful because they helped cement the electoral dominance of the Tories. Privatization created a new set of property owners in Britain, and these individuals were more likely to vote Conservative in the next election (Garrett 1993; Boix 1998). Keynesian policies of demand management played a similar role for the Left throughout the OECD (Przeworksi 1985, chapter 5). The Left's new "supply side agenda" may be less effective over time in this respect and therefore may become less attractive to left-wing governments. If one takes the literature on class voting seriously, active labor market policies that generate human capital may actually undermine electoral support for left-wing parties in the long run through their effects on emergent class structures (Evans 1993, 2000; Oesch 2006), although they seem to have worked for the Left in the short term in some countries (Boix 1998).

Another problem is that active labor market policies benefit labor "outsiders" in ways that may undermine political support of "insiders," which some argue are the core constituency of left-wing parties (Rueda 2005).[18] In theory, insiders are more likely to oppose ALM programs when their jobs are secure, the elasticity of labor demand is low, and unemployment benefits are modest (Saint-Paul 1998). Despite well-known examples like Blair's Britain, Rueda finds no systematic empirical relationship between partisanship and spending on ALM programs (2005, 2006). Also, the political reaction of employers, which matters greatly for the viability of active labor market policies, is highly contingent on the design of these programs. Employers may support training for low-skilled workers, but oppose retraining for highly skilled workers, particularly in industries that face highly cyclical demand for their products (Hall and Soskice 2001; Swenson 2002; Mares 2003).

It may not be developing skills per se that is problematic for the Left, but rather the type of skills that ALM programs promote among workers. Work by Iversen and Soskice (2001) on the relationship between workers' skill sets and attitudes toward social policy suggests that the design of active labor market policies is critical in determining their effect on support for government spending and interventionist policies, which has significant political implications for left-wing parties. Programs that increase workers' skill specificity are likely to increase support for government spending on things like unemployment insurance, health care, and pensions, while those that provide general skills are likely to undermine support for government spending.[19] This is because workers with specific skills are much more likely than those with general skills to experience long spells of unemployment. Thus, the Left may have a political incentive to provide training to enhance specific skills. Indeed, Kitschelt and Rehm (2004) show that, *ceteris paribus,* workers with sector-specific skills are more likely to support left-wing parties.[20]

ALM programs that provide workers with general skills could also change the underlying nature of trade politics in a way that has unintended consequences for foreign economic policy making. If they provided general skills to workers, retraining programs would increase the degree of intersectoral mobility, making it more likely that the major trade cleavages among producers would fall along class instead of sector lines (Hiscox 2001; Hiscox 2002). This could move trade policy from the realm of pressure politics to partisan politics (Verdier 1994), which, in turn, would make it more difficult for chief executive officers, particularly ones from left-wing parties, to pursue free trade policies. Countries like the United States have delegated authority over trade policy to the executive branch of government as a way to depoliticize trade. This strategy becomes much less effective when the degree of intersectoral mobility is high.[21] Moreover, it is important to note that not everyone benefits equally from training. According to Kletzer (2004, 740), workers displaced from trade are not ones who tend to be successful in retraining programs. This is consistent with the empirical results from chapter 2 that suggest active labor market programs do not increase support for trade among those employed in tradable sectors of the economy. Finally, general education policies are unlikely to benefit workers soon enough to "save globalization" (Scheve and Slaughter 2007).

To summarize, even if ALM programs work and promote economic efficiency in the aggregate, there may be political costs for left-wing parties and politicians who support free trade policies. Like trade itself, labor mobility across sectors of the economy generates both winners and losers. To save embedded liberalism, policies must adequately compensate trade's losers without creating a new group of political opponents.

PASSIVE LABOR MARKET POLICIES: INSURANCE AND COMPENSATION

Countries with competitive labor markets could simply redesign and expand their unemployment insurance and compensation programs. The problem with unemployment insurance is that these programs create incentives for people to stay out of work and this makes them too costly. Therefore, these programs would need to be designed to minimize their labor market distortions (e.g., Baily 1978; Shavell and Weiss 1979; Brander and Spencer 1994; Hopenhayn and Nicolini 1997; Kletzer and Litan 2001; Kletzer 2004). Otherwise, they will not be politically sustainable.

Unemployment insurance can lead to problems of moral hazard. If a worker's search effort is endogenous, insurance may reduce his or her incentive to find a job.[22] Empirically, Kraft (1998) finds that passive labor market policies, defined as spending on unemployment benefits and assistance, decrease aggregate employment. In their review of the literature on unemployment insurance, Fredriksson and Holmlund (2006) note that there are three basic ways to improve the social efficiency of unemployment insurance programs: adjusting the duration and over-time profile of benefit payments; monitoring and enforcement; and adding "workfare" requirements. These are discussed, in turn, below.

In his seminal paper on optimal unemployment insurance, Baily (1978) argued for a lump sum "redundancy" payment that would not distort the search efforts of unemployed workers combined with weekly payments. Shavell and Weiss (1979) focus on the optimal payment of benefits over time. They argue that benefit payments should decline monotonically to encourage a more active job search. Building on this work, Hopenhayn and Nicolini (1997) consider the possibility of a wage tax after reemployment that increases with the duration of the unemployment spell. With declining benefits and an increasing tax, there are two policies generating incentives to minimize the duration of unemployment. The same search effort can be induced with a smoother consumption path over the unemployment spell, which makes both the government and the unemployed individual better off than under a system where only declining benefit levels are possible. Wang and Williamson (1996) argue initial benefit payments should be small to discourage on-the-job shirking, which increases the probability of unemployment.

The theoretical case for monitoring and sanctions is straightforward. Enforcing a minimum level of search effort among recipients can be welfare enhancing, even when these enforcement actions are costly. On balance, the evidence suggests that monitoring with sanctions effectively shortens the duration of unemployment spells (Fredriksson and Holmlund 2006, 373–376). Workfare and training requirements can reduce the costs of benefit programs and make these programs welfare enhancing because high-ability individuals and those who suffer little disutility from unemployment will choose not to participate (Fredriksson and Holmlund 2006, 377–380). Job search assistance may also be effective (Forslund and Krueger 2008).

Wage insurance, which pays displaced workers a proportion of their lost income upon reemployment, has received much attention recently in policy-oriented academic circles (Lawrence and Litan 1986; Brander and

Spencer 1994; Kletzer and Litan 2001; and Kletzer 2004). While unemployment benefits typically encourage unemployed workers to stay unemployed, wage insurance has the opposite effect, creating incentives for taking jobs, even jobs below one's reservation wage. From a purely economic point of view, the main problem with wage insurance is that, because the benefits are conditional on employment, it distorts labor market decisions, and leads to inefficient over-employment (Brander and Spencer 1994). As a potential solution to the globalization dilemma that governments face, wage insurance has a significant advantage. Those most adversely affected by trade (high-wage individuals whose disutility from work is low) receive the largest benefit payments. This has the effect of targeting workers who are likely to be the strongest opponents of trade liberalization. (Wage insurance does better if judged as compensatory program with minimal (negative) efficiency consequences.)

Economically Efficient and Politically Feasible Policies

To save embedded liberalism, governments need to adequately compensate trade's losers and, at the same time, promote economic adjustment. However, it can be politically costly to promote too much adjustment too quickly. Labor mobility can be increased in two different ways: by generating incentives for workers to move into new sectors of the economy or removing existing disincentives to stay put. ALM programs would promote labor mobility by making it easier for workers to switch sectors of employment. Passive labor market policy reform would improve labor mobility by removing disincentives. The latter approach is likely to be more politically feasible. ALM programs could anger labor "insiders," expose workers in traditionally non-traded sectors to new trade pressures, and burden firms recovering from cyclical downturns by draining their pools of reserve workers.

The literature on optimal insurance suggests that benefits should be unconditional (i.e., the benefits should be paid regardless of whether an individual takes a job or not), proportional (i.e., the size of the benefits payment should depend on an individual's income while employed), and declining in the length of an unemployment spell. An integrated system of unemployment and wage insurance with benefits declining in the duration of unemployment would achieve these objectives.[23] Several countries have adopted declining rates of unemployment insurance benefits. With declining wage insurance benefits, the percentage of the wage differential covered becomes smaller the longer an individual waits to take a job. An integrated system of this kind would have many of the same advantages as the Hopenhayn and Nicolini (1997) optimal unemployment insurance program that combines declining benefits with a wage tax after reemployment. Under both schemes, one's net income after reemployment declines with the duration of unemployment. This would encourage workers who are not likely to be reemployed in industries facing cyclical downturns—for example, older workers and workers with marginal skills—to move quickly into new sectors of the economy while maintaining incentives for those who are likely to be reemployed—young, highly skilled workers, for example—to stay put.

CONCLUSION

The globalization dilemma is real and likely to exert significant pressure on governments in the not-too-distant future. For those who are concerned about the future of the global economy, a new commitment to strengthening the bargain of embedded liberalism offers hope. In the long run, it may be desirable to "take embedded liberalism global" (Ruggie 2002, 2007). In the short run, it is both possible and desirable to save embedded liberalism at the national level. To this end, there may be room for some old-style Keynesian macroeconomic policy and redistribution (Katpstein 1996, 1999; Scheve and Slaughter 2007), but a new strategy is needed as well, one that promotes economic adjustment and is, at the same time, sensitive to the political constraints faced by left-wing governments. The costs of adjustment should be spread over time, and the process should be largely determined by market forces. What governments can and should do is redesign their insurance and compensatory programs to minimize morally hazardous behavior. The challenge for the Left is to increase the levels of protection provided to those who are vulnerable and, at the same time, decrease the extent to which these protective policies distort market-driven adjustment.

6

Conclusion

Globalization is not inevitable. The continued integration of national markets and growth of the global economy depend on domestic political support, the bases of which are inadequately understood. My objective in the preceding chapters has been to elucidate as much as possible the politics behind the strong anti-globalization sentiment in a number of the world's most economically important and politically influential countries, focusing on the Anglo-American democracies in particular. The political situation is serious. Based on the ISSP survey data presented in chapter 2, all five of these countries—Australia, Canada, New Zealand, the United Kingdom, and the United States—have majorities that support limiting imports to protect the domestic economy. The significance of this fact is highlighted when compared with other countries. In Sweden and Norway, for example, these percentages are approximately 36% and 35%, respectively. The trends in the United States are particularly shocking, as noted by Scheve and Slaughter in their timely *Foreign Affairs* article "A New Deal for Globalization":

> Several polls of U.S. public opinion show an alarming rise in protectionist sentiment over the past several years. For example, an ongoing NBC News/ Wall Street Journal poll found that from December 1999 to March 2007, the share of respondents stating that trade agreements have hurt the United States increased by 16 percentage points (to 46 percent) while the "helped" share fell by 11 points (to just 28 percent). A 2000 Gallup poll found that 56 percent of respondents saw trade as an opportunity and 36 percent saw it as a threat; by 2005, the percentages had shifted to 44 percent and 49 percent, respectively. The March 2007 NBC News/Wall Street Journal poll found negative assessments of open borders even among the highly skilled: only 35 percent of respondents with a college or higher degree said they directly benefited from the global economy (2007, 42).

As I described in chapter 1, trade policy politics in the United States and elsewhere seems to have shifted in an anti-trade direction that reflects these attitudes. These changes are distressing, as they put the future of the international economy in doubt. The possible contraction or even collapse of the global economy is one of the most threatening prospects facing the international community today. The stakes are incredibly high. Expanding trade has been a source of international peace and prosperity for many years now.

In this final chapter, I recap and pull together the main theoretical arguments and the most important pieces of empirical evidence presented throughout this study. I conclude with a few comments about recent trends in the international economy and possible policy responses for governments in the Anglo-American democracies.

Drawing on Rodrik's globalization dilemma, I started with the premise that globalization is a potential source of crisis for the bargain of embedded liberalism. I focused on how political and economic institutions both make conditions ripe for backlash and shape how governments are able to respond to globalization pressures. The extent to which growing trade and increased international capital mobility strain embedded liberalism depends greatly on a country's political and economic institutions. These institutions influence the demand for protection from international shocks as well as the ways governments will supply it.

I have tried to bridge some important divisions in the academic literature on the politics of globalization. My argument, which is novel on many fronts, draws on the analytical strengths of both the optimists' and pessimists' views of globalization politics. I have argued that countries with liberal market economies and majoritarian polities (e.g., the United States and the United Kingdom) will face the most serious political and policy challenges as a result of economic globalization, not countries with corporatist institutions and generous welfare programs (e.g., Austria and Sweden). I have reemphasized the importance of consensual politics to the economic success of corporatism, something that was stressed in the early literature, but seems to have been forgotten more recently, and I have provided a way to reconcile seemingly contradictory views about the partisan biases of PR and majoritarian electoral systems by pointing out that the "constraints" imposed by PR can actually be enabling for the left-wing parties because they allow the Left to make credible commitments to long-term investment-friendly policies.

In my empirical work, I corrected for two methodological limitations in the existing research: I included analyses of individual-level survey data as a way to evaluate micro-level assumptions and modeled directly the spatial interdependence in macro-panel data using techniques and estimators from spatial econometrics. I have stressed that the levels of economic integration that we observe today are not unprecedented, nor is the emergence of a backlash, and that to get an idea of the significance of today's political opposition to globalization, it is important to consider the historical precedents.

RECAPPING THE ARGUMENTS AND EVIDENCE

The outlook of globalization pessimists is far too gloomy, especially when it comes to the future of the welfare state, corporatism, and social democracy.

The Austro-Nordic democracies, where these things flourish, are well-suited to respond to globalization in ways that preserve their political-economic uniqueness. These countries have economic institutions that allow coordinated responses to economic shocks when times are bad. Their politics are characterized by policy stability in the short run with consensus-driven adaptation, including institutional change, in the long run.

Globalization optimists, on the other hand, see the relationship between national-level politics and the world economy through rose-colored glasses and downplay globalization's challenges, particularly concerning the Anglo-American democracies. At the moment, these countries are poorly equipped to weather the globalization storm. Economic shocks to product markets are directly transmitted to the labor market in the liberal market economies. Moreover, trade is increasing labor demand elasticity, which magnifies the employment consequences of all shocks whether they are domestic or international in origin. This makes the labor market more volatile, increasing the risk for workers. In the Anglo-American democracies, I estimated that an exogenous 1% increase in labor compensation leads to a 1.35% decrease in employment in industries at the median level of trade openness. The expected decrease in employment is 1.65% in industries at the 90th percentile of trade openness. In other words, trade makes the labor demand curve flatter, increasing the sensitivity of employment outcomes to changes in wages. Trade has direct employment consequences as well: a 1% decrease in the exports to value added ratio, a proxy for global demand, leads to a .74% decrease in employment in industries at the median wage level, and the effect is stronger at lower wage levels.

Between 1990 and 2000 the average level of trade openness among the Anglo-American democracies went from approximately 40% of GDP to a little more than 56% of GDP. For countries with competitive labor markets, I estimate that an increase of this magnitude will raise the variance in employment volatility by about .4 units. To get a better sense of the size of this effect, if the annual change in employment is around 1.25%—the average for the Anglo-American democracies at the beginning of the 1990s—then, all else being equal, a 16% increase in trade openness would increase the expected annual change to 1.4%. Historically speaking, the systematic component of employment volatility, the part over which governments can be expected to have some control, did not increase in the Anglo-American democracies, but it did remain fairly constant over the 1990s, while in other countries this volatility declined. Growing trade openness seems to explain why these countries did not experience the declines in employment volatility that other countries, particularly the Austro-Nordic democracies, experienced over the same period. As a result, workers in the Anglo-American democracies are more vulnerable to the next round of recessionary shocks.

At the same time, governments in the Anglo-American democracies are unable to credibly commit to capital taxes that are significantly below their short-run revenue maximizing levels. In majoritarian democracies, pre-investment low-tax promises are not credible *ex post*. This "time inconsistency" problem has two significant consequences. First, it makes it difficult for these countries to stimulate employment through tax cuts. The returns on employment generating investment come in the long run, and there is no guarantee that employment-friendly tax policy changes will be sustained over the long term. Second, it makes these countries relatively more dependent on capital taxes than other countries. If low capital taxes do not generate employment, the second-best option for the Anglo-American democracies is to use these taxes to generate revenue. With greater international capital mobility, however, this dependence constrains their ability to finance spending and compensate those who are adversely affected by globalization. In other words, rising levels of international capital mobility take away their second-best option. I estimate that, in capital-rich majoritarian democracies, a 1% increase in financial openness leads to a .39% decrease in the capital tax rate in the long run and a .49% increase in capital-poor consensus democracies. To better understand these estimates, it helps to apply them to a specific historical case of tax reform. In 1988, the last year it restricted international financial transactions, New Zealand's capital tax rate was 49.3%. By 1996, the year New Zealand adopted its proportional representation electoral system, the capital tax rate was 37.7%. According to my estimates, approximately 3.6% of this 11.6% drop in capital taxes, nearly one-third of the reduction, can be explained by New Zealand's removal of capital controls.

For the Anglo-American democracies and other countries that rely heavily on capital taxation, the combination of increased trade exposure and capital mobility, to the extent the former increases employment volatility and the latter decreases revenues, could lead to significant budgetary pressures. By my estimates, a permanent one-unit increase in employment volatility for a country with Britain's 2000 capital tax rate increases the deficit by 1% after two years and raises the steady-state deficit by 2.8% of GDP.

SAVING EMBEDDED LIBERALISM

What can be done to address strong anti-globalization sentiment in the Anglo-American democracies? Doing nothing is a possibility. The hope behind this "strategy" is that, as employment in manufacturing and agriculture declines, opposition to trade will recede. This is probably not a good idea. It is certainly true that employment in tradable industries has continued to decline through the 2000s (see table 6.1). The average percentage of workers employed in

Table 6.1 Exposure and Sensitivity to External Risk, 2000–2006

	Employment in Tradables			Terms of Trade Volatility			Import Penetration			Financial Openness		
	2000	2006	Average (00–06)	2000	2006	Average (00–06)	2000	2006	Average (00–06)	2000	2006	Average (00–06)
Liberal Market Economies:												
Australia	18.66	18.30	18.04	3.41	3.88	3.36	22.45	28.23	24.85	2.00	1.19	1.42
Canada	18.21	17.92	17.96	3.13	1.44	2.92	42.26	41.38	40.38	2.54	2.54	2.54
New Zealand	22.82	22.67	22.74	2.59	3.31	3.12	34.41	38.09	36.61	2.54	2.54	2.54
United Kingdom	18.84	16.38	17.46	1.51	1.54	1.58	29.33	34.68	31.11	2.54	2.54	2.54
United States	16.93	15.27	15.94	2.35	1.05	1.61	14.55	16.22	14.91	2.54	2.54	2.54
Average:	*19.09*	*18.11*	*18.43*	*2.60*	*2.24*	*2.52*	*28.60*	*31.72*	*29.57*	*2.43*	*2.27*	*2.32*
Corporatist Economies:												
Austria	24.81	23.64	23.63	0.86	0.47	0.69	44.67	55.18	49.74	2.54	2.00	2.42
Denmark	22.52	20.44	20.93	0.59	1.24	0.81	43.16	54.14	47.28	2.54	2.54	2.54
Finland	22.63	21.13	21.59	2.37	0.66	1.72	37.51	44.04	39.34	2.54	2.00	2.42
Norway	20.10	18.42	19.09	13.83	5.48	9.34	35.50	37.89	36.10	2.54	2.54	2.54
Sweden	19.65	17.53	18.32	0.88	1.51	1.24	43.00	47.95	43.73	2.54	2.00	2.42
Average:	*21.94*	*20.23*	*20.71*	*3.71*	*1.87*	*2.76*	*40.77*	*47.84*	*43.24*	*2.54*	*2.22*	*2.47*

Other:

Belgium	16.99	16.40	16.40	1.01	0.79	0.76	84.18	90.07	86.63	1.73	2.00	2.19
France	17.27	16.21	16.69	2.06	0.57	1.51	27.91	31.08	28.87	2.54	2.54	2.54
Germany	23.74	21.63	22.46	2.81	0.71	1.81	33.14	44.32	37.05	2.54	2.00	2.42
Ireland	23.93	22.94	23.09	0.77	0.47	0.80	98.08	95.49	97.50	2.54	2.54	2.54
Italy	20.33	20.42	20.54	4.27	2.27	3.01	26.37	28.41	26.83	2.54	2.54	2.54
Japan	27.08	24.61	25.33	3.34	1.76	2.45	9.67	11.39	10.33	2.54	2.00	2.42
Netherlands	16.95	16.63	16.66	0.63	0.28	0.61	68.33	80.36	72.34	2.54	2.54	2.54
Portugal	34.31	30.65	32.39	2.23	1.45	1.58	36.66	40.38	37.55	2.54	2.27	2.46
Spain	21.18	22.36	21.9	2.36	0.55	1.53	31.19	35.50	32.86	2.54	2.00	2.42
Switzerland	25.51	23.14	23.9	2.39	0.91	2.14	43.17	50.06	45.06	2.54	2.00	2.42
Average:	22.73	21.5	21.94	2.19	0.98	1.62	45.87	50.71	47.5	2.46	2.24	2.45

Notes: The deindustrialization, terms of trade volatility, and import penetration variables reported in this table are the same ones considered in Chapters 1 and 3. As in Table 3.1, I report the Chinn and Ito (2007) measure of financial openness (instead of Quinn's measure) because it is available through 2006. The correlation between the Quinn and Chinn and Ito measures is .84.

tradable sectors of the liberal market economies over the 2000–2006 period was 18.4%, down from 19.7% in the 1990s. However, workers employed in service sectors of the economy are no longer sheltered from international competition to the extent they were ten to twenty years ago. Moreover, both terms-of-trade volatility and import penetration have increased from their average levels in the 1990s. The standard deviation in the logged difference in the ratio of export to import prices increased by more than 6% (from 2.36 in the 1990s to 2.52 in the 2000s), and the average level of import penetration increased from 23.6% in the 1990s to 29.6% in the 2000s.

Given these trends in the international economy and public attitudes toward globalization, a policy response of some kind is necessary. (The bargain of embedded liberalism is as politically relevant today as at any time during the Bretton Woods era.) In fact, Jeffry Frieden has described this as *the* challenge of global capitalism in the twenty-first century, "to combine international integration with politically responsive, socially responsible government." He goes on to write, "Contemporary ideologues of many stripes . . . argue that this combination is impossible or undesirable. But theory and history indicate that it is possible for globalization to coexist with policies committed to social advance. It remains for governments and people to put the possible into practice" (2006, 476).

There seems to be a growing sense that something radical needs to be done to address Frieden's challenge, whether it is taking embedded liberalism global, building social market institutions, or providing significant economy-wide income redistribution. The problem with most of the recommended solutions is that they fail the political feasibility test. International political realities make a global approach to embedded liberalism unlikely in the near term, and majoritarian politics at the national level make the task of building social market institutions, particularly corporatist institutions, in the countries that do not already have them almost impossible. Income redistribution along the lines suggested by Scheve and Slaughter, if the threshold for tax relief is adjusted to include the median voter, is the most plausible approach to rebuilding embedded liberalism in the United States and would allow the Democratic Party to recommit to policies of economic openness.

The type of policy recommendations that I have made are far less sweeping and ambitious than these. In chapter 5, I considered policies targeted at workers who experience trade-related job loss in light of the literature on optimal insurance. This research leads to the conclusion that benefits should be unconditional (i.e., the benefits should be paid regardless of whether an individual takes a job or not), proportional (i.e., the size of the benefits payment should depend on an individual's income while employed), and declining in the length of an unemployment spell. An integrated system of unemployment and wage insurance with benefits declining in the duration of unemployment would achieve these objectives. With declining wage insurance benefits, the percentage of the wage differential covered becomes smaller the longer an individual waits to take a job. This would encourage workers who are not likely to be reemployed in industries facing cyclical downturns to move quickly into new sectors of the economy while maintaining incentives for those who are likely to be reemployed to stay put.

In the United States, it would not take much reform to create a system like this. The Trade Act of 2002 initiated a pilot wage insurance program for workers over age fifty. This could be extended to all workers experiencing trade-related job losses. The existing program has proportional benefits (capped at $10,000), but they are not declining with the length of unemployment in any meaningful sense. Anyone who finds employment within 26 weeks of losing his or her job is currently eligible for benefits equal to 50% of the difference between their old and new salaries. This could be changed without much difficulty to minimize the moral hazard problem. For example, coverage rates could be reduced after every two months of an unemployment spell.

It is possible that the growing tide of opposition to trade and globalization more generally is too strong to be turned by minor reforms to existing trade adjustment assistance programs. Of course, there is usually no reason (other than cost) that programs targeted for workers adversely affected by trade cannot be extended to all unemployed workers. And unemployment insurance reforms like those that I and others have suggested could be coupled easily with redistributive tax reform along the lines proposed by Scheve and Slaughter. There are many options available. In the end, what is important, if we hope to successfully rebuild the bargain of embedded liberalism, is that policies be evaluated not only by their consequences for economic efficiency but also in terms of their political feasibility.

Notes

CHAPTER ONE

1. There is a large and growing literature on globalization in political science. Keohane and Milner (1996), Cohen (1996), Garrett (1998b), Berger (2000), Brune and Garrett (2005), and Kayser (2007) provide excellent reviews. Frieden and Martin (2003) place recent studies of globalization at the frontier of international political economy research. See Guillen (2001) for the major globalization debates in sociology.

2. Oftentimes, this debate is boiled down to two simple competing hypotheses: efficiency versus compensation (e.g., Garrett 2001; Mosley 2003). The efficiency hypothesis states that free trade and international capital mobility have compelled governments to scale back their spending, lower their tax rates, and deregulate their economies. The compensation hypothesis says that national governments are still responsive to powerful interests that want to insulate the domestic economy from international competition, and that governments will redistribute the gains from free trade and other policies of economic openness to placate these groups. There is no logical reason that both hypotheses cannot be true simultaneously. It is likely that governments feel both efficiency and compensation pressures, yet most research designs in political science—because they focus on the sign of a single regression coefficient—do not allow for this possibility.

3. This division of the literature can be found in works such as Garrett (1998a), Burgoon (2001), Iversen (2001), and Castles (2004), among others.

4. This argument is often labeled the convergence thesis. For a more recent discussion of the limits that globalization may impose on popular sovereignty, see Freeman (2002). Hellwig (2001) and Hellwig and Samuels (2006) find that economic globalization reduces the likelihood that voters will hold their politicians accountable for national economic performance. One way to interpret this empirical finding is that globalization restricts the scope of democratic governance and accountability. Another, more hopeful position is that globalization simply shifts the scope of democratic governance to a new set of issues (Bernhard and Leblang 2006). Some argue that there was never a democratic choice reflected in meaningful partisan differences in economic policy. According to this view, *partisan* convergence is an inherent feature of democratic capitalism (Clark 2003).

5. The difference in focus reflects the second-image / second-image-reversed distinction made frequently in the international relations and comparative politics research (Waltz 1959; Gourevitch 1978). One group is interested in the internal consequences of globalization across different national political-economic contexts while

the other is primarily concerned about the impact that domestic anti-globalization politics will have on the international economy.

6. See Kitschelt et al. (1999), Hall and Soskice (2001), Huber and Stephens (2001), and Castles (2004).

7. Jensen (2006), for example, argues that fiscal policies are largely ignored by multinational firms when making their production location decisions and therefore governments' taxation and expenditure choices are not highly constrained by the globalization of production.

8. Swank's division between inclusive and exclusive electoral systems corresponds closely with Lijphart's consensus-majoritarian typology that I use throughout this book.

9. It is probably more accurate to say these choices tell us something about the preferences of politically influential groups. For example, Swank's (2002a) argument is not that the preferences of low-skilled workers and other groups harmed by globalization differ across countries but rather that these groups have more political influence in countries with inclusive electoral systems. For a related argument about the ability of right wing governments to enact neoliberal policy reforms, see King and Wood (1999).

10. It is important to note that the labels of globalization "optimist" and "pessimist" do not identify one's normative view of economic globalization. There are plenty of globalization pessimists who think, on balance, economic globalization is a good thing and many optimists who disagree.

11. See, for example, Scheve and Slaughter (2001, 2004, 2006).

12. The United States not only comes the closest to a pure market system, it is also, politically speaking, the most important country in the world when it comes to governing the global economy. This makes the United States a very important case.

13. It is tempting to attribute these changes in public opinion to the 9/11 terrorist attacks. The events of 9/11 certainly contributed to anti-globalization sentiment, particularly in the United States, but later analysis shows that they are unlikely to be the sole determinant. In chapter 2, I demonstrate that these attitudes when they are held have clear connections to individual-level economic conditions. Moreover, at the aggregate country level, we observe very different patterns. For example, the largest anti-globalization change in public opinion occurred in New Zealand. Spain, on the other hand, experienced a large increase in support for trade and globalization over the same period. There is simply too much variation, across individuals and countries, to be explained by a single historical event.

14. See Hiscox (2006) for a critical view of survey research in this area. His main point is that support for (and opposition to) trade is highly contingent on how survey questions are framed.

15. This legislation reflects the political importance of tying domestic compensation to policies that increase a country's exposure to trade, which is all the more notable in this case because it runs counter to the overall trend toward less social protection.

16. For research on the connection between free trade and compensatory policies in the U.S. Congress, see Rickard (2007).

17. For a more recent treatment, see Ruggie 1994, 1995, 1997, and 2003. In addition to Ruggie, those who have argued that government policies, by neutralizing the

negative effects of trade, can deliver pro-trade majorities include Adsera and Boix 2002, Boix 2002, and Mares 2004, 2005. For a discussion of embedded liberalism and disembedded neoliberalism, see Blyth (2002).

18. This is Nelson's (1988) terminology, which has become popular in the literature.

19. See Ruggie (1997) also.

20. Again, protection may come in many forms, including insurance, adjustment assistance, and tariffs.

21. See Katzenstein (1985, 52).

22. Rodrik 1997, chapter 2.

23. Hoover Europe's move from Burgundy to Scotland, BMW's move to Spartanburg, South Carolina, and Mercedes-Benz's decision to locate production in Alabama are typically cited as examples of the ease with which foreign labor in one OECD country can be substituted for domestic labor in another. Trade may also increase the elasticity of the demand for labor by making product markets more competitive (Slaughter 2001).

24. Rodrik argues that this change is particularly important to understanding the impact that globalization has had on low skilled labor in the developed democracies because most trade by OECD countries is with other OECD countries. Trade between economies with similar factor endowments is not likely to shift the labor demand curve, but it is likely to make it flatter. See Rodrik 1997, 26.

25. Of course, not all historically minded scholars share this concern. Pahre (2008), for example, argues that the historical experience of rapid trade expansion in the nineteenth century, driven by a growing network of treaties, suggests that the GATT/WTO regime can sustain today's liberal international economy.

26. Critical realignments are not so rare in American history. Nardulli identifies six between 1828 and 1984. Baumgartner and Jones (1993) make a similar argument about the potential for large-scale change in their Punctuated Equilibrium theory of the American policy-making process.

27. Currently, policy decisions disproportionately represent the interests of those who benefit the most from globalization. This reflects low voter turnout among groups at the bottom end of the income scale (e.g., Franzese 2002; Hansen 1998). However, there are reasons to expect turnout to increase as labor market performance deteriorates, particularly if voters blame the government (e.g., Southwell 1996; Arceneaux 2003).

28. For Britain, see Robinson (1996) and King and Wood (1999). For a discussion of labor market deregulation in Australia under the Howard government, see Hancock (1999).

29. Garrett notes that the relative weakness of the left in the United States and Canada make these countries poor candidates for corporatist labor market reform. This is not to say that major realignments are impossible or even unlikely, but there are other policy options that would be politically viable in the absence of dramatic changes to electorates and party systems.

30. Insiders are workers with secure jobs while outsiders include the unemployed and workers with very little or no job security.

31. Hall and Soskice (2001) also make this point.

CHAPTER TWO

1. Ruggie 1982, 1994, 1997, and 2003.

2. See Blyth 2002. Blyth argues that liberal capitalism has become less embedded since the Reagan and Thatcher period, but the changes, in his view, do not amount to a return to pre-WWI policies. Others argue that the significance of the Reagan and Thatcher "revolutions" has been exaggerated—for example, Pierson 1994.

3. See, for example, Cameron 1978, Stephens 1979, Katzenstein 1985, and Rodrik 1998.

4. Rodrik 1997, 1998; Adserà and Boix 2002; Boix 2002; Swank 2002a; and Mares 2004, 2005.

5. By short-term I mean changes in trade at time t-1 have a discernible effect on government spending at time t.

6. Garrett and Mitchell 2001.

7. Garrett and Mitchell 2001, 163. I believe both short-term and long-term histori-cal forces are operating, and the empirical analysis bears this out.

8. In fact, they find that the relationship is negative and statistically significant.

9. See table 4.2 and figure 4.2, 80–84.

10. Iversen and Cusack 2000.

11. In addition to trade openness, Garrett and Mitchell include the value of imports from low wage countries in their analysis. They find these imports are weakly posi-tively correlated with higher government spending and transfers, 169–170. They do not examine the effects of total imports on spending and transfers.

12. This is true unless one is interested in measuring a country's exposure to exter-nal risk. To do this, one would interact a country's trade openness—a measure of how exposed it is to the international economy—with a measure of external risk like its terms-of-trade volatility. See Rodrik 1997, 1998. By itself, trade openness is not a good measure of risk.

13. The *ceteris paribus* condition is important. I assume that the ability of those employed in traded industries to organize remains constant regardless of their group size. Because small groups may find it easier to engage in collective action, they are often able to exert political influence that is disproportionate to their numbers. For a discussion of the importance of collective action issues in trade policy politics, see Alt and Gilligan 1994 and Ehrlich 2007.

14. See Scheve and Slaughter 2001; O'Rourke and Sinnot 2002; Mayda and Rodrik 2005; and Mayda, O'Rourke, and Sinnot 2007.

15. Both Aldrich et al. (2002) and Brune and Garrett (2005) recognize the macro-level literature on globalization and government spending rests on untested micro-level assumptions and call for empirical evaluations of these microfoundations.

16. I included all the OECD countries reporting occupational categories that include a respondent's industry of employment.

17. See Alt and Gilligan 1994; Hiscox 2002.

18. These models tell us the direct effect of trade on income earned from employ-ing different factors of production. It is also possible that trade affects the wealth and (unearned) income of asset owners. For example, Scheve and Slaughter (2001) find that home owners who live in import competing regions of the United States are, *ceteris pari-bus,* more likely to oppose trade than renters. Unfortunately, the data that I would need to test this and similar hypotheses on a cross-national basis is not readily available.

19. Local currencies were converted into dollars using the appropriate exchange rate; 2003 dollars were converted to 1995 dollars; and monthly income was converted to annual income when necessary. This is the same income measure used by Hiscox and Burgoon 2003.

20. The industries are: (1) agriculture, hunting, forestry, and fishing, (2) mining and quarrying, (3) food products, beverages, and tobacco, (4) textiles, textile products, leather, and footwear, (5) wood and products of wood and cork, (6) paper and paper products, (7) publishing, printing, and reproduction of recorded media, (8) chemical, rubber, plastics, and fuel products, (9) other non-metallic mineral products, (10) basic metals, and (11) machinery and equipment. Mayda and Rodrik (2005) also infer sector of employment from the occupation variable in the ISSP survey, but they use industry classifications from the World Trade Analyzer Dataset.

21. Unfortunately, at the time of writing, the 2003 numbers were not yet available. See tab. 3.1, 30, for the 1995 net replacement rates and tab. 3.1b, 95, for 2002 rates.

22. The 2004 edition of *Benefits and Wages* also provides net replacement rates for families with above average incomes (150% of the average). However, since my income (capital) variable is dichotomous and the above average income net replacement rates are not available for 1995, I do not use this data.

23. In terms of research design, this variable is an improvement over countrywide measures of unemployment protection because it allows the analyst to incorporate fixed country effects into the regressions. The fixed-effects model allows us to control for unobservable or otherwise omitted country-level factors that correlate with a country's average net replacement rate, which makes it a useful model for convincing skeptics that a causal relationship exists. The primary disadvantage of fixed-effects estimators is that they are inefficient (Beck and Katz 2001; Plümper and Troeger 2007) and suffer from attenuation bias if the right-hand-side variables are measured with error (Griliches and Hausman 1986), and this is particularly true when most of the sample variance is between countries. To see the (potential) problem, remember that each individual in the sample contributes to the total sample variance in net replacement rates, and this contribution can be decomposed into the difference between the individual's net replacement rate and the average net replacement rate in his or her country and the difference between his or her country's average net replacement rate and the average overall (full sample) net replacement rate. When we say that most of the variance in net replacement rates is between countries, we mean that more than half of the total variance is attributable to differences between country-average net replacement rates and the overall mean net replacement rate. We can also decompose the sample variance in support for trade into within and between country variance. Almost certainly, some part of the between-country variance in support for trade is explained by the between-country variance in net replacement rates, but this effect is zeroed out in the fixed-effects model. This is inefficient since the estimator is ignoring sample information about the relationship between net replacement rates and support for trade. Moreover, if there is random measurement error in net replacement rates at the individual level—and this is the case since I am using an imperfect imputation strategy—the sample information relating country-average net replacement rates and country-average support for trade is likely to have a higher signal-to-noise ratio than the mean-differenced data. This is the source of the attenuation bias with the fixed-effects estimator. For these reasons, the fixed-effects estimator is likely to give us

coefficient estimates biased toward zero with inflated standard errors relative to the pooled model with robust standard errors. If there are statistically significant effects in the model with country and year dummies, it should be taken as strong evidence of a causal relationship between net replacement rates and support for trade.

24. OECD 2004.

25. This measure has its limitations. Political conservatives, for example, might not say they are proud of their country's social security system even if it offers generous protection. However, if conservatives are more supportive of trade, this will bias against finding a positive relationship between this subjective evaluation and support for free trade.

26. Iversen and Soskice 2001; Hiscox and Burgoon 2003.

27. McKelvey and Zavoina 1975.

28. For a discussion, see Moulton 1990 and Steenbergen and Jones 2002.

29. The cut-point estimates are omitted from the table to save space.

30. Technically, it is the relationship between the continuous *net exports* variable and the latent continuous variable in the ordered probit that is nonlinear (See, for example, Long 1997, chapter 5 for an introduction to ordered probit models). This makes a trichotomous dummy variable approach to modeling the relationship the most parsimonious and straightforward one. My results are stronger with higher order polynomials in *net exports*, but much more difficult to interpret given the added non-linear transformation.

31. In fact, the ratio of sector imports to value added is higher on average for industries above the 75th percentile in the *net exports* distribution than the same ratio for industries in the middle 50% of the distribution. Sectors that export a lot also face substantial import competition.

32. Along these same lines, Scheve (2000) finds that spending on labor market programs reduces the size of the skill cleavage individual-level support for European integration.

33. Many believe that globalization and deindustrialization are interdependent processes in the sense that expanding trade explains the decline of manufacturing among the OECD economies. Iversen and Cusack reject this argument. See Iversen and Cusack 2000, 339–345. I am not arguing that trade causes deindustrialization but rather that deindustrialization conditions the effect of trade on government spending. A similar argument is made by Mares (2004).

34. Economic Outlook database.

35. Their measure is 100 minus the workers employed in manufacturing and agriculture as a percentage of the working age population.

36. This data is from the OECD's Economic Outlook database.

37. The sources are Economic Outlook, Franzese 2002, and Swank 2002b.

38. See, for example, Pierson 2001.

39. Imports cluster spatially in my analysis if countries that share territorial borders are more similar with respect to levels of imports than countries that do not share borders.

40. A few exceptions to the territorial border rule were made. France, Belgium, and the Netherlands were coded as contiguous with Britain; Denmark was coded as contiguous with Sweden; and Australia was coded as contiguous with New Zealand.

41. Franzese and Hays (2007, 2008) discuss the benefits and costs of using a serially lagged spatial lag variable. Since the endogeneity of the spatial lag is relatively easy to address in the specification of the likelihood function, I use a contemporaneous spatial lag.

42. This is similar to Mares' finding for the interwar period that both terms-of-trade and unemployment volatility have a larger impact on the coverage of unemployment insurance when the percentage of the workforce employed in manufacturing is high. See Mares 2004.

43. For the experiments, I used regression model (1).

44. The sample low and high deindustrialization values for Germany, found at the beginning and end of the series respectively, are 60% and 75%. Since the import variable is logged, a 1-unit positive shock amounts to a 100% increase.

45. The original Iversen and Cusack results are presented in Table 3 (200, 333).

46. For an excellent discussion of spatial multipliers, see Anselin (2003).

47. The counterfactual addressed here is usually the steady-state effect of *permanent* shocks since, given stationarity, the long-run steady-state effect of a temporary shock is zero.

CHAPTER THREE

1. For Pontusson and Swenson, corporatism is defined by "institutional arrangements for collaborative or tripartite governance of labor markets by representatives of capital, labor, and the state" (1996, 224).

2. For example, the Iversen, Pontusson, and Soskice (2000) volume was originally motivated by changes to the "Swedish model" of corporatism.

3. Wallerstein and Golden (2000) argue that Sweden is the only Nordic country that has experienced significant decentralization. In Denmark, in particular, they argue that the formation of supraindustrial bargaining cartels have offset the decentralizing changes highlighted by Iversen (1996) and others. Since their analysis only covers the period up to 1992, they do not consider the changes to the Finnish system that are discussed in Niemela (1999).

4. The empirical relationship between bargaining centralization and wage equality is very strong (e.g., Iversen 1996, 1999). The theoretical argument is that, in highly centralized systems, low-skill low-wage workers can veto inegalitarian agreements.

5. These are applications of the first and second Hicks-Marshallian laws of derived demand, respectively (See Hamermesh 1993, 24–25).

6. Equation (3.7) is typically called the Slutsky equation (see Silberberg and Suen 2001, 276–282). The first term represents the change in leisure consumption that results from sliding a linear budget constraint along a fixed indifference curve. Since utility is held constant, this is a pure substitution effect caused by a change in relative price of leisure. The second term gives the change in leisure consumption resulting from a parallel outward shift in the budget constraint. Since prices are held constant, this is a pure income effect.

7. In this case, a positive shock to labor demand leads to less of an increase in employment because workers value leisure relatively more (compared to when the supply is elastic) and a negative shock to labor demand would lead to a lesser decline in employment because workers value leisure relatively less. Hence, employment

outcomes are more stable. The same conditions lead to greater volatility in wages, however.

8. This is a slightly modified version of the utility function in Summers et al. (1993). The differences between my function and theirs stem partly from the fact that there is no labor income taxation and government spending in my model. I also add γ as an exponent to L. Summers et al. (1993) assume that the number of union members is fixed. While some may view this assumption as problematic, it is merely an analytical convenience, albeit one with some justification. One way to think about N is as the optimal union size. There are large literatures on the optimal size of firms, clubs, and even nations. It is not unreasonable to think that there is an optimal union size beyond which union leaders do not want to grow due to various diseconomies of scale. There is also a historical justification since one of the original purposes of corporatism was to limit the competition among employers for labor, see, for example, Swenson's (2002) discussion of solidarism in Sweden. Again, this implies an exogenous employment/membership limit, this time systemic in origin, beyond which union leaders may not want to grow.

9. To keep the notation as simple as possible, I do not subscript these utilities.

10. This raises an obvious question about union representation. Why do workers not choose leaders who share their preferences? One answer to this question is that there are organizational imperatives that make this impossible. Union leadership and the rank-and-file have different objectives and therefore will never share exactly the same preferences. There is an inherent principal-agent problem. Another, more pleasing, answer is that workers may have an incentive to choose leaders with different preferences. I do not develop rigorously the microfoundations of this argument, but it would be similar to Rogoff's (1985) point about appointing conservative central bankers. The model would have multiple periods and a time-inconsistency element to it. One possibility is to introduce a government that funds public goods with a distortionary tax on labor. *Ex ante* workers would like to commit to higher levels of work effort in the future in order to minimize tax rates in the present, but the commitment is not credible so they benefit from delegating authority to union leaders with stronger preferences for employment over leisure.

11. Lange et al. also examine the German case, but they note its systems and practices differ significantly from the other five countries in their study.

12. I cannot effectively test the effects of trade on the elasticity of labor demand in the corporatist countries because the identification strategy is undermined by coordinated wage bargaining (discussed below).

13. One partial exception is Scheve (2000), who looks at support for European integration across skill cleavages conditional on a respondent's country's labor market institutions. He finds the skill gap in support for the European Union is smaller in countries with centralized wage bargaining, presumably because corporatism attenuates trade's effect on domestic labor markets.

14. Since most of his second stage estimation uses the constant output (own price) labor demand elasticity, I will focus on this elasticity.

15. These aggregated sets of industries are: (1) food and tobacco, (2) textiles, apparel, and footwear, (3) wood products and printing, (4) chemicals and petroleum products, (5) transportation, (6) primary and fabricated metals, (7) machinery, (8) instruments and miscellaneous products.

16. He uses long-differences of three, five, and ten years.

17. The industries are: (1) mining and quarrying of energy producing material, (2) mining and quarrying except energy producing materials, (3) food products, beverages, and tobacco, (4) textiles, textile products, leather, and footwear, (5) wood and products of wood and cork, (6) pulp, paper, paper products, printing, and publishing, (7) chemical, rubber, plastics, and fuel products, (8) other non-metallic mineral products, (9) basic metals, metal products, machinery, and equipment, (10) basic metals and fabricated metal products, (11) machinery and equipment, (12) transport equipment, and (13) manufacturing not elsewhere classified (nec).

18. Fixed effects provide a conservative method to control for alternative explanations for the cross-national and inter-temporal patterns of manufacturing employment that we observe in the data (e.g., deindustrialization).

19. This is especially true when the business cycles of the importing countries are not correlated. Kim (2007) makes a similar argument. Her careful empirical analysis shows no link between trade openness and aggregate income, consumption and investment in a panel of 175 countries over fifty-three years (1950–2002). The main difference between her analysis and mine is that I focus on employment outcomes in OECD countries with competitive labor markets. There seems to be a strong connection between trade and employment volatility in these cases.

20. One reason industries that trade might face more price volatility than industries that produce for domestic markets is that trade involves transactions in multiple currencies. To the extent that things like short-term capital flows drive exchange rate fluctuations, workers in tradable industries are subject to risks that workers in purely domestic industries are not. For a good discussion of how producer groups in tradable industries are affected by exchange rates, see Frieden (1991). Iversen and Cusak do not consider this possibility.

21. Note that this turns Iversen and Cusak's argument around. They contend that deindustrialization produces labor market uncertainty because workers are forced to cross skill boundaries. To the extent that trade generates labor market volatility, deindustrialization may also reduce uncertainty by moving workers from tradable to non-tradable sectors of the economy. This is similar and related to the argument in chapter 2: deindustrialization conditions the effect of trade on government spending.

22. There has been much debate about whether elected politicians are more sensitive to dispersed or concentrated costs and benefits among the citizenry. It is probably fair to say that the answer depends on the political institutional context. Political institutions are the focus of chapter 4, but it is worth noting that the political institutions in most countries with competitive labor markets enhance the sensitivity of politicians to precisely the kinds of risks that these markets generate.

23. See Rodrik (2000) for a similar analysis.

24. Krugman, "The Trouble with Trade." (*NYT*, December 28, 2007).

CHAPTER FOUR

1. In the appendix to this chapter, I also present a stylized model of capital tax competition from Persson and Tabellini (2000) to show the importance of strategic policy interdependence across countries. Exogenous changes in the capital tax policies of one country will affect the policies of its competitors. This interdependence, in turn, has important implications for empirical analysis.

2. For empirical evidence that there is a globalization dilemma, see Rodrik (1997). For research concluding that globalization does not impose significant tax constraints, see Swank (1998, 2002), Swank and Steinmo (2002), and Garrett and Mitchell (2001). For a review of the economic literature, see Hines (1999).

3. For a survey of the tax competition literature, see Wilson (1999), Oates (2001), and Wilson and Wildasin (2004). Competition leads to convergence in the net return to capital, but very little can be said about how capital mobility affects overall levels of taxation. A model of fiscal competition that can support either a race to the bottom or a race to the top (or efficient levels of taxation) in equilibrium is provided in Wooders, Zissimos, and Dhillon (2001) and Lockwood and Makris (2006). The assumptions one makes are critical. In models where governments tax a single source like capital, an increase in the interjurisdictional mobility of this source pushes tax rates down. Oates (2001) discusses the importance of this assumption (i.e., a limited range of tax instruments).

4. The data are from Volkerink and de Haan (2001) and Carey and Rabesona (2002). These studies update the estimates originally provided in Mendoza, Razin, and Tesar (1994, 1997). The OECD countries included in the sample are Australia, Austria, Belgium, Canada, Denmark, Finland, France, Germany, Ireland, Italy, Japan, Netherlands, New Zealand, Norway, Portugal, Spain, Sweden, Switzerland, the United Kingdom, and the United States.

5. See Rodrik (1997), Mendoza, Razin, and Tesar (1994, 1997), and Winner (2005).

6. Kitschelt, Lange, Marks, and Stephens (1999, 444).

7. In addition to Garrett, recent research that makes the divergent paths argument includes Swank (2002), Kitschelt et al. (1997), Pierson (2001), and Hall and Soskice (2001).

8. The years considered in Table 4.1 (1966–1990) represent the time period for which Garrett codes political-economic coherence.

9. Summers et al. (1993) also find a negative relationship between corporatism and capital taxes.

10. For the connection between corporatism and consensus democracy, see Lijphart and Crepaz (1991).

11. There is a similar relationship between consensus democracy and the capital tax rate. Also, the bivariate relationship is robust when alternative measures of consensus democracy are used—for example, Crepaz's (1996) measures of government "encompassment." Garrett and Mitchell (2001) also find (controlling for a large number of economic variables) that majoritarian democracies like Canada, the United Kingdom, and the United States tax capital at a higher rate than other countries. In chapter 12 of their textbook, Persson and Tabellini (2000) note the same relationship.

12. For a similar argument, see Meltzer and Richard (1981).

13. Other explanations are large country market power, imperfectly mobile capital, and economic rents (Mutti 2003; Slemrod 2004).

14. According to Rodrik (1997, 90), these costs include, among other things, establishing a business in an unfamiliar environment, communicating with subsidiaries, and shipping goods back to the home economy. Thus, the capital flows in this model represent foreign direct investment rather than portfolio investment.

15. In other words, my model is a pure model of income redistribution. Shareholders are taxed and wage earners are subsidized. In this way, the model resembles those of both Rodrik and Becker.

16. Becker (1983, 377).

17. See Olson (1965). It may seem that collective action should be endogenous in the model, given the size differences between shareholders and wage earners. Wage earners should face severe collective action difficulties tipping the balance of influence in favor of shareholders. This is certainly true in consensus democracies, where the cost of collective action in equilibrium is high. These costs should create a strong incentive for individual wage earners to "free ride" off the efforts of other workers. However, since I argue that wage earners have more political influence in majoritarian democracies, modeling the collective action problem would only strengthen my main result. This is discussed in more detail below.

18. Boix (1999). Of course, the view that proportional representation constrains labor power is controversial. I discuss the debate over the partisan biases of electoral systems below.

19. Clausing (2007) finds that the average OECD revenue maximizing tax rate for corporations is about 33% and that this tax rate is systematically lower for countries that are more deeply integrated into the global economy.

20. Slemrod favors the "backstop" explanation for the corporate tax. Governments tax corporations to prevent individuals from relabeling their labor income as business income to avoid taxes. According to this view, the trends in corporate taxes are explained by changes in the top marginal income taxes, which he sees as a purely domestic source of change. Some would argue that much of the change we observe in top marginal income tax rates is driven by international pressures, which are driven by both the globalization of financial markets and the mobility of labor, particularly in Europe (see, e.g., Genschel 2002).

21. The data needed to compute these tax rates are available from the OECD's *Revenue Statistics* and *National Accounts: Detailed Tables*. The Mendoza et al. capital tax rates have been used by Rodrik (1997), Garrett (1998a), Garrett (1998b), Garrett and Mitchell (2001), Swank and Steinmo (2002), and Swank (2006), among others.

22. In short, while there is a strong secular trend in the degree to which countries restrict financial transactions, the correlation between time and capital controls is far from perfect. Every country in the sample changed its capital and financial controls policy over the period of analysis, however. These changes were relatively large for countries like the United Kingdom, Norway, Finland, and New Zealand and relatively small for countries like Japan, Switzerland, the United States, and Germany.

23. Quinn's broad measure of financial openness reflects restrictions on both capital and current account transactions. Other measures of capital mobility like capital flows can be problematic. Low flows between two countries, for example, do not imply low capital mobility, if the return to capital is the same in both countries. For a discussion of these measurement issues, see O'Rourke and Williamson (1999) and Hallerberg and Basinger (1998). The secular trend is an imperfect proxy for technological change. The estimated coefficients will include the effect of any trended variable. Technological innovation is probably the most important of these, but it is not likely to be the only trended variable. Nevertheless, the time trend provides a good starting point for the empirical analysis.

24. This data is provided in the Penn World Table, the data source used by Quinn and Inclan (1997) to examine the impact of capital endowments on financial liberalization. In the theoretical model, the impact of globalization on capital tax rates is a

function of the initial capital endowment rather than the relative endowment of capital to labor. This is because I assume the labor supply is fixed and therefore does not affect the return to capital. In the empirical analysis, it is important to account for the fact that countries have different labor endowments.

25. For partisanship, I use the percentage of cabinet seats held by leftist parties provided in Duane Swank's (2002b) *21-Nation Pooled Time-Series Dataset, 1950–1999*. For labor market institutions, I use union density. The Single European Act—which established a common European market by eliminating all obstacles to the movement of goods, services, labor, and capital—was signed in 1986. The EU dummy variable takes a value of 1 starting in 1986 for the countries that were members of the European Union when the Single European Act was signed. For Austria, Sweden, and Finland the dummy variable takes a value of 1 starting in 1995.

26. Note that period dummies cannot be included in the regression that has a deterministic time trend. These two effects are not separately identifiable.

27. See, for example, Blonigen et al. (2007), Guerin (2006), and Abreau and Melendez (2006).

28. There are large theoretical and empirical literatures that connect proportional representation to bigger governments (e.g., Austen-Smith 2000, Tavits 2004, Franzese and Hays 2008), and this relationship might lead one to expect higher capital taxes in consensus democracies. Of course, empirically speaking, we know this is not the case.

29. These biases seem to depend on fairly strong assumptions. In the majoritarian case, voters are unable to distinguish extreme and moderate leaders ex ante (before elections) and unable to punish leaders who renege on campaign promises ex post (after elections). In the proportional representation case, regressive redistribution is not allowed by assumption, which eliminates the bases for left-right and center-right coalitions to form. If we relax these assumptions, majoritarianism would produce center-biased economic policies that benefit the median voter, while proportional representation would produce tail-protected economic policies (that is, policies that protect both the rich and poor). Given the fact that the majoritarian democracies tax capital at high rates and many of the European countries with proportional representation electoral systems rely heavily on consumption taxes, it is clear that the simple partisan biases described by Iversen and Soskice do not completely determine the tax systems that we observe.

30. Others who study the consequences of globalization for domestic economic and social policy have made similar arguments—e.g., Rodrik (1997, 38). Dehejia and Genschel (1999) use the EU to test the predictions of their tax competition model.

31. Lijphart (1999).

32. Dehejia and Genschel (1999).

33. This assumption is common in the literature—for example, Garrett (1998a) makes this assumption.

34. For excellent surveys of Conservative tax reform in Britain, see King and Robson (1993) and Leape (1993).

35. For a good discussion of the end of imputation in Britain, see Gammie (1997).

36. For a hypothetical illustration of the revenue consequences, see Hughes (1998). For actual revenue estimates, see OECD (2000a).

37. Due to missing data for the operating surplus of private unincorporated enterprises, I am not able to extend this chart beyond 1998.

38. Quoted from the official English translation of the PvdA's 1998 election manifesto. See Partij van de Arbeid (1998).

39. For a good discussion, see OECD (2000b) and Cnossen and Bovenberg (2000).

40. Cnossen and Bovenberg (2000)

41. OECD (200b).

42. The international dimension is important. The reforms made Britain a more attractive location for investment by foreign firms, in particular, French and German firms. As for capital outflows, the survey evidence suggests that British firms are sensitive to cross-national differences in tax rates (e.g., Devereux and Pearson 1989).

43. These numbers were calculated using data from the IMF's *International Financial Statistics.* The sample includes Australia, Austria, Canada, Denmark, Finland, France, Germany, Ireland, Italy, Japan, Netherlands, New Zealand, Norway, Spain, Sweden, Switzerland, United Kingdom, and United States.

44. Ministry of Finance (2000).

45. OECD (2000b).

CHAPTER FIVE

1. Berman (2006) comes to a similar conclusion. She believes that social democracy's approach to managing economic globalization in the 21st century must involve international organizations like the EU, IMF, and WTO.

2. Although they are not directly concerned with possibility of a backlash against globalization, both Kenworthy (2004) and Pontusson (2005) have argued that progressive economic policy reform is both possible and desirable in liberal market economies.

3. Adding the chapter 2 variables to the regressions does not change, in a qualitative sense, any of the inferences drawn from the analysis.

4. Note that the relationship between employment volatility and government spending (government consumption and social benefits spending) is unconditional: when employment volatility increases, theory tell us that spending goes up, regardless of tax constraints. The increase in spending can be financed either by taxes or borrowing. Thus, the conditional relationship implied by the interaction term only makes sense when modeling deficit spending. When capital taxes are high the increase in spending driven by employment volatility is more likely to be financed by borrowing, which, in turn, contributes to a negative budget balance.

5. Note that the interaction term also implies that the effect of capital taxation on the budget balance is conditional on employment volatility. The marginal revenue gain from raising capital taxes is lower when the economy is turbulent. In other words, the Laffer curve constraints discussed in chapter 4 are stronger when the economy is performing poorly.

6. While recognizing the importance of institutional and policy complementarity, both Kenworthy and Pontusson argue that this logic can be taken too far. They argue that there are plenty of progressive policies that can achieve egalitarian outcomes in the liberal market economies.

7. See, for example, Wallerstein (1990, 1999).

8. For Britain, see Robinson (1996) and King and Wood (1999). For a discussion of labor market deregulation in Australia under the Howard government, see Hancock (1999).

9. Garrett notes that the relative weakness of the Left in the United States and Canada make these countries poor candidates for corporatist labor market reform. This is not to say that major realignments are impossible or even unlikely, but there are other policy options that would be politically viable in the absence of dramatic changes to electorates and party systems.

10. The phrase "fair and reasonable," which comes from the 1907 Harvester decision, set the precedent for decades of award decisions.

11. Wailes and Lansbury (1999) divide the post-1986 period into three subperiods they call managed decentralism (1987–1991), coordinated flexibility (1991–1996), and fragmented flexibility (1996–present).

12. The changes are described in Hancock (1999, 47–48).

13. Cusack et al. (2007) focus on the economic determinants of electoral systems. They argue that, in those economies where employers and workers had a common interest in developing industry specific skills, the need for cross-class cooperation in both the economy and the polity created incentives for political parties to adopt proportional representation electoral institutions and develop modes of non-market coordination. Martin and Swank (2008) examine the political determinants of systems of industrial relations, arguing proportional multi-party political systems are more conducive to the development of peak business associations, which are necessary for coordinated capitalism.

14. A recent paper by Davidson, Matusz, and Nelson (2007) is exceptional in this respect. They argue that compensation might induce the median voter to support trade liberalization, but only if compensation occurs before trade is liberalized.

15. These effects, discussed in Calmfors et al. (2001), are the main ways that ALM programs can unexpectedly contribute to unemployment by reducing its opportunity cost. Program participants or potential participants either choose not to take jobs that they would have taken absent training or choose jobs in sectors where unemployment is more likely. In the first instance, participants directly choose continued training over a job. They "lock in" to the program and refuse to exit even when a job is available. In the second, training increases productivity and consequently the wage that makes a job seeker indifferent between taking a job and remaining unemployed (i.e., the reservation wage). Increased productivity can affect reservation wages either through augmented income potential from grey and black market opportunities or by raising aspirations. Education-training arbitrage is considered in Fukushima (2001). In his model, young people equate the expected returns from ordinary higher education and a standard education with the possibility for training later in life. Training raises the expected return from a standard education and leads to more unskilled workers entering the low productivity sector of the economy. Since the demand for unskilled workers is unaffected by training programs and the wage is typically fixed by legislation, the level of employment is fixed and the inflow of unskilled workers generates unemployment.

16. Displacement occurs when employers substitute subsidized workers for unsubsidized workers in their hiring. Subsidies crowd out regular employment.

17. Although Forslund and Krueger (2008) conclude that Sweden's ALM programs did not aid its recovery from the negative employment shock experienced during the early 1990s.

18. Insiders are workers with secure jobs while outsiders include the unemployed and workers with very little or no job security.

19. Hall and Soskice (2001) also make this point.

20. At the same time, given that sector-specific training is the type of training firms are likely to provide privately—because the risk of poaching with sector specific workers is lower—it is not clear that public spending on these programs would be socially efficient.

21. There is an active debate about the extent to which trade is or will become a partisan issue again. The evidence from congressional roll-call votes is mixed. Hiscox (2002a, 2002b) finds that sectoral politics explains these votes relatively well, while Ladewig (2006) finds that partisan politics does better, at least for the recent past.

22. Of course, the flip side of this argument is that insurance encourages workers and employers to take risks on high wage / high productivity jobs, which in theory could expand output (Acemoglu and Shimer 1999).

23. Interestingly, in the U.S. case, this would not require much change to existing policy.

References

Abreau, Maria and Jose Melendez. 2006. "Spatial Determinants of Foreign Direct Investment." Paper presented at the Fourth Annual Conference of the Euro-Latin Study Network on Integration and Trade (ELSNIT). An initiative of the Inter-American Development Bank Paris, France, October 20–21, 2006.

Acemoglu, Daron and Robert Shimer. 1999. "Efficient Unemployment Insurance." *Journal of Political Economy* 107(5):893–928.

Adserà, Alicia and Carles Boix. 2002. "Trade, Democracy, and the Size of the Public Sector: The Political Underpinnings of Openness." *International Organization* 56(2):229–262.

Alderson, Arthur S. 1999. "Explaining Deindustrialization: Globalization, Failure, or Success?" *American Sociological Review* 64:701–721.

———— and Francois Nielsen. 2002. "Globalization and the great U-Turn: Income Inequality Trends in 16 OECD Countries." *American Journal of Sociology* 107(5): 1244–1299.

Aldrich, John H., Claire Kramer, Peter Lange, Renan Levine, Jennifer Merolla, Laura Stephenson and Elizabeth Zechmeister. 2002. In Pursuit of the Missing Link: Do Voters Make the Connection Between Macroeconomic Change and Welfare State Growth? Paper presented at the Annual Meeting of the American Political Science Association, August 29 to September 1.

Alesina, Alberto and Howard Rosenthal. 1995. *Partisan Politics, Divided Government, and the Economy.* New York: Cambridge University Press.

Alt, James and Michael Gilligan. 1994. "The Political Economy of Trading States: Factor Specificity, Collective Action Problems and Domestic Political Institutions." *The Journal of Political Philosophy* 2(2):165–192.

Andrews, David M. 1994. "Capital Mobility and State Autonomy: Toward a Structural Theory of International Monetary Relations." *International Studies Quarterly* 38(2):193–218.

Andrews, Josephine T. and Robert W. Jackman. 2005. "Strategic Fools: Electoral Rule Choice Under Extreme Uncertainty." *Electoral Studies* 24(1):65–84.

Angell, Norman. 1914. *The Great Illusion: A Study of the Relation of Military Power to National Advantage.* London: William Heinemann.

Anselin, Luc. 2003. "Spatial Externalities, Spatial Multipliers, and Spatial Econometrics." *International Regional Science Review* 26(2):153–166.

Arceneaux, Kevin. 2003. "The Conditional Impact of Blame Attribution on the Relationship between Economic Adversity and Turnout." *Political Research Quarterly* 56(1):67–75.

Austen-Smith, David. 2000. "Redistributing Income under Proportional Representation." *Journal of Political Economy* 108(6): 1235–1269.

—— and Jeffrey Banks. 1988. "Elections, Coalitions, and Legislative Outcomes." *American Political Science Review* 82(2):405–422.

Baily, Martin N. 1978. "Some Aspects of Optimal Unemployment Insurance." *Journal of Public Economics* 10:379–402.

Basinger, Scott and Mark Hallerberg. (2004). "Remodeling the Competition for Capital: How Domestic Politics Erases the Race to the Bottom." *American Political Science Review* 98(2):261–76.

Baumgartner, Frank and Bryan Jones. 1993. *Agendas and Instability in American Politics*. Chicago: University of Chicago Press.

Bawn, Kathleen. 1999. "Money and Majorities in the Federal Republic of Germany: Evidence for a Veto Players Model of Government Spending." *American Journal of Political Science* 43(3): 449–476.

Beck, Nathaniel and Jonathan N. Katz. 2001. "Throwing Out the Baby with the Bath Water: A Comment on Green, Kim, and Yoon." *International Organization* 55(2):487–495.

Becker, Gary. 1983. "A Theory of Competition among Pressure Groups for Political Influence." *The Quarterly Journal of Economics* 98(3):371–400.

Berger, Suzanne. 2000. "Globalization and Politics." *Annual Review of Political Science* 3:43–62.

Berman, Sheri. 2006. *The Primacy of Politics: Social Democracy and the Making of Europe's Twentieth Century*. New York: Cambridge University Press.

Bernhard, William and David Leblang. 2006. *Democratic Processes and Financial Markets: Pricing Politics*. New York: Cambridge University Press.

Besley, Timothy and Stephen Coate. 1997. "An Economic Model of Representative Democracy." *The Quarterly Journal of Economics* 112(1):85–114.

Blais, André, Agnieszka Dobrzynska and Indridi H. Indridason. 2005. "To Adopt or Not to Adopt Proportional Representation: The Politics of Institutional Choice." *British Journal of Political Science* 35(1):182–190.

Blanchard, Olivier and Justin Wolfers (2000). "The Role of Shocks and Institutions in the Rise of Euopean Unemployment: The Aggregate Evidence." *The Economic Journal* 110(March):C1–C33.

Blau, Francine D. and Lawrence M. Kahn. 2002. *At Home and Abroad: U.S. Labor-Market Performance in International Perspective*. New York: Russell Sage Foundation.

Blonigen, Bruce A., Ronald B. Davies, Glen R. Waddell and Helen T. Naughton. 2007. "FDI in Space: Spatial Autoregressive Relationships in Foreign Direct Investment." *European Economic Review* 51(5):1303–1325.

Blyth, Mark. 2002. *Great Transformations: Economic Ideas and Institutional Change in the Twentieth Century*. Cambridge: Cambridge University Press.

Boix, Carles. 2002. "Between Protection and Compensation: The Political Economy of Trade." Unpublished Manuscript. University of Chicago.

——. 1999. "Setting the Rules of the Game: The Choice of Electoral Systems in Advanced Democracies." *American Political Science Review* 93(3):609–624.

——. 1998. *Political Parties, Growth and Equality: Conservative and Social Democratic Economic Strategies in the World Economy*. Cambridge, U.K.: Cambridge University Press.

———. 1997. "Political Parties and the Supply Side of the Economy: The Provision of Physical and Human Capital in Advanced Economies, 1960–90." *American Journal of Political Science* 41(3):814–845.

Bordo, Michael D., Alan M. Taylor, and Jeffrey G. Williamson. *Globalization in Historical Perspective*. Chicago: The University of Chicago Press, 2003.

Bowman, John R. 2002. "Employers and the Persistence of Centralized Wage Setting: The Case of Norway." *Comparative Political Studies* 35(9):995–1026.

Brander, James A. and Barbara J. Spencer. 1994. "Trade Adjustment Assistance: Welfare and Incentive Effects of Payments to Displaced Workers." *Journal of International Economics* 36(3–4):239–261.

Brennan, Geoffrey and Jonathan Pincus. 2002. "Australia's Economic Institutions." In *Australia Reshaped: 200 Years of Institutional Transformation*, ed. Geoffrey Brennan and Francis G. Castles. Cambridge, UK: Cambridge University Press.

Bretschger, Lucas and Frank Hettich. 2002. "Globalisation, Capital Mobility and Tax Competition: Theory and Evidence for the OECD." *European Journal of Political Economy* 18:695–716.

Brown, Courtney. 1988. "Mass Dynamics of U.S. Presidential Competitions, 1928–1936." *American Political Science Review* 82(4):1153–1181.

Brune, Nancy and Geoffrey Garrett. 2005. "The Globalization Rorschach Test: International Economic Integration, Inequality, and the Role of Government." *Annual Review of Political Science* 8:399–423.

Burgoon, Brian. 2001. "Globalization and Welfare Compensation: Disentangling the Ties That Bind." *International Organization* 55(3):509–552.

Calmfors, Lars, Anders Forslund and Maria Hemstrom. 2001. "Does Active Labour Market Policy Work? Lessons from the Swedish Experiences." *Swedish Economic Policy Review* 8(2):61–124.

——— and J. Driffill. 1988. "Coordination of Wage Bargaining." *Economic Policy* 6(1): 14–61.

Cameron, David. 1978. "The Expansion of the Public Economy: A Comparative Analysis." *American Political Science Review* 72(4):1243–1261.

Carey, David and Josette Rabesona. 2002. "Average Effective Tax Rates on Capital, Labour, and Consumption," Venice Summer Institute Workshop on Measuring the Tax Burden on Capital and Labour (July).

Castles, Francis G. 2004. *The Future of the Welfare State: Crisis Myths and Crisis Realities*. Oxford, U.K.: Oxford University Press.

Cerny, Philip G. 1995. "Globalization and the Changing Logic of Collective Action." *International Organization* 49(4):595–625.

Clark, William Roberts. 2003. *Capitalism, Not Globalism: Capital Mobility, Central Bank Independence, and the Political Control of the Economy*. Ann Arbor: University of Michigan Press.

Clausing, Kimberly A. 2007. "Corporate Tax Revenues in OECD Countries." *International Tax and Public Finance* 14:115–133.

Cline, William R. 1997. *Trade and Income Distribution*. Washington D.C.: Institute for International Economics.

Cnossen, Sijbren and Lans Bovenberg, "Fundamental Tax Reform in the Netherlands." Working Paper No. 342. Munich, Germany: CESifo, 2000.

Cohen, Benjamin. 1996. "Phoenix Risen: The Resurrection of Global Finance." *World Politics* 48(2):268–296.

Collins, Susan M. 1998. "Economic Integration and the American Worker: An Overview." In *Imports, Exports, and the American Worker,* ed. Susan M. Collins, 3–45. Washington, D.C.: Brookings Institution.

Crepaz, Markus L. 1998. "Inclusion versus Exclusion: Political Institutions and Welfare Expenditures." *Comparative Politics* 31(1):61–80.

———. 1996. "Constitutional Structures and Regime Performance in 18 Industrial Democracies: A Test of Olson's Hypothesis." *European Journal of Political Research* 29(1):87–104.

Cusack, Thomas R., Torben Iversen and David Soskice. 2007. "Economic Interests and the Origins of Electoral Systems." *American Political Science Review* 101(3):373–391.

———, Torben Iversen and Philipp Rehm. 2006. "Risks at Work: The Demand and Supply Sides of Government Redistribution." *Oxford Review of Economic Policy* 22(3):365–389.

Dahlberg, Matz and Anders Forslund. 2005. "Direct Displacement Effects of Labour Market Programmes." *Scandinavian Journal of Economics* 107(3):475–494.

Davidson, Carl, Seven J. Matusza and Douglas R. Nelson. 2007. "Can compensation save free trade?" *Journal of International Economics* 71(1):167–186.

Dehejia, Vivek H. and Philipp Genschel. 1999. "Tax Competition in the European Union." *Politics and Society* 27(3):403–430.

Devereux, Michael and Mark Pearson. 1989. "Corporate Tax Harmonization and Economic Efficiency." Report series No. 35. London: Institute for Fiscal Studies.

Ehrlich, Sean D. 2007. "Access to Protection: Domestic Institutions and Trade Policy in Democracies." *International Organization* 61(3):571–605.

Eichengreen, Barry and Torben Iversen. 1999. "Institutions and Economic Performance: Evidence from the Labour Market." *Oxford Review of Economic Policy* 15(4): 121–138.

Elliott, Kimberly Ann, Debayani Kar and J. David Richardson. 2004. "Assessing Globalization's Critics: 'Talkers Are No Good Doers?' " In *Challenges to Globalization: Analyzing the Economics,* ed. Robert E. Baldwin and L. Alan Winters, 17–60. Chicago: The University of Chicago Press.

Engle, Robert F. 1982. "Autoregressive Conditional Heteroscedasticity with Estimates of the Variance of United Kingdom Inflation." *Econometrica* 50(4):987–1007.

Erikson, Robert S., Michael B. Mackuen and James A. Stimson. 2002. *The Macro Polity.* New York: Cambridge University Press.

Estevao, Marcello M. 2003. "Do Active Labor Market Policies Increase Employment?" (December 1). IMF Working Paper No. 03/234 Available at SSRN: http://ssrn. com/abstract=481182 or DOI: 10.2139/ssrn.481182.

Evans, Geoffrey. 2000. "The Continued Significance of Class Voting." *Annual Review of Political Science* 3:401–417.

———. 1993. "Class, Prospects and the Life-cycle: Explaining the Association between Class Position and Political Preferences." *Acta Sociologica* 36(3):263–276.

Fischer, Stanley. 1980. "Dynamic Inconsistency, Cooperation, and the Benevolent Dissembling Government." *Journal of Economic Dynamics and Control* 2:93–107.

Forslund, Anders and Alan Krueger. 1997. "An Evaluation of the Swedish Active Labor Market Policy: New and Received Wisdom." In *The Welfare State in Transition: Reforming the Swedish Model,* ed. Richard Freeman, R. Topel, and B. Swedenborg, 267–298. Chicago: University of Chicago Press.

Franzese, Robert J. and Jude C. Hays. 2008. "Empirical Models of Spatial Interdependence." In *Oxford Handbook of Political Methodology*, ed. Janet Box-Steffensmeier, Henry Brady, and David Collier, 570–604. Oxford, U.K.: Oxford University Press.

———— and Jude C. Hays. 2008. "Inequality and Unemployment, Redistribution and Insurance, and Participation: A Theoretical Model and an Empirical System of Endogenous Equations." In *Democracy, Inequality, and Representation*, ed. P. Beramendi and C. Anderson, 232–277. New York: Russell Sage Foundation.

———— and Jude C. Hays. 2007. "Spatial-Econometric Models of Cross-Sectional Interdependence in Political-Science Panel and TSCS Data." *Political Analysis*, 2007, 15(2):140–164.

———— and Jude C. Hays. 2006. "Strategic Interaction among EU Governments in Active Labor Market Policy-making: Subsidiarity and Policy Coordination under the European Employment Strategy." *European Union Politics* 7(2):167–189.

————. 2002. *Macroeconomic Policies of Developed Democracies*. Cambridge: Cambridge University Press.

Fredriksson, Peter and Bertil Holmlund. 2006. "Improving Incentives in Unemployment Insurance: A Review of Recent Research." *Journal of Economic Surveys* 20(3):357–386.

Freeman, John R. 2002. "Competing Commitments: Technocracy and Democracy in the Design of Monetary Institutions." *International Organization* 56(4):889–910.

————. 1990. "Banking on Democracy? International Finance and the Possibilities for Popular Sovereignty." Unpublished Manuscript. University of Minnesota.

Frieden, Jeffry. 2006. *Global Capitalism: Its Fall and Rise in the Twentieth Century*. New York: W.W. Norton.

————. 1991. "Invested Interests: The Politics of National Economic Policies in a World of Global Finance." *International Organization* 45(4):425–451.

Frieden, Jeffry and Lisa Martin. 2003. "International Political Economy: Global and Domestic Interactions," in *Political Science: The State of the Discipline*, ed. Ira Katznelson and Helen Milner. New York: W.W. Norton, 2003.

Fukushima, Yoshihiko. 2001. "Active Labour Market Programmes, Education and Unemployment." Department of Economics, Stockholm University.

Gammie, Malcolm. 1997. "The End of Imputation: Changes in UK Dividend Taxation." *Intertax* 25:333–341.

Garrett, Geoffrey. 2001. "Globalization and Government Spending around the World." *Studies in Comparative International Development* 35(4):3–29.

————. 1998a. *Partisan Politics in the Global Economy*. Cambridge: Cambridge University Press.

————. 1998b. "Global Markets and National Politics: Collision Course or Virtuous Circle?" *International Organization* 52(4):787–824.

————. 1993. "The Politics of Structural Change: Swedish Social Democracy and Thatcherism in Comparative Perspective." *Comparative Political Studies* 25(4): 521–547.

————, and Peter Lange. 1991. "Political Responses to Interdependence: What's 'Left' for the Left?" *International Organization* 45(4):539–564.

————, and Deborah Mitchell. 2001. "Globalization, Government Spending and Taxation in the OECD." *European Journal of Political Research* 39(3):145–178.

Genschel, Philipp. 2002. "Globalization, Tax Competition, and the Welfare State." *Politics and Society* 30(2):245–275.

Gilpin, Robert. 2000. *The Challenge of Global Capitalism: The World Economy in the 21st Century.* Princeton, N.J.: Princeton University Press.

Goodman, Alissa and Steven Webb. 1994. "For Richer, For Poorer: The Changing Distribution of Income in the UK, 1961–91." *Fiscal Studies* 15(4):29–62.

Gordon, Roger H. 1986. "Taxation of Investment and Savings in a World Economy." *The American Economic Review* 76(5):1086–1102.

Gourevitch, Peter. 1978. "The Second Image Reversed: The International Sources of Domestic Politics." *International Organization* 32(4):881–912.

Griliches, Zvi and Jerry A. Hausman. 1986. "Errors in Variables in Panel Data." *Journal of Econometrics* 31:93–118.

Guerin, Selen S. 2006. "The Role of Geography in Financial and Economic Integration: A Comparative Analysis of Foreign Direct Investment, Trade and Portfolio Investment Flows." *World Economy* 29(2):189–209.

Guillen, Mauro F. 2001. "Is Globalization Civilizing, Destructive or Feeble? A Critique of Five Key Debates in the Social Science Literature." *Annual Review of Sociology* 27:235–60.

Hall, Peter and Robert J. Franzese, Jr. 1998. "Central Bank Independence, Coordinated Wage Bargaining and European Monetary Union." *International Organization* 52(2):505–535.

——— and David Soskice. 2001. *Varieties of Capitalism: The Institutional Foundations of Comparative Advantage.* New York: Oxford University Press.

Hallerberg Mark and Scott Basinger. 1998. "Internationalization and Changes in Tax Policy in OECD Countries: The Importance of Domestic Veto Players." *Comparative Political Studies* 31(3):321–352.

Hamann, Kerstin and John Kelly. 2007. "Party Politics and the Reemergence of Social Pacts in Western Europe." *Comparative Political Studies* 40(8):971–994.

Hamermesh, Daniel S. 1993. *Labor Demand.* Princeton, N.J.: Princeton University Press.

Hampson, Ian and David E. Morgan. 1998. "Continuity and Change in Australian Industrial Relations: Recent Developments." *Industrial Relations* 53(3):564–591.

Hancock, Keith. 1999. "Labour Market Deregulation in Australia." In *Reshaping the Labour Market: Regulation, Efficiency and Equality in Australia,* ed. Sue Richardson, 38–85. Cambridge: Cambridge University Press.

Hansen, John Mark. 1998. "Individuals, Institutions, and Public Preferences over Public Finance." *American Political Science Review* 92(3):513–531.

Harding, Ann. 1997. "The Suffering Middle: Trends in Income Inequality in Australia, 1982 to 1993–1994." *The Australian Economic Review* 30(4):341–58.

Harvey, A. C. 1976. "Estimating Regression Models with Multiplicative Heteroscedasticity." *Econometrica* 44(3):461–465.

Hays, Jude C. 2003. "Globalization and Capital Taxation in Consensus and Majoritarian Democracies." *World Politics* 56(1):79–113.

———, Sean D. Ehrlich and Clint Peinhardt. 2005. "Government Spending and Public Support for Trade in the OECD: An Empirical Test of the Embedded Liberalism Thesis." *International Organization* 59(2):473–494.

Heckman, James J., Robert J. LaLonde, and Jeffrey A. Smith. 1999. "The Economics and Econometrics of Active Labor Market Programs." In *Handbook of Labor Economics,* ed. Orley Ashenfelter and David Card, 1865–2097. Vol. 3a, Amsterdam: Elsevier.

Hellwig, Timothy. 2001. "Interdependence, Government Constraints, and Economic Voting." *The Journal of Politics* 63(4):1141–1162.

———— and David Samuels. 2006. "Voting in Open Economies: The Electoral Consequences of Globalization." *Comparative Political Studies* 40(3):283–306.

Hines, James R. 1999. "Lessons from Behavioral Responses to International Taxation." *National Tax Journal* 52(2):305–322.

Hiscox, Michael. 2006. "Through a Glass and Darkly: Attitudes Toward International Trade and the Curious Effects of Issue Framing." *International Organization* 60(3):755–780.

————. 2002. *International Trade and Political Conflict: Commerce, Coalitions, and Mobility.* Princeton, N.J.: Princeton University Press.

————. 2001. "Class versus Industry Cleavage: Inter-industry Factor Mobility and the Politics of Trade." *International Organization* 55(1):1–46.

———— and Brian Burgoon. 2003. Trade Openness and Political Compensation: Explaining Labor Demands for Adjustment Assistance. Unpublished Manuscript. Cambridge, MA.: Harvard University.

Hopenhayn, Hugo A. and Juan Pablo Nicolini. 1997. "Optimal Unemployment Insurance." *Journal of Political Economy* 105(2):412–438.

Howe, John, Richard Mitchell, Jill Murray, Anthony O'Donnell and Glenn Patmore. 2005. "The Coalition's Proposed Industrial Relations Changes: An Interim Assessment." *Australian Bulletin of Labour* 31(3):189–209.

Huber, Evelyne and John D. Stephens. 2001. *Development and Crisis of the Welfare State: Parties and Policies in Global Markets.* Chicago: University of Chicago Press.

Hughes, David. 1998. "United Kingdom: Recent Changes to the UK Tax Credit Regime, the Abolition of ACT, and Certain Related Matters." *Bulletin for International Fiscal Documentation* 52(1):19–23.

Ito, Hiro and Menzie Chinn. 2007. "A New Measure of Financial Openness." Unpublished Manuscript, University of Wisconsin.

Iversen, Torben. 2001. "The Dynamics of Welfare State Expansion: Trade Openness, Deindustrialization, and Partisan Politics." In *The New Politics of the Welfare State,* ed. Paul Pierson, 45–79. New York: Oxford University Press.

————. 1999. *Contested Economic Institutions: The Politics of Macroeconomics and Wage Bargaining in Advanced Democracies.* New York: Cambridge University Press.

————. 1996. "Power, Flexibility, and the Breakdown of Centralized Wage Bargaining: Denmark and Sweden in Comparative Perspective." *Comparative Politics* (July): 399–436.

———— and Thomas R. Cusack. 2000. The Causes of Welfare State Expansion: Deindustrialization or Globalization? *World Politics* 52:313–349.

———— Jonas Pontusson and David Soskice. 2000. *Unions, Employers, and Central Banks: Macroeconomic Coordination and Institutional Change in Social Market Economies.* New York: Cambridge University Press.

———— and David Soskice. 2001. "An Asset Theory of Social Policy Preferences." *American Political Science Review* 95(4):893–893.

———— and David Soskice. 2006. "Electoral Institutions and the Politics of Coalitions: Why Some Democracies Redistribute More than Others." *American Political Science Review* 100(2):165–181.

——— and Anne Wren. 1998. "Equality, Employment, and Budgetary Restraint: The Trilemma of the Service Economy." *World Politics* 50:507–546.

James, Harold. 2001. *The End of Globalization: Lessons from the Great Depression.* Cambridge, MA: Harvard University Press.

Jensen, J. Bradford and Lori G. Kletzer. 2005. "Tradable Services: Understanding the Scope and Impact of Services Offshoring." In *Offshoring White-Collar Work—The Issues and the Implications,* ed. Lael Brainard and Susan M. Collins. Brookings Trade Forum.

Jensen, Nathan M. 2006. *Nation-States and the Multinational Corporation: A Political Economy of Foreign Direct Investment.* Princeton: Princeton University Press.

Kapstein, Ethan B. 1999. *Sharing the Wealth: Workers and the World Economy.* New York: W.W. Norton & Company.

———. 1996. "Workers and the World Economy." *Foreign Affairs* 75:16–37.

Katzenstein, Peter. 1985. *Small States in World Markets: Industrial Policy in Europe.* Ithaca, NY: Cornell University Press.

Kayser, Mark A. 2007. "How Domestic Is Domestic Politics." *Annual Review of Political Science* 10:341–362.

Kenworthy, Lane. 2004. *Egalitarian Capitalism: Jobs, Incomes, and Growth in Affluent Countries.* New York: Russell Sage Foundation.

Keohane, Robert. 1984. "The World Political Economy and the Crisis of Embedded Liberalism." In *Order and Conflict in Contemporary Capitalism,* ed. John H. Goldthorpe, 15–38. Oxford: Clarendon Press.

——— and Helen Milner. 1996. *Internationalization and Domestic Politics.* Cambridge: Cambridge University Press.

Kim, So Young. 2007. "Openness, External Risk, and Volatility: Implications for the Compensation Hypothesis." *International Organization* 61(1):181–216.

King, Desmond and Stewart Wood. 1999. "The Political Economy of Neoliberalism: Britain and the United States in the 1980s." In *Continuity and Change in Contemporary Capitalism,* ed. Herbert Kitschelt, Peter Lange, Gary Marks, and John D. Stephens, 371–397. New York: Cambridge University Press.

King, Mervyn A. and Mark H. Robson. 1993. "United Kingdom." In *Tax Reform and the Cost of Capital: An International Comparison,* ed. Dale W. Jorgenson and Ralph Landau. Washington D.C.: The Brookings Institution.

Kitschelt, Herbert, Peter Lange, Gary Marks and John D. Stephens. 1999. *Continuity and Change in Contemporary Capitalism.* New York: Cambridge University Press.

——— and Philipp Rehm. 2004. "Socio-Economic Group Preferences and Partisan Alignments." Paper prepared for the 14th Conference of the Council of European Studies.

Kletzer, Lori. 2004. "Trade-related Job Loss and Wage Insurance: A Synthetic Review." *Review of International Economics* 12(5):724–748.

———, and Robert E. Litan. 2001. "A Prescription to Relive Worker Anxiety." *Brookings Policy Brief,* No. 73.

Kraft, Kornelius. 1998. "An Evaluation of Active and Passive Labour Market Policy." *Applied Economics* 30: 783–793.

Kurzer, Paulette. 1993. *Business and Banking.* Ithaca, NY: Cornell University Press.

Ladewig, Jeffrey W. 2006. "Domestic Influences on International Trade Policy: Factor Mobility in the United States, 1963 to 1992." *International Organization* 60(1): 69–103.

Lange, Peter. 1984. "Unions, Workers, and Wage Regulation: the Rational Bases of Consent." In *Order and Conflict in Contemporary Capitalism,* ed. John H. Goldthorpe, 98–123. New York: Oxford University Press.

———, Michael Wallerstein and Miriam Golden. 1995. "The End of Corporatism? Wage Setting in the Nordic and Germanic Countries." In *The Workers of Nations: Industrial Relations in a Global Economy,* ed. Sanford M. Jacoby. New York: Oxford University Press.

Layard, Richard, Stephen Nickell, and Richard Jackman. 1991. *Unemployment: Macroeconomic Performance and the Labour Market.* New York: Oxford University Press.

Leape, Jonathan I. 1993. "Tax Policies in the 1980s and 1990s: The Case of the United Kingdom." In *Taxation in the United States and Europe,* ed. Anthonie Knoester. New York: St. Martin's Press.

Lee, Woojin and John E. Roemer. 2005. "The Rise and Fall of Unionised Labour Markets: A Political Economy Approach." *The Economic Journal* 115(January):28–67.

Lijphart, Arend. 1999. *Patterns of Democracy: Government Forms and Performance in Thirty-Six Countries.* New Haven: Yale University Press.

——— and Markus Crepaz. 1991. "Corporatism and Consensus Democracy in Eighteen Countries: Conceptual and Empirical Linkages." *British Journal of Political Science* 21(2):235–246.

Lockwood, Ben and Miltiadis Makris. 2006. "Tax Incidence, Majority Voting and Capital Market Integration." *Journal of Public Economics* 90:1107–1025.

Long, J. Scott. 1997. *Regression Models for Categorical and Limited Dependent Variables.* Thousand Oaks, CA: SAGE Publications, Inc.

Maier, Charles S. 1984. "Preconditions for Corporatism." In *Order and Conflict in Contemporary Capitalism,* ed. John H. Goldthorpe. New York: Oxford University Press.

Mares, Isabela. 2006. *Taxation, Wage Bargaining, and Unemployment.* New York: Cambridge University Press.

———. 2005. "Social Protection around the world: External insecurity, state capacity and domestic political cleavages." *Comparative Political Studies* 38(6):623–651.

———. 2004. "Economic insecurity and social policy expansion: evidence from inter-war Europe." *International Organization* 58(4):745–774.

———. 2003. *The Politics of Social Risk: Business and Welfare State Development.* New York: Cambridge University Press.

Martin, Cathie Jo and Duane Swank. 2008. "The Political Origins of Coordinated Capitalism: Business Organizations, Party Systems, and State Structure in the Age of Innocence." *American Political Science Review* 102(2):181–198.

Martin, John P. 2000. "What Works Among Active Labour Market Policies: Evidence from OECD Countries' Experiences." *OECD Economic Studies* 30(1):79–113.

———, and David Grubb 2001. "What Works and for Whom: A Review of OECD Countries' Experiences with Active Labour Market Policies." Working Paper Series 2001:14, IFAU—Institute for 26 Labour Market Policy Evaluation.

Mayda, Anna Maria, Kevin H. O'Rourke and Richard Sinnott. 2007. "Risk, Government and Globalization: International Survey Evidence." *IIIS Discussion Paper* No. 218. Available at SSRN: http://ssrn.com/abstract=980939.

Mayda, Anna Maria, Kevin H. O'Rourke and Richard Sinnott and Dani Rodrik. 2005. "Why Are Some People (and Countries) More Protectionist Than Others?" *European Economic Review* 49(6):1393–1430.

McGann, Anthony. 2006. *The Logic of Democracy: Reconciling Equality, Deliberation, and Minority Protection.* Ann Arbor: The University of Michigan Press.

McKelvey, Richard and William Zavoina. 1975. Statistical-Model for Analysis of Ordinal Level Dependent Variables. *Journal of Mathematical Sociology* 4(1):103–120.

Meltzer, Allan H. and Scott F. Richard, "A Rational Theory of the Size of Government." *Journal of Political Economy* 89(5):914–927.

Mendelsohn, Matthew and Robert Wolfe. 2001. "Probing the Aftermyth of Seattle: Canadian Public Opinion on International Trade, 1980–2000." *International Journal* 56(2):234–260.

Mendoza, Enrique, Assaf Razin, and Linda Tesar. 1997. "On the Ineffectiveness of Tax Policy in Altering Long-Run Growth: Harberger's Superneutrality Conjecture." *Journal of Public Economics* 66(1):99–126.

———, Assaf Razin and Linda Tesar. 1994. "Effective Tax Rates in Macroeconomics: Cross-Country Estimates of Tax Rates on Factor Incomes and Consumption." *Journal of Monetary Economics* 34(3):297–323.

Milesi-Ferretti, Gian Maria, Roberto Perotti and Massimo Rostagno. 2002. "Electoral Systems and Public Spending." *The Quarterly Journal of Economics* (May):609–657.

Milner, Helen V. and Benjamin Judkins. 2004. "Partisanship, Trade Policy, and Globalization: Is There a Left-Right Divide on Trade Policy?" *International Studies Quarterly* 48:95–119.

Ministry of Finance. 2000. *The Budgetary Policy of the Second Kok Government.* Amsterdam: Central Information Directorate, October.

Moe, Terry M. and Michael Caldwell. 1994. "The Institutional Foundations of Democratic Government: A Comparison of Presidential and Parliamentary Systems." *Journal of Institutional and Theoretical Economics* 150(1):171–195.

Moses, Jonathan. 1994. "Abdication from National Policy Autonomy: What's Left for the Left to Leave?" *Politics and Society* 22:125–148.

Mosley, Layna. 2003. *Global Capital and National Governments.* Cambridge, U.K.: Cambridge University Press.

Moulton, Brent R. 1990. "An Illustration of the Pitfall in Estimating the Effects of Aggregate Variables on Micro Units." *The Review of Economics and Statistics* 72(2):334–338.

Mutti, John H. 2003. *Foreign Direct Investment and Tax Competition.* Washington, D.C.: Institute for International Economics.

Nardulli, Peter. 1995. "The Concept of a Critical Realignment, Electoral Behavior, and Political Change." *American Political Science Review* 89(1):10–22.

Nelson, Douglass. 1988. "Endogenous Tariff Theory: A Critical Survey." *American Journal of Political Science* 32:796–839.

Niemelä, Jukka. 1999. "Organised Decentralisation of Finnish Industrial Relations." Paper presented at the 21st Conference of the International Working Party on Labour Market Segmentation, Bremen, Germany, September 9–11.

Oates, Wallace E. 2001. "Fiscal Competition or Harmonization? Some Reflections." *National Tax Journal* 54(3):507–512.

Oesch, Daniel. 2006. "Coming to Grips with a Changing Class Structure: An Analysis of Employment Stratification in Britain, Germany, Sweden, and Switzerland." *International Sociology* 21(2):263–288.

Ohmae, Kenichi. 1995. *The End of the Nation State: The Rise of Regional Economies.* New York: The Free Press.

Olson, Mancur. 1965. *The Logic of Collective Action.* Cambridge, MA: Harvard University Press.

Organization for Economic Cooperation and Development. 2004. *OECD Employment Outlook.* Paris: OECD.

———. 2000a. *OECD Economic Surveys: United Kingdom.* Paris: OECD.

———. 2000b. *OECD Economic Surveys 1999–2000: Netherlands.* Paris: OECD.

———. 1998. *Benefit Systems and Work Incentives.* Paris: OECD.

O'Rourke, Kevin H. and Jeffrey G. Williamson. 1999. *Globalization and History: The Evolution of a Nineteenth-Century Atlantic Economy.* Cambridge, MA: The MIT Press.

——— and Richard Sinnott. 2002. "The Determinants of Individual Trade Policy Preferences: International Survey Evidence." In *Brookings Trade Forum: 2001,* ed. Susan M. Collins and Dani Rodrik, 157–206. Washington D.C.: Brookings Institute.

Oswald, Andrew J. 1993. "Efficient Contracts are on the Labour Demand Curve: Theory and Facts." *Labour Economics* (1):85–114.

———. 1985. "The Economic Theory of Trade Unions: An Introductory Survey." *Scandinavian Journal of Economics* 87(2): 160–193.

Pahre, Robert. 2008. *Politics and Trade Cooperation in the Nineteenth Century: The "Agreeable Customs" of 1815–1914.* New York: Cambridge University Press.

Partij van de Arbeid. 1998. *Eenwereld te Winnen.* Amsterdam: PvdA.

Peetz, David. 1998. *Unions in a Contrary World: The Future of the Australian Trade Union Movement.* Cambridge: Cambridge University Press.

Persson, Torsten, Gerard Roland and Guido Tabellini. "Comparative politics and public Finance." *Journal of Political Economy* 108(6):1121–1161.

Pierson, Paul. 1994. *Dismantling the Welfare State? Reagan, Thatcher, and the Politics of Retrenchment.* Cambridge: Cambridge University Press.

———. 2001. "The Dynamics of Welfare State Expansion: Trade Openness, De-industrialization, and Partisan Politics." In *The New Politics of the Welfare State,* ed. Paul Pierson, 80–104. New York: Oxford University Press.

——— and Guido Tabellini. 2000. *Political Economics: Explaining Economic Policy.* Cambridge, MA: The MIT Press.

Pierson, Paul. 2001. *The New Politics of the Welfare State.* New York: Oxford University Press.

Polanyi, Karl. 1944. *The Great Transformation: The Political and Economic Origins of Our Time.* Boston: Beacon Press.

Pontusson, Jonas. 2005. *Inequality and Prosperity: Social Europe vs. Liberal America.* Ithaca, N.Y.: Cornell University Press.

——— and Peter Swenson. 1996. "Labor Markets, Production Strategies, and Wage Bargaining Institutions: The Swedish Employer Offensive in Comparative Perspective." *Comparative Political Studies* 29(2):223–250.

Plümper, Thomas and Vera E. Troeger. 2007. "Efficient Estimation of Time-Invariant and Rarely Changing Variables in Finite Sample Panel Analyses with Unit Fixed Effects." *Political Analysis* 15(2):124–139.

Przeworski, Adam. 1985. *Capitalism and Social Democracy.* Cambridge: Cambridge University Press, 1985.

Quinn, Dennis and John Woolley. 2001. "Democracy and National Economic Performance: The Preference for Stability." *American Journal of Political Science* 45(3): 634–657.

—— and Carla Inclan. 1997. "The Origins of Financial Openness: A Study of Current and Capital Account Liberalization." *American Journal of Political Science* 41(3):771–813.

Rhodes, Martin. 2001. "The Political Economy of Social Pacts: 'Competitive Corporatism' and European Welfare Reform." In *The New Politics of the Welfare State,* ed. Paul Pierson. New York: Oxford University Press.

Rickard, Stephanie J. 2007. "Compensating the Losers: Evidence of Policy Responses to Globalization from Congressional Votes." Paper presented at the 2nd Annual Meeting of the International Political Economy Society, Stanford University, November 9–12.

Robinson, Peter. 1996. *Labour Market Studies. United Kingdom.* Luxembourg: Office for the Official Publications of the European Communities.

Rodrik, Dani. 1997. *Has Globalization Gone Too Far?* Washington, D.C.: Institute for International Economics.

——. 1998. "Why Do More Open Economies Have Bigger Governments?" *Journal of Political Economy* 106(5):997–1032.

——. 2000. "Participatory Politics, Social Cooperation, and Economic Stability." *The American Economic Review* 90(2):140–144.

Roemer, John E. 1998. "Why the Poor Do not Expropriate the Rich: An Old Argument in New Garb." *Journal of Public Economics* 70(3):399–424.

Rogoff, Kenneth. 1985. "The Optimal Degree of Commitment to an Intermediate Monetary Target." *The Quarterly Journal of Economics* 100(4):1169–1189.

Rokkan, Stein. 1970. *Citizens, Elections, and Parties: Approaches to the Comparative Study of the Processes of Development.* Oslo: Universitetsforlaget.

Rowthorn, Robert and Ramana Ramaswamy. 1999. "Growth, Trade, and Deindustrialization." *IMF Staff Papers* 46(1):18–41.

Rueda, David. 2006. "Social Democracy and Active Labour-Market Policies: Insiders, Outsiders and the Politics of Employment Promotion." *British Journal of Political Science* 36(3):385–406.

——. 2005. "Insider-Outsider Politics in Industrial Democracies: The Challenge to Social Democratic Parties." *American Political Science Review* 99(1):61–74.

—— and Jonas Pontusson. 2000. "Wage Inequality and Varieties of Capitalism." *World Politics* 52(3):350–383.

Ruggie, John Gerard. 2007. "Global Markets and Global Governance: The Prospects for Convergence." In *Global Liberalism and Political Order: Toward a New Grand Compromise?,* ed. Steven Bernstein and Louis W. Pauly. Albany, NY: SUNY Press.

——. 2003. "Taking Embedded Liberalism Global: the Corporate Connection." In *Taming Globalization: Frontiers of Governance,* ed. David Held and Mathias Koenig-Archibugi, 93–129. Cambridge, UK: Polity.

——. 1997. "Globalization and the Embedded Liberalism Compromise: The End of an Era?" Max Planck Institut fur Gesellschaftsforschung, Cologne, Working Paper 97/1.

——. 1995. "At Home Abroad, Abroad at Home: International Liberalization and Domestic Stability in the New World Economy." *Millennium: Journal of International Studies* 24(3):507–26.

———. 1994. "Trade, Protectionism, and the Future of Welfare Capitalism." *Journal of International Affairs* 48(1):1–11.

———. 1982. "International Regimes, Transactions, and Change: Embedded Liberalism in the Postwar Economic Order." *International Organization* 36(2): 379–415.

Saint-Paul, Gilles. 1998. "A Framework for Analyzing the Political Support for Active Labour Market Policy." *Journal of Public Economics* 67:151–165.

Scharpf, Fritz W. 1991. *Crisis and Choice in European Social Democracy* Ithaca, NY: Cornell University Press.

Scheve, Kenneth. 2000. "Comparative Context and Public Preferences over Regional Economic Integration." Unpublished Manuscript. New Haven, CT: Yale University.

——— and Matthew J. Slaughter. 2007. "A New Deal for Globalization." *Foreign Affairs* 86(4):34–47.

——— and Matthew Slaughter. 2006. "Public Opinion, International Economic Integration, and the Welfare State" In Samuel Bowles, Pranab Bardhan, and Michael Wallerstein (eds.), *Globalization and Egalitarian Redistribution*. Princeton: Princeton University Press.

——— and Matthew Slaughter. 2004. "Economic Insecurity and the Globalization of Production." *American Journal of Political Science* 48(4):662–674.

——— and Matthew Slaughter. 2001. *Globalization and the Perceptions of American Workers*. Washington, D.C.: Institute for International Economics.

Shavell, Steven and Laurence Weiss. 1979. "The Optimal Payment of Unemployment Insurance Benefits over Time." *Journal of Political Economy* 87(6):1347–1362.

Silberberg, Eugene and Wing Suen. 2001. *The Structure of Economics: A Mathematical Analysis*. New York: McGraw-Hill.

Skolnikoff, Eugene B. 1993. *The Elusive Transformation: Science Technology, and the Evolution of International Politics*. Princeton: Princeton University Press.

Slaughter, Matthew J. 2001. "International Trade and Labor-Demand Elasticities." *Journal of International Economics* 54:27–56.

Slemrod, Joel. 2004. "Are Corporate Tax Rates, or Countries, Converging?" *Journal of Public Economics* 88:1169–1186.

Soskice, David. 1990. "Wage Determination: The Changing Role of Institutions in Advanced Industrial Countries." *Oxford Review of Economic Policy* 6:36–61.

Southwell, Priscilla L. 1996. "Economic Salience and Differential Abstention in Presidential Elections." *American Politics Quarterly* 24(2):221–236.

Steenbergen, Marco R. and Bradford S. Jones. 2002. "Modeling Multilevel Data Structures." *American Journal of Political Science* 46(1):218–237.

Steigum, Erling. 1984. "Intersectoral Transfer of Labour in a Small Open Economy." *European Economic Review* 24:225–237.

Steinmo, Sven. 1994. "The End of Redistribution? International Pressures and Domestic Policy Choices." *Challenge* 37(6):9–19.

Strom, Kaare. 1990. *Minority Government and Majority Rule*. New York: Cambridge University Press.

———. 1985. "Party Goals and Government Performance in Parliamentary Democracies." *American Political Science Review* 75(3):738–754.

Summers, Lawrence, Jonathan Gruber and Rodrigo Vergara. 1993. "Taxation and the Structure of Labor Markets: The Case of Corporatism." *The Quarterly Journal of Economics* (May):385–411.

Sundquist, James. 1988. "Needed: A Political Theory for the New Era of Coalition Government in the United States." *Political Science Quarterly* 103(4):613–635.

Swank, D. 2006. "Tax Policy in an Era of Internationalization: Explaining the Spread of Neoliberalism." *International Organization* 60(4):847–882.

———. 2002a. *Global Capital, Political Institutions, and Policy Change in Developed Welfare States* Cambridge, UK: Cambridge University Press.

———. 2002b. 21-NATION POOLED TIME-SERIES DATA SET, 1950–1999, mimeo. Marquette University.

———. 1998. "Funding the Welfare State: Globalization and the Taxation of Business in Advanced Market Economies." *Political Studies* 46(4):671–692.

——— and Sven Steinmo. 2002. "The New Political Economy of Taxation in Advanced Capitalist Democracies." *American Journal of Political Science* 46(3):642–655.

Swenson, Peter. 2002. *Capitalists against Markets: The Making of Labor Markets and Welfare States.* New York: Oxford University Press.

Tavits, Margit. 2004. "The Size of Government in Majoritarian and Consensus Democracies." *Comparative Political Studies* 37(3):340–359.

Thörnqvist, Christer. 1999. "The Decentralization of Industrial Relations: The Swedish Case in Comparative Perspective." *European Journal of Industrial Relations* 5(1): 71–87.

Traxler, Franz. 2004. "The Metamorphoses of Corporatism: From Classical to Lean Patterns." *European Journal of Political Research* 43:571–598.

———. 1995. "Farewell to Labour Market Associations? Organized versus Disorganized Decentralization as a Map for Industrial Relations." In *Organized Industrial Relations in Europe: What Future?*, ed. C. Crouch and F. Traxler. Aldershot, UK: Avebury.

——— and Bernhard Kittel. 2000. "The Bargaining System and Performance: A Comparison of 18 OECD Countries." *Comparative Political Studies* 33(9): 1154–1190.

Tsebelis, George. 2002. *Veto Players: How Political Institutions Work.* Princeton: Princeton University Press.

——— and Eric C. C. Chang. 2004. "Veto Players and the Structure of Budgets in Advanced Industrial Countries." *European Journal of Political Research* 43(3):449–476.

Verdier, Daniel. 1994. *Democracy and International Trade: Britain, France, and the United States, 1860–1990.* Princeton: Princeton University Press.

Volkerink, Bjørn and Jakob de Haan. 2001. "Tax Ratios: A Critical Survey." OECD Tax Policy Studies No. 5 (November).

Wailes, N. and Lansbury, R. D. 1999. *Collective Bargaining and Flexibility: Australia.* International Labour Organisation (available at http://www.ilo.org).

Wallerstein, Michael. 1999. "Wage-Setting Institutions and Pay Inequality in Advanced Industrial Societies." *American Journal of Political Science* 43(3):649–680.

———. 1990. "Centralized Bargaining and Wage Restraint." *American Journal of Political Science* 34(4):982–1004.

——— and Miriam Golden. 2000. "Postwar Wage Setting in the Nordic Countries." In *Unions, Employers, and Central Banks: Macroeconomic Coordination and Institutional Change in Social Market Economies,* ed. Torben Iversen, Jonas Pontuson, and David Soskice, 107–137. New York: Cambridge University Press.

Waltz, Kenneth. 1959. *Man, the State, and War: A Theoretical Analysis.* New York: Columbia University Press.

Wang, Cheng and Stephen D. Williamson. 1996. "Unemployment Insurance with Moral Hazard in a Dynamic Economy." *Carnegie-Rochester Conference Series on Public Policy* 44:1–41.

Webster, Elizabeth. 1999. "Labour Market Programs and the Australian Beveridge Curve: 1978 to 1997." *The Economic Record* 75:405–16.

Western, Bruce. 1995. "A Comparative Study of Working-Class Disorganization: Union Decline in Eighteen Advanced Capitalist Countries." *American Sociological Review* 60(2):179–201.

Wilson, John D. 1999. "Theories of Tax Competition," *National Tax Journal* 52(2):269–304.

———, and David E. Wildasin. 2004. "Capital Tax Competition: Bane or Boon?" *Journal of Public Economics* 88: 1065–1091.

Winner, Hannes. 2005. "Has Tax Competition Emerged in OECD Countries? Evidence from Panel Data." *International Tax and Public Finance* 12:667–687.

Winner, Langdon. 1977. *Autonomous Technology: Technics-out-of-Control as a Theme in Political Thought.* Cambridge, MA: The MIT Press.

Wooden, Mark. 2005. "Australia's Industrial Relations Reform Agenda." Paper presented at the 34th Conference of Economists, University of Melbourne, September 26–28.

Wooders, Myrna H. Ben Zissimos and Amrita Dhillon. 2001. "Tax Competition Reconsidered." Warwick Economic Research Paper no. 622. Coventry, UK: Warwick University.

Wriston, Walter B. 1992. *The Twilight of Sovereignty: How the Information Revolution Is Transforming Our World.* New York: Charles Scribner's Sons.

Young, Garry. 1999. "The Influence of Foreign Factor Prices and International Taxation on Fixed Investment in the UK." *Oxford Economic Papers* 51(2):355–373.

Index